# FAME

# FAME

## WHAT THE CLASSICS TELL US ABOUT OUR CULT OF CELEBRITY

### Tom Payne

PICADOR

NEW YORK

www.picadorusa.com

Picador® is a U.S. registered trademark and is used by St. Martin's Press under license from Pan Books Limited.

For information on Picador Reading Group Guides, please contact Picador.
E-mail: readinggroupguides@picadorusa.com

Book design by Jonathan Bennett

Grateful acknowledgment is given for permission to use material from the following:

*The Republic* by Plato, translated and with an introduction by Desmond Lee. Penguin Classics, 1955, fourth revised edition, 2002. Copyright © 1953, 1974, 1987, 2002 by H.D.P. Lee.

*Confessions* by Saint Augustine, translated and with an introduction by R. S. Pine-Coffin. Penguin Classics, 1961. Copyright © 1961 by R. S. Pine-Coffin.

*Roman Erotic Elegy* by Paul Veyne. Originally published as *L'élége érotique romaine: L'amour, la poésie et l'Occident.* Copyright © 1983 by Editions du Seuil. Reprinted by permission of Georges Borchardt, Inc., on behalf of Editions du Seuil.

"Photography and Electoral Appeal" from *Mythologies* by Roland Barthes, translated by Annette Lavers. Translation copyright © 1972 by Jonathan Cape Ltd. Reprinted by permission of Hill and Wang, a division of Farrar, Straus and Giroux, LLC.

"Lament for Ignacio Sánchez Mejías" from *Collected Poems* by Federico García Lorca, translated by Christopher Maurer. Translation copyright © 1991 by Christopher Maurer. Reprinted by permission of Farrar, Straus and Giroux, LLC.

Library of Congress Cataloging-in-Publication Data

Payne, Tom.
    Fame : what the classics tell us about our cult of celebrity / Tom Payne. — 1st Picador paperback ed.
        p. cm.
    ISBN 978-0-312-42993-5
    1. Fame—Social aspects.   2. Celebrities.   3. Popular culture.   4. Civilization, Classical.   5. Heroes in literature.   6. Hero worship—History—To 1500.   I. Title.
    BJ1470.5.P39 2010
    302'.1—dc22

                                                                                    2010030959

This book was originally published in Great Britain, in different form, by Vintage.

First U.S. Edition: November 2010

10   9   8   7   6   5   4   3   2   1

For Louise

# CONTENTS

# Contents

I see the temples

of the deaths

of the bodies of Gods.

I see the old signifiers.

—WALT WHITMAN,

"Salut au Monde!"

*Leaves of Grass*, 1856

# FAME

# Introduction: Them and Us

On one of her visits to Wembley Arena, northwest London, Mariah Carey began to sign enormous balls and toss them into the audience. These gifts bestowed her fame upon her fans, who could keep the spheres to show that, one night, something of Mariah Carey's bounced their way. But what if you were already famous? One of the people who caught the balls was the late Jade Goody, a star of reality television who came to represent the unlikely celebrity, and who was, in her brief, brash life, loved and loathed, often by the same people, and at the same time. Certainly she inspired revulsion when she caught one of these balls (it helped that she was standing on her chair). The woman next to her said, "You don't need that! You can get one anytime." To this onlooker, all fame felt the same. But Jade felt like an outsider herself, and managed to retain a sense of wonder throughout her exposure to the glamorous. When she recalled the brush with Mariah Carey in her memoirs, she wrote, "I was looking at her like she was God or something."

This is a book about fame; but the problem with writing about fame is that everyone knows all about it already. That's what fame means, after all. But more and more, we all know different things. We each of us have our own way of interacting with famous people, and even if our way of interacting with them is to avoid knowing much about them at all, well, that's still a response to them. I remember being surprised when, after a supper with friends I admire for their braininess, we all sat down to watch *I'm a Celebrity, Get Me Out of Here!* Since this was the first season of the original British version, I was witnessing something that would soon become an international brand. Not that I appreciated it at the time. Back then, in 2002, I comforted myself with the fact that I could watch the finals with none of the endless reality before it. Still, I guess I learned something that night: I learned that I had a lot to learn. And already I was having my own relationship with the famous, however disinterested I claimed to be. No one puts the problem better than Catullus, the smartest poet of the Roman Republic:*

> *Caesar, I want no more to do you right*
> *than I am bothered if you're black or white.*†

Even in this dismissal, Caesar rates a name-dropping. The joke appears to be that Caesar was hard to miss, unless you'd spent the last decade in Parthia. All Caesar's ambition, Rubicon crossing, and attempts to organize his own deification ended up making him seem try-hard. The Romans had what they called a course of honors, a hierarchy of possible promotions, and Caesar had reached the top of it. Still, you could always rely on poets to pooh-pooh the whole process.

This cool stance might strike us as familiar, just as we look at a new intake for *Celebrity Apprentice* and ask ourselves, Who the—? But is it so familiar? We're constantly hearing easy formulations such as, "We have become obsessed with celebrity. Children now look to celebrities as role models. Honestly, you can get to be famous for doing nothing these days. We're living with a cult of celebrity." In this book, I ask the question, Is this anything new? And, ultimately, Is our obsession with fame really such a bad thing? Authors queue up to tell us that our vapid preoccupations presage the end of civilized life. But it's possible to see our fascination with even the most fleeting stars as something that bonds us, and which expresses something about how our civilization works.

There are risks in this approach. It will involve a lot of flipping from one culture to another, in a search for shared human responses to history. As we dip in and out of different times and different cultures (mostly Western, admittedly, with a fairly consistent em-

---

* Or, perhaps, anywhere ever. This is Poem 93.
† It's tempting to translate that second line as "than it matters to me if you're black or white," in homage to Michael Jackson's song.

phasis on Greece and Rome), we will find things that feel similar to our own experience of fame. Sometimes they do provide equivalents for our own preoccupations; but we need to remember that sometimes they show a completely different way of dealing with famous people. For example, if we look at Stone Age burial practices, we find ourselves in a world where modern ideas of fame don't apply at all: Rather than celebrating individuals who are different and removed from us in some way, earlier societies would honor and trust members of a community whose diverse skills made them part of a coherent whole. Some of their bones might even be replaced with the equivalent bone of some other deceased dignitary.

This in itself sounds nostalgic, as though we're looking back wistfully to the fourth millennium B.C. Still, if we look at the distinctions between then and now—after all, there can be nothing but distinctions from an age as remote as that—we find that the story of fame is a story that concerns all of us. Famous people have occupied different positions in society during different ages, and I offer this as a way of looking at human history. On the face of it, the study of celebrities doesn't tell us much about what appear to be the really important things in life. Nothing about grain supply or industry; not much about irrigation and the three-field system; very little, directly, about the laws of thermodynamics. For these reasons, plenty of historians, particularly in the late twentieth century, have tried to move away from the "Great Man" theory of history—the idea that the past is usefully studied through kings and countries, or that heroes and villains have made us who we are. In shunning all this, historians have hoped to discover truths about what really matters.

This book says phooey to all that. We shouldn't rule out heroes and villains. Even if they don't really explain how things are today, it's still important that we made heroes and villains out of them; and that tells us so much about us. I remember listening to lectures delivered by the provocative professor of ancient history Keith Hopkins, who would argue that what mattered to people wasn't so much what was true in the world around them, but what they believed to be true. If we look at myths and stories or novels, these are as revealing about us as anything, because they tell later generations what seemed possible. The same has always applied to our interest in the famous. To pick a random example: Michael Jackson did not sleep in an oxygen chamber. He pretended he did, to see how fun it would be to start a rumor. The problem is, he could have come up with things much weirder than that, and we still would have nodded, mmm-hm. From this we learn, first, that Michael Jackson had absolutely no idea of how we saw him, and what we were prepared to believe of him; and second, that we have adjusted ourselves to the weirdness of his world. In a completely different time and place, and for completely different reasons, Cimon, the Athenian general and statesman, pretended he wasn't dead. Plutarch writes of the episode,

> As he was dying he told his companions to conceal the fact of his death and sail back home straight away. And so they managed to get back home safely without either the enemy or the allies realising what had happened, "under Cimon's command," as Phanodemus puts it, "even though he had been dead for thirty days."

This piece of propaganda enabled him to keep his allies together and his enemies afraid. As a distinguished commander, he managed to fulfill his functions; as a private person, he was able to settle into an eternal rest. What we learn from this is that Cimon had achieved a mighty reputation, and that people wanted to be led by him. It might also suggest that without him, his forces would have been factious and ill disciplined.

So even the credence we place in flimflam tells us something about who we are, and how (or if) we have changed. We need to know why we take all this stuff so seriously. We should examine why Katie Couric is supposed to have said this:

> Everybody I know, they were very upset this weekend about this. . . . And I actually called our newsdesk on Saturday and said: "I know that we have this tsunami going on, and—and all

*these people, but is it true that they [Brad & Jennifer] broke up?" . . . I can't believe I'm so invested in this, but I just feel bad.*

Yes, this is an alarming response to a shrinking planet, but we do need to know how we got here. Clearly, there are needs that famous people fulfill, and not just for Katie Couric.

Sages inveigh against our willingness to put faith in things and dreams that aren't permanent, and castigate our reliance on diverting rubbish. Perhaps this is to make us feel dumber than they are; but really, we're all in this together. In his book *The Cult of the Saints,* Peter Brown looks at the early church and deals with a prevalent argument about the nature of popular religion. Historians and thinkers, he says, have instilled in us the belief that a select few fine souls are able to contemplate the spiritual world and to grasp abstract ideas, whereas the rest of us are infected by superstition and cults. He sets about demonstrating that often, the leadership of the church was just as happy to think and act in these ways. By analogy, we aren't really being true to ourselves when we blame others, such as gossips, or when we say, "The media are to blame." The media, they're us. Or at least, the media are the people who buy newspapers and magazines, and advertisers have done enough research on these people, who we may or may not be, to know who we— they—are. And if we didn't read the articles, there would be no advertisements, and with no advertisements, no newspapers. I say this because our tastes and desires affect how we take in the world around us, and although our increased media literacy has made us savvy to how that works, we still need to stay vigilant.

Now, a couple of words about the "we," the "us," and the "our." First of all, it might seem a little rich for an author who's spent his entire life in Britain to start binding an American readership into a vision of our relationship with fame. In fact, Britain and America's two relationships with fame—our relationships with the special— will always be subtly different. It is too tempting to generalize, or to rely on some commonplace such as America's admiration of success and Britain's culture of embarrassment. (Even so, there may be something in this: Simon Cowell and Sharon Osbourne have earned much of their kudos from judging talent shows, which, translated, means sniffing in a British way about Americans who aspire to succeed.) Still, if I could add a caricature of my own, I'd say that we're catching up with you. Britons may prefer to show you their homes in the back pages of *Vogue* rather than on *MTV Cribs,* but if the model Jordan (or Katie Price, depending on how famous she feels) wants to marry in a hurry, she goes to Las Vegas. And although there are substantive differences, such as stricter libel laws in Britain, both countries can now consider their journalists to be more intrusive (more, certainly, than continental Europe).

And in any case, I'll be using "we" in a way that I hope will test what many cultures share: a sense of the difference between the ordinary and the numinous. I have come to think that it's extremely hard to separate oneself from this situation. I'm aware that not everybody reads *National Enquirer,* and it's understandable that sensitive readers might not want to feel bundled into the collective entity that worries about Angelina Jolie's weight loss, however alarming it is. I see it as a necessary shorthand, though, to distinguish famous people from the rest of us. After all, to be famous is to be prominent in a way that not everyone can be. If too many people were famous, then we wouldn't be able to remember who they were, or at least, they wouldn't be able to stand out so well from the rest of us. Elizabeth Hurley puts this so neatly when she talks about "civilians."★ The word suggests that famous people offer us service; they suffer and expose themselves for us. To be famous is to be different, and even if you're famous for something quite ordinary, you're still distinguished by the property of fame itself. In France one word for a celebrity is "people." For example, a headline in French *Elle* reads, "LILY ALLEN: *boot people.*" When this is translated into English it becomes something like "Lily Allen, a celebrity who wears [a range of] boots." It can be used as an adjective: The French for "You look like a celebrity" is *"T'as un look people."* One effect of this is to make the cult of celebrity look like an Anglo-Saxon idea; but it's still an idea that's somehow cool, just as France has a sense of chic among the non-

---

★ Clive James points out that he used this epithet before Liz Hurley did.

French. In sounding cool, what the word really does is to put a gulf the size of an ocean between *les people* and *la peuple,* or the populace.

This goes to the heart of a concern that many have about fame: that the "them" in the equation—the stars, the resplendent rulers—have become pointlessly numerous, and seem now to be picked randomly from the ranks of the "us" end of the lollipop. (It's tempting to see ours as the fuzzier end, but this notion becomes harder to sustain the more we contemplate how rough fame can be.) The idea that there's more room at the top shows us that we often do try to make sense of our world by looking at how we regard the luminaries among us. It tells us about developments in technology, such as the Internet, and about changes in society, such as the growth of democracy. Important things.

But then, some things do end up looking the same in any age. For example, although some today go about saying that you can become famous for doing nothing, it's not a new concern. Admittedly, when Chaucer wrote his lines on the subject, he was working through a number of responses to fame; but here (more or less) is how he imagines the exchanges between two groups of layabouts and the queen who bestows celebrity:

> *And they said, "Mercy, Lady dear!*
> *To tell it certain, as it is,*
> *We have done neither that nor this*
> *but spent our lives in idle play.*
> *Nevertheless, we come to pray*
> *that we should have as good a fame,*
> *and great renown, and well-known name*
> *as those who have done noble deeds*
> *and who have satisfied their needs*
> *for love and every other thing. . . ."*

To this group, she gives fame, no questions asked. The next group of petitioners is not as lucky:

> *The seventh crowd came and appealed,*
> *and everyone among them kneeled*

*to say, "My lady, grant us soon*
*the same thing; give the self-same boon*
*that this last company has got."*
*She said, "Shame on you, you whole lot,*
*you sluggish swine, you idle scum*
*whose faculties are slow and dumb!*
*What? you false thieves. Why should I serve*
*you the good fame you don't deserve*
*because you've not achieved a thing?*
*You are the sort who ought to swing,*
*because you're like the lazy cat*
*who wants a fish but, fancy that,*
*he doesn't want to wet his claws.*
*So may bad luck befall your jaws. . . ."*

Saint Augustine was worried about something similar. As a young man, he was a writer and orator who sought fame, and admired those who had already attained it. Only after soul-searching does he realize the problems attending fame:

> *I know now, and confess it as the truth, that I admired Hierius more because others praised him than for the accomplishments for which they praised him. I know this because those same people, instead of praising him, might have abused him.*

This looks like an early example of famous for being famous. It isn't exactly—Hierius was clearly worth celebrating—but even here, fame is seen as something to attain for its own sake, and as something that becomes a guide on how we see people.

From this, we can assume that there always have been people whose fame has snowballed as if from nothing. The problem is that we don't often know who they were, since the snow has long since melted. And similarly, we don't clearly know which luminaries from our own age will drip away or turn to slush. If the result is that schoolchildren are as familiar with P. Diddy as they are with Charles Darwin or Winston Churchill, this really shouldn't alarm us; future schoolchildren might never hear of P. Diddy, let alone

T-Pain. This means that we can look at fame as a kind of constant—something that is present throughout most of human history. It really is like the house Chaucer imagines (following from the cave Ovid imagines). You can be in it or out of it, but the structure will always be there.

For sure, human beings change, and history changes them, and we will often see how that has happened; but even though it is full of stories, and is about stories, the history of fame is not a straightforward narrative. There are narrative elements, and sometimes it is tempting to see it as "one damned thing after another": We could begin with those primitive burial customs and consider the significance of how writing developed in Mesopotamia before discussing the innovations of the Greeks; moving to the personality-worshipping Romans; skipping over the Dark Ages as being just too dark; emerging in the Middle Ages with a new, more intimate sort of theology and a growing middle class; and then lighting on the revolution of the Renaissance, from which point everything would be plain sailing: Man asserts his place in the universe at last, and anyone can be a fascinating genius; even more so in the Romantic era, that time of exhilarating social turmoil that brought us so tantalizingly close to our own world via the Victorians, a transitional phase that is surely good for a few anecdotes.

Tempting, but it's even more tempting not to. This would surely be a pretty frustrating book if there were whole chapters in which the reader had little chance of meeting Kate Winslet or Tom Cruise or whomever.

This means that, inevitably, there will be gaps. An ideal edition of this book would have extra-wide margins, and the reader would have plenty of room to scribble in glosses such as, "Why doesn't he mention troubadours?" or "What about Sharon Osbourne?" These are both fair questions and everyone will know something worth adding to what follows. But if you start looking at the world in a certain way, then absolutely everything has something to do with fame. In every interview, the subject is asked how he or she has coped or will cope with fame, from Russell Brand, who would listen to Donald Trump's motivational tapes as a child in his eagerness to learn how to make it; to Katie Holmes, who from childhood dreamed of marrying Tom Cruise and living with him in a mansion "where she would start the day by sliding from her bedroom into her own swimming pool"; to Ricky Gervais, who knows he's famous but goes to bed early; and on to a not quite famous Norwegian songwriter called Annie, who goes about saying such things as, "I wish they could either hate me or like me, as long as they've heard of me."★

So my best hope for this book is that it gives you some kind of framework in which, or against which, you can form your own views on the subject, and to work out where "you," rather than "we," stand in relation to those famous people, "them." In saying this, I don't want to preclude the possibility that you, the reader, are famous. I'd love that.

★ I'm on the like side of Anne Lilia Berge Strand, however ridiculous she can sound: Just before this, she told the interviewer, "Actually, I find it really annoying if, for example, I take a cab and they notice I have all my instruments around me, and they say, 'Ah, so you do music?' And I say, 'Yeah, I'm Annie!' but then they're just like, 'I've never heard of you' "(Alex McPherson, "North Star," *The Guardian,* July 4, 2008).

# A Certain Sacrifice: What Was Britney Telling Us When She Cut Her Own Hair?

> You do have to sacrifice your freedom when you're in this business, but it's a small price to pay for all the good.

> —BRITNEY AND LYNNE SPEARS
> *Britney Spears Heart to Heart* (2000)

---

> And shall my life, my single life,
> Obstruct all this?

> —IPHIGENIA IN EURIPIDES'
> *Iphigenia at Aulis*

### i. Hey, Britney, I hear you want to lose control

At 7 P.M., Tarzana, California, was getting dark.* It was that sinister time the French call *entre chien et loup,* when the world turns onto its wilder side. Esther's Hair Salon had shut for the night. That didn't stop Britney Spears. She strode up to the door and demanded admission. When Esther Tognozzi recognized the singer, she opened the shop. Britney Spears entered, trailing long, mucky, black locks and, behind them, a couple of tall bodyguards.

In Tognozzi's account, Britney comes across as solemn. She asked the hairdresser to shave her head. The hairdresser said that she would rather not, and proposed what she later called "less drastic solutions."

---

* The place takes its name from Tarzan, Lord of the Apes, whose creator, Edgar Rice Burroughs, owned the land.

She was concerned about being sued, but seems unintimidated nonetheless, and said, "Please, let's not have a hormonal moment." Still, "She was on a mission," said Tognozzi. "She had made up her mind that she was shaving her head before she came in."

So what happened next was completely up to Britney Spears. Tognozzi even tried good-cop interrogation techniques to make her reconsider, such as talking about babies; but babies have always been a tricky subject for Britney. According to J. T. Tognozzi, Esther's husband, "She grabbed the shears and just started shaving her head." As she did so, a crowd gathered outside to watch. When she was halfway through, like a monk with a mullet, she turned to her audience, some of whom had cameras ready, and beamed a sustained smile.

It is that smile that has convinced so many, including Esther Tognozzi, that the whole thing was a performance, a publicity stunt. If so, was Britney seeking publicity for its own sake, or trying to tell us something? It led others to speculate on the cultural history of women with shaven heads. One journalist, Patrick Barkham, invoked Joan of Arc's spirit, and another, Lisa Appignanesi, recalled Théroigne de Méricourt, the courtesan who became a symbol of French revolutionary fervor but who ended up in an asylum, bald as a victim on the guillotine's scaffold. Barkham offers the precedent of Greek slaves.

Does any of this explain why Britney Spears did what she did that night? Was it something apparently spontaneous, and yet for public consumption, along the lines of the sex tapes that are leaked with the connivance of those having the sex? Britney has been capable of similarly desperate ploys, and, according to Vanessa Grigoriadis, went so far as to conceal the existence of her second child, Jayden; as the journalist put it, she was "hoping for a big payday."★ (So no wonder she wasn't going to talk to a hairdresser about babies.) It might well have been a performance. But did it really mean that much? Maybe she really needed a haircut. Esther Tognozzi

---

★ *Rolling Stone*, February 21, 2008.

thought so, and pointed out that Britney had "about four inches" of real hair beneath her extensions: "Maybe she just got sick and tired of all the extensions and chemicals in her hair, and maybe she just want[ed] a new beginning," she said. "It's only hair. It grows back." This sounds pretty convincing (if inconsistent with the other Tognozzi theory). But was it so urgent that Britney needed to batten on Esther's locked door when she was sweeping up clippings or counting change?

It's worth seeing if there's anything in those comparisons with the tonsures of the past. She might not have said, "I want to go with a Théroigne de Méricourt look for a bit," nor have had Joan of Arc much in mind. But the urgency of it, and the openness of it, does suggest something subconscious and irrational—Britney losing control.

So either her head needed a fresh start, or else she really *was* trying to tell us something. To suggest that Britney's gesture was an attempt to communicate with her audience is to make stalkers out of all of us. By this definition, fans and detractors alike would be looking at celebrities' actions and constructing intimate messages. He's wearing that tie. It's the tie I like best on him. He loves me back.

But is this so silly in Britney's case? What if we could, collectively, be stalkers? In so many ways, society can and does act as a faceless beast. It is how we come to call ourselves a society. Émile Durkheim, the French thinker often considered to be a founding father of sociology, wrote, "It is through common action that society becomes self-aware. . . . The collective feelings and ideas that determine its unity and character must be maintained and confirmed at regular intervals." If this weren't true, fame wouldn't work. People are famous when lots of people know about them. It helps if the famous people wanted the fame in the first place; but once they're in our hands, we decide just how famous, and for how long.

Certainly this was true when the word was invented. In Latin, *fama* has a spectrum of meanings, not many of them polite.★ It is closest to the idea of Rumor. The word itself comes from the Greek word *pheme*, meaning speech; and the Greek word for fame is *kleos*, meaning something heard. This allows for a whole game of telephone, and of misunderstandings; but ultimately, the result is some kind of consensus. "Gossip" is one English equivalent for *fama*, although there's also a sense that this is the kind of gossip crowds agree to be true.

In Virgil's *Aeneid*, when the African queen Dido begins her affair with Aeneas, up pops Fame to spread the news. Her techniques are as lethal as TMZ:

> *No other malice goes faster than fame;*
> *growing with movement, strengthening as it goes,*
> *first little, fearful, soon striding the winds,*
> *it treads the earth, but hides its head in clouds . . .*
> *the horrid huge monster has many wings,*
> *beneath which, strange to say, are vigilant eyes,*
> *and each eye has a pricked ear, tongue and voice.*

Before long, a story coheres, and Fame has done her work: "Foul fame spreads this to people's mouths *passim*."

This creature was doing its work as it spotted the happenings in Tarzana and strode about the globe; the only difference these days is that it doesn't start off little and fearful. Once a tale has been uploaded or bought by a network, Fame has all the confidence it needs. And then, even quicker than before, the same talk is on mouths everywhere. Before long, we reach a kindred feeling about Britney; we feel like society as Durkheim defined it. We can feel as one, and we feel as convinced as a stalker that what we feel is true. We could do this with the guidance of the media, who have been apt to link her action with suicide attempts. We could do it by consulting bloggers who believe these reports. We could do it

---

★ If the Romans wanted to talk about fame in a good sense, they would use some other word: Lewis and Short's *Latin Dictionary* offers such peaches as *gloria, laudatio, plausus,* and *dignitas.*

by blogging for ourselves. And we could end up agreeing with whoever it is on YouTube, calling him or herself saobsidian, whose comment on the footage of Britney's number-one cut is, "Don't you love seeing someone self-destruct in the fast lane? muaHA-HAHA!"

So we think (don't we?) that Britney Spears *is* telling us something. She might be; she might not be. The matter seems to be out of her control. We pick up the signals emitted by luminaries, and do what we want with them. What great ones do, the less will prattle of. The result is myth. But we have to ask ourselves what myth is. Myths, after all, tell us little about anything that really happened in the universe ever, and yet they do tell us almost everything about ourselves. They tell us the grim truths about humanity that we would struggle to express otherwise—those desires so unspeakable that we have to evolve a kind of code.

And if we link Britney's haircut to her self-destruction, what are we learning about our own needs?

Our needs might not always be like those of the ancient Greeks, those shavers of slaves; but they knew a lot about control and the irrational. They were at once sophisticated thinkers and prey to primitive urges. They managed to analyze the disturbing rituals and actions of the past, and to preserve vestiges of them. And in common with other societies, they placed enormous importance on hair.

## ii. *Like a virgin*

In the age of legends and heroes, there was a young mortal man called Hippolytus, who hated the idea of sex. He poured all his energies into hunting. Aphrodite, the goddess of love, took such offense at this that she accused him of "consorting with Artemis," the goddess of hunting, and of not having sex, and quickly resolved to kill him. Artemis could do nothing to stop this; but when the hero's body lay heaving its last, having been gored by a bull from the sea—a symbol of bottomless, surging energy—she offered him a lasting fame. That fame was to take the form of a cult:

*To you, poor man, instead of these travails,*
*I give great honors in the Trozen town:*
*throughout deep time, before their wedding days*
*unyoked maidens will cut their hair for you;*
*the great grief of their tears shall be your tribute.*

In his play *Hippolytus,* the tragedian Euripides slips in this passage to explain an ancient custom his audience would have known about, and he is linking the practice to a character whose celibacy made him famous. But what about the practice itself? Other writers picked up on it, because it really did last a long time. The travel writer and historian Pausanias was writing about it in the second century A.D., roughly six hundred years after Euripides' play: "Each virgin cuts her hair before the marriage, and bears up the snips, carrying them to the temple." The fate of Britney's locks would be to arrive at that new kind of public site of worship, eBay. Lucian, also writing in the second century, says that men would cut their hair, too. There is more than an echo of this in Orthodox Jewish wedding ceremonies, in which the bride cuts her hair, and covers her head with a wig, called a sheytl. Only her husband is allowed to see the hair that grows in its place.★

To offer one's hair is a rite of passage. There are instances of this from all over the world: Fiji, Cambodia, Assam, Central America, and some tribes in Africa. Among Eastern European Jews, there would be a party to celebrate a child's first haircut. Like nail clippings and foreskins, hair is believed to contain the owner's personality, even when it's cut off. The women celebrating Hippolytus are sacrificing a part of themselves, and saying good-bye to it.

Now, Britney's career has been a rapid sequence of good-byes— not just to her children, with whom the courts do not trust her, nor to her husband, Kevin Federline. As Vanessa Grigoriadis reported in *Rolling Stone:*

---

★ There was a space for weeping in the proceedings, too: In traditional services around the Yiddish-speaking world, a man called a *badkhn* would make up verses with the aim of making the bride cry, then laugh. An album by Budowitz called *Wedding without a Bride* re-creates some of this gloriously, with excellent liner notes.

*She has pushed away her family: her brother and father, her sister, Jamie Lynn, whom she speaks to on the phone and sees rarely; and her mother, Lynne, whom Britney considers poisonous.*

Well, to say good-bye to your hair is really a proxy for saying good-bye to something else; and if haircuts are as important as all that, then in Tarzana Britney was delivering more than a kiss-off to her coiffeuse. Unlike the maids weeping at the shrine of Hippolytus, the entertainer never really gave her chastity a decent farewell.

You could argue that the hair came off rather late—a long, long time after the Justin Timberlake tryst, for example—but the transition that other singers have handled in so practical, even formulaic a way was a much more muddled business with Britney. Nelly Furtado announced that she was no longer "like a bird" with her song "Maneater"; Christina Aguilera demurred in "Genie in a Bottle," with her body saying yes but her heart the opposite, but was unambiguous in "Dirrty," where the heart has little to tell someone who is "sweating till [her] clothes come off." And what could be clearer than when Rihanna (or her people) called a transitionary album *Good Girl Gone Bad*? One waits for the next crop of pop starlets to grow up in this formulaic display of public image metamorphosis.

The affair of Britney Spears, on the other hand, was tenebrous from the start. She began her singing and dancing life as a card-carrying member of the Mickey Mouse Club. In a book she and her mom composed together, she ends up saying, "I've been in a couple of clubs where people are drinking a lot and doing drugs and I'm like, 'Get me out of here!' I don't understand that behavior— it's just so uncalled for." This book is a tragic document in every sense, in which a mother and daughter appear to be interested in protecting the latter's innocence by placing her firmly by the hearth; and yet this is the time of her very debut album, . . . *Baby One More Time,* in which she presented herself as a mutinous high-school girl who needed a smack. The audience could see that she hadn't sacrificed her hair; they couldn't be so sure that she hadn't sacrificed her virginity. The fact that she was once virginal and innocent is an important part of her act, and she has played with it, by, for example, sporting a top that says, I'M A VIRGIN, BUT THIS IS AN OLD SHIRT.

Given all this ambiguity, there had to be some kind of statement from Britney the artist. It came in 2002, around the time she was turning twenty-one, with the song "Overprotected," which could be read as the beginning of the good-byes—a circular letter to anyone with a stake in her future. It could remind us of the ancient Greek women who, at their marriage ceremonies, would offer their toys, such as balls or tambourines, to Artemis. With hindsight, though, if we take this as having anything to do with her life, it could point to the moment when Britney Spears allowed her life to become chaos.

In any case, it took her further up the hierarchy of things people are prepared to sacrifice for fame in its broadest sense, even if she did it in the wrong order. It should be hair first, then chastity, and then—we shall see. Still, the passage into adulthood can lead to its own kind of renown; with any luck, good renown. For the women mourning and honoring the chaste Hippolytus, the crossing from maid to wife was traumatic and inevitable. But there was at least a sort of fame they could earn from it. The Greeks called it *eukleos*— good reputation. The good reputation came from being married and doing nothing wrong.* In ancient Greece, the standards were already pretty high, and being seen outside was bad enough. Women were expected to marry when they were about thirteen years old, to a man of about thirty. And failure to do this, or to produce children shortly afterward, could produce its own kind of shame. (So people are allowed to be proud, too, and Britney Spears had her own way of showing pride in childbirth: *People* magazine, which had given her $1 million for her wedding photographs, paid

---

* In *Hippolytus*, Aphrodite's plan to kill Hippolytus involves killing his stepmother, Phaedra, too. She's only a little regretful about this: "Phaedra will be *eukleos*, but she dies all the same" (47–48).

her the same again for pictures of her firstborn, Sean Preston; hence, the expectation of a pricey epiphany for her second baby, Jayden.)

This automatic bad fame has been hard to shake. One custom that persisted into the twentieth century in some Mediterranean countries was the displaying of the wedding bedsheets to show that the bride was chaste. This in turn harked back to the passage in Deuteronomy ruling that if a man slandered his new wife, then the father must bring the sheets to the elders. If the groom was lying, he was chastised and fined; if the bride was lying, she was stoned to death.

These days, it isn't so bad to be bad. Madonna let it be known that losing her virginity was a career move. If we take her seriously about this, then we see her sacrificing something in the name of fame itself. The story becomes a part of the process. Unlike Christina Aguilera, or Nelly Furtado, there was no simulacrum of innocence at the start of her career: Her first album included the songs "Borderline" and "Burning Up"; her second album, *Like a Virgin,* reminded us that the chastity she sacrificed can be remembered but not retrieved. She won fame for being sexual, and one of the ways in which she sealed the deal was with sex. It might well be the case that her later dalliances with record producers and musicians, including Prince, were career motivated, and, as she has been eager to explain, mutually beneficial; but this is all part of the Madonna myth. The truth is much too sweet to be well known: She lost her virginity to a man named Russell Long, who now works as a trucker for the United Parcel Service.

All this activity points us toward the highest, most eye-catching sacrifices of all—the sacrifices of the self. In some ways they are interchangeable. The French speak of *la petite mort,* and the use of "die" to indicate a sexual sort of completion litters madrigals and plays from the Renaissance onwards. It provides the double entendres that link the bawdy laughs to the tragedy of *Antony and Cleopatra.* Jokes on the word "die" rely on the play between the impossibility of dying more than once in one sense and the possibility of dying lots of times in the other sense. In a song from his play *Marriage a-la-Mode* (1673), John Dryden offered progressive advice on how repeated mortification can lead to bigger, better deaths:

> *Thus intranc'd they did lie,*
> *Till Alexis did try*
> *To recover new breath, that again he might die:*
> *Then often they died; but the more they did so,*
> *The nymph died more quick, and the shepherd more slow.*

From famous people, we want many things; and famous people become famous because they deliver. They must give of themselves in as many senses as they can. On one level—one sense of dying—we want them to be ours completely, and to know them intimately. On the other, we take some share, and even some satisfaction, in their deaths. A death tells a story that is familiar to all of us, and we want to know the details, however gory. Homer's audience wanted to know just where the spear or arrow struck a victim, and all about the exit wound; the world received daily, then even more frequent updates on the demise of Pope John Paul II; Farrah Fawcett confronted her own death, and shaved off her hair, in front of ten million viewers. It is one reason why obituary pages have such allure: Certainly we grieve for the men and women memorialized there, but this gives us a chance to share that feeling of loss and pain. It brings us together in a way that makes us civilized, however odd that might seem. When civilization itself was still emerging, we brought ourselves together in even more dramatic ways.

### iii. If I die tonight, at least I can say / I did what I wanted to do

If Britney didn't think of herself as Théroigne de Méricourt, even less can she have wanted to be a cow or a goat in some Athenian temple. But let us try looking at what those holy beasts experienced in their last hours, and why the Greeks put them through it; and why people did these things to people.

One of the most gripping accounts of a Greek sacrifice comes from Euripides' tragedy *Electra*. In Euripides' plays, whenever we hear of sacrifice, we become aware of grislier precedents, when humans were offered to the gods. Here the echo comes because the man offering the sacrifice, Orestes, uses the occasion to kill Aegisthus. Commenting on the drama, the British classical scholar J. D. Denniston gives a calm account of the usual procedure:

> First, the victim is adorned with crowns, or otherwise beautified. Then barley-meal, crown, and sacrificial knife are put in a basket. . . . The basket is carried around the altar from left to right. The sacrificer then takes a brand from the altar fire, dips it in the bowl of lustral water, and sprinkles the altar, the victim, and the whole company. This action dedicates the victim to death. . . . After this, the [barley-meal is] scattered on the altar fire and on the head of the victim. The sacrificer then cuts a lock of hair from the victim and throws it into the fire, again symbolizing the dedication of the victim to death. After or before this action, or simultaneously with it, he utters a prayer, in which the congregation join. Finally, to the accompaniment of flute music, he slays the victim. Its blood flows into the sacrificial bowl. The tongue is cut out and the body is flayed and cut up. Certain portions are reserved for the gods: part of the rest is consumed by the congregation.

This account misses out the joyful procession that serves as a prelude to the ceremony, which is a vital part of it. But note the hair. In his book *Homo Necans,* a study of why men kill that focuses on ancient Greece, the formidable classicist Walter Burkert writes: "This is another, though more serious act of beginning, just as the water and barley grains were a beginning. Blood has not yet been spilled and no pain whatsoever has been inflicted, but the inviolability of the sacrificial animal has been abolished irreversibly."

It misses out something else that Burkert mentions: "Generally it is hoped that the animal will follow the procession compliantly or even willingly." He quotes a phrase of Aeschylus about a willing bull.★ To create the effect of agreement, some of the water is sprinkled on the animal's head. The idea is to make the victim

---

★ *Agamemnon,* 1297: "Yet, if you have true foreknowledge / Of your own death, why, like an ox for sacrifice, / Move thus towards the altar with intrepid step?"

shake itself, as if nodding. Apollo's oracle at Delphi pronounced, "That which willingly nods at the washing of hands I say you may justly sacrifice." By showing compliance, the victim makes itself acceptable unto God.

Yes, this was a pretense. After all, the knife was hidden from them. In *The Restaurant at the End of the Universe*, Douglas Adams does create a cow that has been specially bred not only to die happily to be on your plate but also to advise on which parts will be tastiest; but real animals don't do this. The slaughterer had to be subtle and quick. Oxen would be felled with an axe; smaller animals would have their throats cut above the altar. Amid the blood, women were obliged to scream.

With human beings, though, the possibility of consent exists, if not the likelihood. In the first war the Athenians fought, Othonia agreed to be sacrificed so that her father, Erechtheus, could be sure of victory over Eleusis. The Trojan War began with a maiden sacrifice. No wind was blowing on the island of Aulis, where the Greek fleet was marooned. The oracle Calchas told their king, Agamemnon, that the gods would gladly send the army and navy on their way to Troy, so long as Agamemnon sacrificed his daughter Iphigenia. In Euripides' play about the myth, Iphigenia is distraught when she first becomes aware of her fate. She thinks she is in Aulis to marry Achilles, but what might have been a wedding night is set to be her last. She is outraged. Soon, though, she resolves to die. She reasons that if she doesn't, then the Greeks will be unable to fight and so earn their own glory:

> *Shall thousands, when their country's injured, lift*
> *Their shields, shall thousands grasp the oar, and dare,*
> *Advancing bravely against the foe, to die*
> *For Greece? And shall my life, my single life,*
> *Obstruct all this?*

We will see the relevance of that collective glory, with all its benefits to the community, later on. What concerns us here is the singular glory that comes to Iphigenia. And Euripides makes her want it. When her mother, Clytemnestra, suggests that she is lost,

Iphigenia replies, "Not lost, but saved: you will be famous through me." The chorus chimes in shortly afterward: "And for this, immortal fame, / Virgin, shall attend thy name." Even though Achilles vows to prevent the act, he cannot: The Greek soldiers in their thousands will stone him to death and Iphigenia if he tries to save her. In this image, we see the whole crisis of fame. In a way, it's an ideal situation that Euripides creates, even as he looks back to the horrors of the Bronze Age. The crowd wants something, and an individual is prepared to give it to them.

Put this way, it looks like a metaphor that could sum up our own relationship with famous people, from whom we demand so much. But the more we look at our acts of collective cruelty and puzzle at the generosity—ironically enough, at the selflessness—of these famous characters, this becomes something much more than a metaphor: It becomes the ritual that lies behind what we are doing.

When Walter Burkert wrote *Homo Necans* in 1971, he was writing before the deaths of Kurt Cobain, or Michael Hutchence, or Heath Ledger; before David Hasselhoff's daughter filmed him scrabbling for a burger as she begged him to stop drinking; before we saw pictures of Amy Winehouse's self-abused body; before *Celebrity Rehab.* Maybe he didn't have Janis Joplin in mind, even as she sang, "Take another little piece of my heart now, baby." But he clearly thought that his study of ancient sacrifice had some relevance for our times. In the book's last paragraph, he writes:

> *The modern world, whose pride is in the full emancipation of the individual, has gradually allowed the ritual tradition to break down. At the same time, it has relegated death to the fringes of existence and thought. As the idealistic tradition deteriorates, however, secret societies, ecstatic behavior, love of violence and death spring up all the more wildly and destructively amid seemingly rational orders. . . . In the end, societal forms in which man's archaic psyche will be granted its rights will presumably assert themselves.*

We beautify people with crowns; we celebrate them, and let them feast; then, as Leonard Cohen suggests, we tie them to the kitchen chair, we break their crowns, we cut their hair, and above it all we sound a shrill shriek. In the West these days, few of us are directly involved in armed combat—that trauma in which men bond, and in which they are prepared to die for a people's collective identity; that bloodshed in which men work as one body, but do what they can to commemorate the individuals who are lost in it. Instead, we have smaller, overstretched armies whose stated aim is to keep peace, and which try to do this remotely if possible. We don't go to stonings or gladiatorial fights to the death or hangings; but we do try to learn as much as possible about those whose status in society makes them more likely to die before the rest of us.

In later chapters, we will examine how famous people came to be the outlet for these violent urges, rather than, say, cock-fighting; and we will look to earlier societies to see if there are elements of what many call "the cult of celebrity." But for now, let us continue to look at sacrifices, to see if there is any explanation for our behavior.

First of all, why were there sacrifices? As Burkert explains, for most of mankind's development, we have been hunters. From the moment when we could both walk erect enough and make wood sharp enough to do damage, we have lived off animal flesh. But the hunt has come to be seen as a way of diverting the natural violence human beings have wanted to perpetrate on their own species. This impulse has been observed in the higher primates.* In human beings, it seems, the instinct to survive prevailed over the instinct to slaughter. And yet where that instinct for collective violence has risen, it has been directed toward top people—people who could be kings, patriarchs, or, nowadays, people who think they've got something over us.

---

* Burkert quotes an account of an orangutan who killed his foster sister, witnessed by B. M. F. Galdikas (*National Geographic* 157 [1980]. "He studiously avoided looking into [the victim's] direction. After some time . . . he slowly approached. Then, standing on two legs, he raised both arms over his head and brought them down, fluttering, in front of him . . . [like] a shaman . . . performing rituals of obsequiousness to his god."

If we look again at the accounts of sacrifices, we see something liturgical, with priests and routines that end up feeling right to their participants because they are used to them, and have been from an early age. In the bloodshed and the howls, congregants would have experienced the shock and thrill of death, no less than spectators at a bullfight do now. Most important, they would have shared that shock with each other. Any guilt or dismay at shedding the blood of an adorned, bleating kid would be felt more dimly the wider the circle. The effect was to bond people closer together. Feelings of guilt would have been attenuated; a feeling of togetherness, of complicity, would have taken their place. (Anyone who has read to the end of *Perfume* will have encountered something like this; anyone who doesn't want the end spoiled should avoid the footnote below.*) If people feel bad about seeing Amy Winehouse on TMZ after a night of putting syringes between her toes, at least they have the consolation that it really isn't just them.

This need is as urgent as the need to belong, and to break bread and more with our fellow humans. In ancient Greece, the best opportunity people would have had to be carnivorous was the sacrifice. Perhaps with this in mind, they made sure they had a full calendar of festivals. Even then, meat wasn't something they would have eaten for fun: They had fish for that. Meat was reserved for special occasions, during which everyone would have a chance to have some. Flesh would be doled out not according to the best cuts but in equal portions, regardless of which cut of the body it came from, and you were as likely to get gristle as side—pieces were decided by lot. At the great Dionysus festival, where the tragedy competition was held, hundreds of beasts would have been offered and consumed in honour of the god of abandon and ecstasy. It was a communal barbecue that also looked to other worlds and other ways of being. After feasting, people would sit to watch plays in

---

* The murderous perfumer Grenouille dies at the hands of a mob that can't get enough of the fragrance he has created. Patrick Süskind's language mixes spontaneity with the known rituals of sacrifice: They encircle him, hack him apart, and eat him. Afterward they feel awkward, but before long they have a shared sense of pride.

which famous individuals—heroes or kings—suffered things that most mortals would be able to avoid.

It's the existence of human sacrifice that makes the link of our destructive relationship with celebrities less metaphorical and more real. One possibility is that animal sacrifice exists as a substitute for human sacrifice, and that, if anything, human sacrifice came more naturally to us at earlier stages of our evolution. Myths commonly relate how human victims are replaced by beasts at the last minute. The episode of Abraham and Isaac in the Book of Genesis is the best-known example. In *Iphigenia at Aulis*, although Iphigenia does agree to her death, she vanishes magically before the knife can harm her, and a deer appears in her place. (In other versions of the myth, she dies.) In Euripides' other play about Iphigenia, *Iphigenia in Tauris*, the heroine is spirited away to the Black Sea, where she ends up having to sacrifice her brother Orestes, and the action concerns the ruse they devise to avoid this. At the Spartan festival of the Karneia, naked men have to pursue a man who is wearing woolen fillets so that he looks like a ram. But when he is caught, he is spared, and must shout out a good wish for Sparta. Herodotus tells us about the actual human sacrifice for which this is a stand-in.★

Through all these retellings and reenactings, the Greeks were preserving the memories of something grislier. In all of this, the stories we tell—and continue to tell—are important; but what is even more important is what we do about those stories: the ritual. After all, the myths can change, or else exist in many different versions; the ritual is repeated and hardens into custom.

But why would human beings sacrifice each other in the first place? One place to look for an answer is James Frazer's extraordinary book *The Golden Bough*. We will be dipping in and out of the work with pangs of fear, not just because it is so often gory and

---

★ The sacrifice has a complicated myth behind it: One Athamas was to be punished for plotting to kill Phrixus, but Phrixus's son Cytissorus rescued Athamas. So now the gods wanted the blood of Phrixus, and Cytissorus, and any of their descendants. From then on, if any of them entered the Council Chamber at Halos, they would die. On attempting escape, they would be led back in solemn procession, with a wreath on their heads. Later accounts of the ritual mention the woolen fillets. (*Herodotus*, Book 1,8.197)

ghoulish, but also because its seriousness as a work of scholarship
has been dismissed over the years; one recent authority has called
it "a vast compendium of bizarre beliefs" that sold well because its
"sensationalism" played well with Victorians. This makes the book
sound lurid and disorganized. Actually, it's a systematic study that
uses a range of evidence—sometimes, admittedly, anecdotal—to
support its central idea. Frazer cheerfully makes links from culture
to culture in ways that modern anthropologists avoid; and even he
might balk at the uses to which his theories are put here. But it is
hard to ignore his illustrations of birth and rebirth, or to cast aside
the array of information he assembled, especially when we are considering our own instinctive and collective actions.

The book looks hard at fertility rituals and sacrifices to the earth
meant to ensure a good harvest. One might have thought that the
agricultural revolution of 10,000 B.C., when land in Mesopotamia
and, gradually, beyond became cultivable, would have been a time
when humans turned away from bloodshed and sacrificing one
another. But no: The earth needed bodies so that life could spring
back up from it. These offerings took place within the rhythms of
sowing seed and harvesting the crop. In *The Golden Bough,* James
Frazer recounts the details of as many of these practices as he can
find. He dwells on the doings of Himalayan peoples: "Among the
Lhota Naga . . . it used to be common custom to chop off the heads,
hands and feet of people they met with, and then to stick up the
severed extremities in their fields to ensure a good crop grain." An
example of the harvest festival comes from Mexico: "When the
first-fruits of the season were offered to the sun, a criminal was
placed between two immense stones, balanced opposite each other,
and was crushed by them as they fell together. His remains were
buried, and a feast and dance followed." Other sacrifices take place
at funerals: Achilles slaughters twelve Trojans to accompany Patro-
clus into the Underworld; the execution is frenzied.

The theme that emerges from so many of these sacrifices is that
they are deaths delivered to ensure the continuation of life. The
myth is primitive, and the ritual part of a magical system devised
by our distant ancestors. The magic is called homeopathic because

it seeks to treat a problem with something similar to it, so a way of appeasing death is with death. And yet, it is the same principle that lies beneath Christianity: Christ is often called a sacrificial lamb; but as a result of this sacrifice, Christians have the possibility of eternal life.

What sorts of people were sacrificed? Criminals would seem like an obvious choice, since nobody would miss them much; and anyway, they tend to pollute a community. In fact, executions in ancient Athens were most often for things that would never count as crimes now, such as messing up religious ceremonies. As Burkert says, "The tabu almost became an excuse to find a victim for releasing the sacred impulses of aggression." And in dispatching a wrongdoer, a society allows him or her to take some of its guilt away. We attach our feelings to them, and we are purged. This helps us to understand why we need famous people to operate outside the realms of what we consider normal or decent: It matters to us that if pop stars die, it's because they're messing with those drugs; that artists are so often seen to make pacts with the devil; that rappers lead a lifestyle that bears as close a resemblance to *Grand Theft Auto* as possible; that Marilyn Manson goes about doing Marilyn Manson things.

But another feature of the victims is that they were transformed into gods. (Christ managed to be executed as if He were a criminal, and to assume His divinity in the process—He ticks all the boxes.) It was the idea of "killing the god" that appealed so much both to James Frazer and to Sigmund Freud. Indeed, for Freud, this idea lay at the root of the Oedipus complex; or at least it helped explain to him why boys would want to kill their fathers. He imagined that primates and primitive people would be driven out of a community by its eventual leader; then they would gang up together and return to eliminate the top ape. Frazer, too, has lots to tell us about how divine kings are killed in this way. Rulers should not be allowed to grow feeble, or else they vitiate a whole tribe. They have to die before they get old.

"Killing the god" is more mysterious. It might seem odd to us that gods die, but they do; or at least, the people who first conceived of them didn't imagine that their creations would live forever. "Man in fact created gods in his own likeness and being himself mortal he naturally supposed his creatures to be in the same sad predicament." As we shall see, a whole range of societies found ways of having gods among them, and with our own hierarchies of divas, goddesses, and sex gods, we manage to do the same. And those societies have always been worried that their gods might become weary. When this is the case, they need dispatching. Pages and pages of Frazer's *The Golden Bough* are devoted to the most gruesome examples of this he could find. Here is one of the tamest:

> . . . no Dinka rain-maker is allowed to die a natural death of sickness of old age; for the Dinka believe that if such an untoward event were to happen, the tribe would suffer from disease and famine, and the herds would not yield their increase. So when a rain-maker feels that he is growing old and infirm, he tells his children that he wishes to die. Among the Agar Dinka a large grave is dug and the rain-maker lies down in it. . . . For many hours, generally for more than a day, the rain-maker lies without eating or drinking. From time to time he speaks to the people, recalling the past history of the tribe, reminding them how he has ruled and advised them, and instructing them how they are to act in the future. Then, when he has concluded his admonition, he tells them that it is finished and bids them cover him up. So the earth is thrown down on him as he lies in the grave, and he soon dies of suffocation.*

The example of the rain-maker gives us a figure in a community who is trusted and honored for his special skills, and these skills give him a divine status. And it shows us someone who knows how valuable he is to his people, but who knows when his time is up. He has a strong sense of self, and yet, for the good of the tribe, he must be selfless.

The gifts that make us fête someone as a hero or a visionary are

---

* The Dinka tribes live in the south of Sudan. Note "it is finished," in which Frazer echoes the last words of Christ.

also the very attributes that make us push them to the edges, and, as with Michael Jackson, wish them into Neverland. Frazer is clear about the benefits this collective action has for the tribe. He describes how the Albanians of the eastern Caucasus kept slaves in the temple of the moon. These slaves were already prophetic, inspired people; but when one was even more inspired and left the temple for the woods, he was captured and maintained in luxury for a year. This luxury and feasting is a regular feature of god killing, and is revealing about the indulgences we demand our celebrities enjoy to excess.* When (or if) we watch programs called *The Fabulous Life of* . . . and lap up tales of lavish weddings or overpriced hotels, we are allowing these quasi-divine people the hedonism that cannot last. They live for us, and we live through them. As Frazer recounts:

> *A man whose business it was to slay these human victims and to whom practice had given dexterity, advanced from the crowd and thrust a sacred spear into the victim's side, piercing his heart. . . . . Then the body was carried to a certain spot where all the people stood upon it as a purificatory ceremony . . . since the man was believed to be possessed by the divine spirit, we have here an undoubted example of a man-god slain to take away the sins and misfortunes of the people.*

Another group of people who appear often in stories of sacrifice are virgins. Stravinsky's ballet *The Rite of Spring* is perhaps the best-known resurrection of this theme: Its subtitle is *Scenes from Pagan Russia*. As Stravinsky explained, the idea behind the music came to him in a dream: "I saw in imagination a solemn pagan rite; sage-elders, seated in a circle, watching a young girl dance herself to death. They were sacrificing her to propitiate the god of Spring." Virgin sacrifices tend to happen at the start of things—the

---

* Nicholas Denyer's lectures on philosophy for the Cambridge Classics course have included a remark that might be relevant here: that Socrates felt he had done such a service to the state that he should be treated as an Olympic victor, and fed at the city's expense for the rest of his life. But they didn't give him the free food, just one free drink.

Trojan war, as we have seen, and at the beginning of the harvest festival. Their deaths usher in a spell of violence, which would be appropriate to the age of man the hunter; or of fertility, for man the farmer.

Just as we see in Madonna's second album, or with Britney Spears's T-shirt, the idea of virginity often carries with it its opposite. The goddess of chastity is also the goddess of birth. In ancient Greece, deaths at childbirth were sometimes attributed to Artemis, goddess of both chastity and hunting, as if she were punishing women for having fallen; and yet she was also seen as the deity who would liberate women from the pangs of labor, with a successful delivery providing the relief. In some rituals, a virgin would be selected so that she could be defiled. An ambassador of the Abbasid Caliph in Baghdad, Ahmad ibn-Fadlan, wrote of a Viking funeral he witnessed. When the chief died, his girls and pages were asked, "Which one of you will die with him?" A maid answered, "I will." But before her death, the girl would go from tent to tent, sleeping with the chief's men; they felt they were doing him honor.

This combination of sex and violence shows ancient customs at their most disturbing. The spontaneous overflow of powerful feelings was institutionalized, perhaps so they seemed less spontaneous and somehow right; but even this suggests an awareness that something was already wrong. Walter Burkert says that human sacrifice is where "religion and morality part company." But some aspects still have more to do with human bonding than divine worship. This is why our devotion to famous people tells us as much about how we relate to each other as it does about how we revere our heroes and heroines.

We have become repelled by these practices, but have something of their roots in our own need to preserve our group identity. It explains why Euripides rigged the story of Iphigenia, so that he wouldn't have to have a messenger reporting a scene of actual virgin sacrifice. Both the myths and their performances often rely on the victim wanting it, whether "it" is defilement or death. And yet a victim would have wanted this as much as the animal victims we encountered earlier. As Ahmad ibn-Fadlan reports of the girl who is to be strangled, then burned with her chief:

> *They gave her strong drink and admonished her to drink it quickly.*
> *After this, the girl seemed dazed. At this moment the men began*
> *to beat upon their shields, in order to drown out the noise of her*
> *cries, which might deter other girls from seeking death with their*
> *masters in the future.*

People clearly don't want to endure this; but they do want to endure fame, no matter how obvious the warnings are. The strong drink, the meals, the drugs, the luxury—are they the reasons why people want to become famous? Or are they the trappings that ameliorate or obliterate the pain of belonging to everybody? Are they an alluring, seductive cocktail, or a date-rape drug?

### iv. Piece of me

We round on people who are gifted or peculiar or who offer us something we can take for ourselves. The important thing is that they are unlike us. More and more of us may be becoming famous, for fewer and fewer good reasons; but when people become famous, they cross the bar, or the red rope with the bouncer in front of it. They might treat us differently, but then, we treat them differently, too. If they weren't different, they wouldn't be famous; and if all that makes them famous is fame itself, well, that's still something the rest of us don't have.

Britney Spears is sufficiently famous that people want to be her. Not just as famous as her; it's Britney or nobody:

> *Crystal is a shy, single 24-year-old Britney Spears lookalike who*
> *lives a normal life. She has a comfy office job but secretly desires*
> *a different lifestyle. Crystal thinks bigger breasts and a nose job*
> *will give her the confidence needed to become a stripper. Because*
> *of her similarities to Britney, Crystal is planning on impersonat-*
> *ing Britney on stage when she becomes a stripper. After surgery,*
> *she can honestly say, she's "Not that innocent!"*

In this episode of *I Want a Famous Face,* an MTV show in which we follow a noncelebrity through his or her journey toward looking like a celebrity, Crystal undergoes the operations that will transform her into Britney. She has the muted support of her mom, or at least she does until she starts posing for glamour shots and sending her portfolio to *Playboy.* The payoff – that now she is "Not that innocent" – suggests that Crystal, like Britney, is toying with the clash of the naive and the naughty. But can "not that innocent" mean that Crystal isn't as innocent as Britney? Certainly the nature of her modeling ambition suggests so. She wants to outdo Britney, or at least to go further in what she's prepared to offer her viewers.

To do that, though, she has to take on the form of Britney. The idea suggests those images in *The Golden Bough* of humans who are sacrificed as gods, then flayed, so that others can climb into the skin and dance. Britney becomes divine not only because she can be in two places at once, and each community can have its own little Britney, but also because if she starts to grow weary or ill or disappoints dramatically at the *MTV Video Music Awards* in September 2007 by putting on a little weight, lip-synching, and/or toppling as a heel breaks, then her public can axe her and demand a new one.

The tragedy of the 2007 performance was that it was her relaunch. This was meant to be the rebirth of the goddess. After all, the hair had come off in February; she had taken leave of her former life. The fact that she ended up being booed showed how little her intentions chimed with those of the public. Then Sarah Silverman began her routine, including some schtick about Britney: She said that Britney's children were the cutest mistakes she'd ever seen. On one level, it was a cruel joke, part of the roasting Silverman was booked to deliver. On the other hand, if we remember that the goddess of chastity either relieves from labor or punishes the lapse, it becomes more forgiving, as if Britney were always the little girl from the Mickey Mouse Club, and her parturition were the unfortunate consequence of some other mistake.

In the face of all this confusion, Britney Spears has again striven to be straight with us. Her song "Piece of Me" reads like an American artist's response to unjust criticism. From the outset, she reminds us that she was "Miss American Dream" aged seventeen; but before long, she is defending herself in terms that other successful but more ordinary women might be proud to use: "And with a kid on my arm, I'm still an exceptional earner." Clearly a significant part of her demographic is juggling child care with career.

Here the singer is using language that describes loss of control, and ultimately dismemberment (as per the song title). It begins to evoke the parceling out of cow chunks at a sacrifice, or the encircling mob at the end of Patrick Süskind's novel. Either Britney is going to give us everything after all, or else she wants to withdraw some of the exposure she's gained. But that is impossible. Her offering has become part of our folk memory.

And so it was with the hair. It has long since grown back, although the tattoos she had done that night are more likely to be there still. For a moment the snippings were for sale on eBay. Then they were taken off the market. A good thing, too. Britney consented to the haircut. She has consented to other things, and her words have sanctioned her transition from innocence into the unpredictable. But her own destruction? Maybe not. It seems for now that subsequent, tolerable success has allowed her a kind of rebirth instead. But she should still be careful about leaving bits of her hair lying around:

> *For the savage believes that the sympathetic connexion which exists between himself and every part of his body continues to exist even after the physical connexion has been broken, and that therefore he will suffer from any harm that may befall the severed parts of his body, such as the clippings of his hair or the parings of his nails. Accordingly he takes care that these severed portions of himself shall not be left in places where they might either be exposed to accidental injury or fall into the hands of malicious persons who might work magic on them to his detriment or*

*death. Such dangers are common to all, but sacred persons have more to fear from them than ordinary people, so the precautions taken by them are proportionately stringent.*

And Britney is sacred; "ordinary people" have made her so. Let us hope that they, or we, allow her to live as healthily and prosperously as any god.

# Temporary Like Achilles:
# Why Do We Reject Our Heroes?

### i. *The bloom of good fortune*

He had quick reactions for an old man. The gun fired, and Linford Christie bolted from the block. He had once said that he started on the "B" of the bang; but according to the judges, he'd gone before the plosive had begun. And that was the second time. Christie appealed on the spot; the appeal was declined. He proposed to run anyway, but left when the judge pointed toward the door that led off the track. One American television commentator said: "That was as poor a show of sportsmanship as I have ever seen." Christie, the captain of the British team, said: "I have lost my title, but I can't say I have been beaten."

But Christie, who had won the gold medal for Britain in the 1992 Olympics, was beaten now. He had anticipated the moment: "You always know one day you are the best in the world, next day you are not and you have to find ways to live with that." Even in so resolute a champion, perhaps there was that instinct to slip, and to be beaten by something other than his declining prowess in his sport. He was thirty-six. He had already identified that his form wouldn't last, and had even anticipated that his fame would lose some of its luster. The reasons why might have had something to do with modern developments such as steroids, but they follow an ancient pattern.

Let's take the modern factors first. He received a two-year ban from the sport following a positive test for nandrolone, and if he was guilty, then it was surely an odd crime. He still denies it. He argued successfully to British athletics officials that he had no motive: He had retired, and was running a sixty-meter sprint in Germany for a bet with his protégés. And it wasn't just a little nandrolone; it was one hundred times the threshold at which there's reasonable doubt. This was hardly a minor infraction of the rules. But then, what if he did do it? Was this a desperate last attempt to save face in front of people who looked up to him? It's like that moment in a British school sports day when fathers race against one another: It reminds us that the contests that seem the most fun are the fiercest fought.

Scientific papers have suggested that there's every chance Christie is innocent in both cases. Researchers in Aberdeen found that "a combination of dietary supplements and vigorous exercise could cause excessive levels of nandrolone"; and as for the second false start, well, certain people in certain circumstances really can react to a stimulus that fast. If he was innocent, then a run of very bad luck had made him seem guilty; and yet Christie has accepted that the reverse was true of his rise to the top. In comparison to his schoolmates in Hammersmith, he has said, "I wasn't the fastest, I was just the luckiest."

Does this suggest that he learned something when the luck ran out? Oedipus, when he exalted that he was the "son of luck," didn't know what he was saying; when he realized who his real father was, and that he had killed him in ignorance, he learned that he was the son of truly terrible luck. In Greek, the word *tuche* covers all this and more—in its very broadest sense, it is "stuff that happens." Oedipus's experience of it, like Linford Christie's, points toward the wheel of fortune—and the inevitability that the only way is down.

There was Carl Lewis saying he would have won; there was the tag of Linford's lunchbox;* the very day he won the gold medal, there was a warrant for his brother's arrest. Later would come the disqualification in Atlanta, the drugs ban, his brother's death from being stabbed on Portobello Road, and a series of exclusions and slights. Lord Coe wrote a snippy piece about him in *The Daily Telegraph* just as the period of his ban was ending;† he played no part in

---

* A judge, Mr. Justice Popplewell, confessed that he had no idea what this meant. He will want to know that the "lunchbox" is a part of Linford that would become more exposed if he were wearing Lycra shorts.
† He came third, and won his place on the scratch card, but there was no reference to this in the speeches made at the card's launch, according to *The Times*, June 25, 2008.

the London Olympic bid; he didn't carry the torch during the 2008 Olympic flame parade. The British Olympic Association won't give him accreditation for the Olympic Games ever again.

In the ancient Olympics there was no drug testing, so victors were less likely to fall from heavenly and political favor.★ All were feasted at the state's expense for life, and some achieved high office; but at least one, Megacles, was ostracized—cast out of the city. When the poet Pindar tells us about this, he is clear that "the abiding bloom of good fortune brings with it both good and bad." Of the exile, Pindar writes, "I grieve that fine deeds are repaid with envy."

Envy could well account for the kind of mass action called an ostracism—when a whole city decides they can do without you for ten years. It could equally account for the "Linford's lunchbox" tag. But it is merely a symptom of our deeper relationship with the famous—the pact by which it is agreed that, when they disappoint us, we will dispense with them. After all, heroes need renewing; we can dismiss them, and even dispatch them, and, once their bloom has faded, or they are under the ground, we can garner more with ever-returning spring.

So often, the bloom that fades is the bloom of youth. One of the peculiar things about the Linford Christie story is that he flourished so late. Sneers about his late development, and what fueled it, led to a libel trial that Christie won. The implication is that he was already too old to be a winner, and that younger, sweeter victors were preferable. The line of travel is more satisfying, because it is easier to spot.

Like Peter Pan, Achilles is a hero because he will never grow old. Unlike Peter Pan, this is because he will die in battle. When he is enraged by Agamemnon, he turns to his mother Thetis for comfort. She recognizes that everything about him, not just his temper, is quick:

---

★ Bribery did happen, though. Cheats at the ancient Olympics were obliged to erect a statue to Zeus, with an inscription explaining the offense. The first of these, which were called *zanes,* records an attempt to ask boxers to take a dive.

> *My child, why did I bear you, bringing you up*
> *so doomed? I wish you'd stay beside the ships*
> *untroubled, tearless—little time is left.*

There are many versions of the Achilles story. In some he makes the choice between a short, glorious existence and a long, quiet one early in life. In Homer's *Iliad* he appears to have more choice in the matter:

> *My mother Thetis of the shining feet*
> *tells me two sorts of death lead to my end.*
> *If I stay here and keep Troy under siege*
> *there will be no return, but deathless fame;*
> *if I head home, to my sweet fatherland,*
> *there'll be no splendid fame, my pride will be*
> *nothing, yet the swift end, the death, withdraws.*

He is constantly aware that his glory comes from action, and that it is the action that will kill him. Once he's in the thick of battle, he has little sympathy for those who haven't reached the same conclusion. When Lycaon begs Achilles to spare his life, Achilles tells him:

> *Nobody will escape his death, no one*
> *whom God puts in my hands in front of Troy,*
> *no Trojans—certainly no sons of Priam.*
> *So, friend, you die as well. Why all the fuss?*
> *Patroclos died, who far surpasses you.*
> *You see how beautiful and great I am?*
> *I'm from a good father, my mother's a goddess,*
> *but death and powerful fate await me too.*
> *There'll be a dawn, or evening, or midday*
> *when somebody in combat takes my life,*
> *either by spear, or arrow from the string.*

Achilles is on a roll. In Greek, this is called an *aristeia*—when you're performing at your peak and slaying so many men you can't always remember their names. But the pattern of *aristeiai* is that they come to an end. Achilles' death falls outside of the *Iliad*—the story of Paris's arrow landing in his heel is one of the myths that come from elsewhere. But, just as Homer has to include the deaths of other men, usually in their prime, so he must anticipate that of Achilles himself. To survive and grow old would be undistinguished. Even Priam must admit that he's past his great days. In the *Iliad* he is a figure of great dignity; but if we flash forward to the fall of Troy, as Virgil recounts it centuries later, he puts on his youthful armor, and his wife, Hecuba, calls out to him, "The time doesn't require this kind of aid, nor such defenses."

The one exception that proves this rule is Nestor. He's extremely old and still fighting, even though he sees himself more in a consultancy role by the time of the Trojan War. Still, even as an exception, he knows how the rule works, and in a revealing aside during one of his extremely long and often inconclusive speeches, he says to the feuding Agamemnon and Achilles:

> *Trust me. You are both younger men than I:*
> *Before, I knew much better men than you . . .* ★

This suggestion haunts the thousands of lines after it, and all human achievement since. However great and praiseworthy you feel, you're not as great as the previous generation. Toward the end of the poem, Homer's audience has another sharp reminder that they're crap, and they know they are:

> *. . . and in his hands Aeneas*
> *picked up a stone (a great task) which would need*
> *two men to lift today. He did it easily.*

The taunt reminds us of the one delivered by Gareth Keenan in the original British version of *The Office*. As the tiebreaker in a pub quiz, Chris Finch decides that throwing should be the means of deciding the winner. When he successfully throws a kettle over the pub, Gareth turns to Luke, whose team are the rightful winners,

---

★ *Iliad* 1.259–261. Nestor's speeches can tend to be about how worth listening to Nestor's speeches are.

and says, "He's thrown a kettle over a pub—what have you done?" It is as if we who are young will never achieve so much. The words show that these accusations are unjust but inevitable.

Still, if Homer's audience is feeble, and in a previous generation there were men finer than Agamemnon and Achilles, where does that put us? Virgil offers us a clue. Virgil tells the story of the same Aeneas, the Trojan who fled the sacked city to found what would become Rome. If we allow that the *Iliad* appeared in written form sometime in the eighth century B.C. and that Virgil was composing his *Aeneid* a little before the birth of Christ, we can see how weak Virgil's readers have become from this account of Turnus's attempt to lob a rock at Aeneas:

> *Without a word more he looked round and his eyes alit on a*
> *    huge stone—*
> *A huge old stone which for years had been lying there on the*
> *    plain*
> *As a boundary mark between fields, to prevent disputes about*
> *    ownership.*
> *Hardly could twelve strong men, of such physique as the earth*
> *Produces nowadays, pick up and carry it on their shoulders.*

If we divide the twelve carrying men of Virgil's time by the two stone lifters in Homer's currency, then we can divide the (say) 700 years between the two writers by six phases of enfeeblement, and reckon on needing two new men to help out every 116.66 years to get anywhere near schlepping it. By now we would need about 31 men. Maybe even more if we consider the humbling fact that Turnus couldn't even throw it very far:

> *Ice-bound were his veins, and his legs felt like water.*
> *So too the stone he hurled, flying through empty air,*
> *Failed to make the distance, fell short of its objective.*

It's almost gratifying that Finchy can achieve what he does. This idea of perpetual decay, as if human endeavor has a kind of nuclear half-life, is hardwired into our brains from ancient times. The Egyptians and the people of the Indus Valley had their own versions. The Greek view of it is enshrined in Hesiod's poem *Works and Days,* written around 700 B.C. The poet tries to explain why men must always toil. In the time of Cronos, the father of Zeus, we lived in a golden age. Fruit and crops grew for us without us having to do anything about it (Ovid adds that it would all be in a plentiful heap in the middle of a field), and when death finally came, we never really noticed it. Then came the silver age, which had the advantage that children took a hundred years to grow up, but the disadvantage that they developed from being not very bright to not very good. Then came the bronze age, which was a time of war; the bronze people harried themselves to extinction.

Oddly, there was an upturn with the next age, to which Hesiod doesn't assign any metal. This was the age of heroes—the age before our own, when men were more like gods again. Half of them were involved in the Theban wars or the Trojan War, while the other half lived by the sea in conditions similar to the golden age. But then came the fifth generation:

> *I wish I weren't among the fifth-age men*
> *but that I'd died before, or been born later.*
> *You see, this race is iron. They do not cease*
> *from toil or pain by day, nor, in the night*
> *from being destroyed. God gave them heavy cares.*
> *But he mixed splendid people with the bad.*
> *Zeus will despatch this race of mortal men*
> *when they are born grey-haired about the temples.*
> *Fathers will row with children; vice versa . . .*
> *Children won't honour their senescing parents,*
> *but blame them, come to them with nasty words,*
> *the fools, not seeing the gods will punish them.*
> *They won't make recompense to the ageing parents*
> *Who reared them. . . .*

Note the two different sorts of age that concern the poet: There's age in the sense of epoch, and age as a stage in somebody's life. In the golden age, life is protracted innocence, and in the silver, arrested development. But the two ideas of age are strongly linked. The farther down the generations we are, the quicker we get old. And, perversely, the quicker we get old, the less we respect the dignity of the previous generation. As Horace put it so crisply:

> *Our parents' time, worse than their parents', bore*
> *us lessers, who in turn will be producing*
> *stock weaker still.*

So now we can dismiss anybody seeking honor on two counts: Either they're not as impressive as the greats who came before them, or else they're going to be past their own prime at any minute. It means that there is an built-in mechanism for tossing and renewing famous people. The common complaint that celebrities aren't glamorous anymore, or that people are celebrities for doing nothing, is inevitable, and we are apt to repeat it whether or not it is true. This means that there are only two hopes for the famous of any age. One, the better one, is to fade away so that, flawed as they are, they become the standard by which we can say how rubbish the new shower is. The German *Nibelungenlied* puts this at its most pleasant (and it's only fairly pleasant) when it depicts a feast at which the old serve the young, just as the old were served in their youth. Here, there is at least some hope of sharing in a new wave of glory: Linford Christie might yet coach a champion, even if the history of sport is full of fine players who have been embarrassing as managers (however good he was as a player, for example, Lou Piniella is now the third most ejected manager of all time). It doesn't matter, so long as people expose themselves to our judgments.

Fading away is one option; the other is to be destroyed in the search for glory.

### ii. *We were all going direct to Heaven, we were all going direct the other way*

As with Achilles, we cherish some sorts of fame really because they are over so fast. These are the talents we remember for as long as we can, because we know that we will never witness them again.

And yet the struggle to remember is hard, and when we forget we don't forgive. Once somebody is out of mind, we move on to somebody else. With perishable sorts of fame, their exponents can disappear either because they stop impressing or they stop altogether. An analogy comes from political careers, which the British parliamentarian Enoch Powell said always end in failure. (Certainly Powell did everything he could to make his own career end in isolation, with a notorious speech about race relations in 1968, and his exit from the Conservative Party to join the Ulster Unionists in 1974.) Powell had a clear view of where the glory really lay. On *Desert Island Discs,* when he was asked how he should like to be remembered, he replied, "I should like to have been killed in the war."

Given the inevitability of loss, failure, and death, why would anybody bother to strive for something as unstable as success? In his lectures on the city of Athens, the great Cambridge scholar of ancient history Paul Millett listed the most prominent statesmen of the fifth century B.C. and noted which had been ostracized or assassinated or executed. When contemplating why these men would go into public life at all, given the prospects, he turned to Homer, and a moment in the *Iliad* when the Trojan ally Sarpedon encourages Glaucus to charge the shield wall:

> *Glaucus, why are we placed high in their minds,*
> *with privileges, meat and glasses filled*
> *in Lycia, where all see us as gods,*
> *and we're given estates on Xanthus' banks,*
> *so blessed with vines and furrows bearing wheat?*
> *Because the first of the Lycians have to stand*
> *and hurl ourselves against the battle's heat*
> *so that some Lycian, armed to fight, can say,*
> *"The kings who rule in Lycia have their fame,*
> *and dine on plump lamb cuts, and drink the best*
> *wine we can offer; but this is the best*
> *'because they fight as first among the Lycians."*
> *My friend, if we could run away from this*

44

*and live always, without old age or death*
*we'd never fight in the front line—I'd never*
*urge you to find your kudos from a war.*
*But since death gathers in a thousand shapes*
*and mortal man can't run away from them,*
*let's give men glory, or else win our own.*

These are lines to bear in mind whenever we wonder why athletes are paid so much, and when we ask if sportsmen now are motivated more by reward than by achievement for its own sake. Sarpedon shows how both can be motivations. Ultimately he tells us that if we are alive, and will one day die, the choice isn't so much death or glory as death with glory or death without glory. The glory has its perks, but those who want it have to struggle for it. That last line reminds us that there is no second place. A warrior must kill or be killed.

We will consider how the soldier's glory has fared throughout the ages shortly; but first, let's look at sports, or, as George Orwell called it, "war minus the shooting." In the ancient Olympics, only one man per event was awarded the crown; some have thought that this crowning reenacted the process by which people become king. In his book on the Olympic Games, the classicist Nigel Spivey compares this to the way Muhammad Ali became "King of the Ring," and we might add the way in which the Tour de France crowns its King of the Mountains. The analogy with kingship holds up well if we contemplate the mystery at the center of *The Golden Bough*. At the heart of that enormous book is a riddle about a priest. This priest would guard the shrine of Diana at Lake Nemi. James Frazer set out to ask why anyone would want the job, considering how he got it and how lousy the retirement plan was. For his epigraph, he quotes from the historian Thomas Babington Macaulay's poem *The Lays of Ancient Rome*:

> *Those trees in whose grim shadow*
> *The ghastly priest doth reign,*
> *The priest who slew the slayer,*
> *And shall himself be slain—*

The successful applicant kills the present incumbent and waits for the inevitable handover. So it is with sports. As Sarpedon says, you either gain glory or you give it to someone else. In sports the argument about death doesn't feel so true, because you can retire; but this doesn't get us very far, for two reasons. For one thing, retiring, even if it's to go off and become a team manager or to run lawn tennis, is still letting somebody else have the glory; and for another, some sports do gain their allure from the possibility of death.

For a start, take running, the most straightforward sport of all. We have already seen how the Spartans turned their running race at the Karneia into a mock hunt and included a gesture toward human sacrifice. We should reflect, too, that the final clash between Achilles and Hector resembles a race:

> *As in a dream, he can't delay the chaser,*
> *and the delayer can't outrun the chased. . . .*

The process of an athletic tournament is unlikely to be lethal, but this does happen, and Olympic runners risked sunstroke. From time to time a competitor was felled by a badly thrown javelin or a discus, both of which are further reminders that, for the Greeks, sport was a method of military training: The discus resembles a shield, and the javelin really is a javelin. Health may have been on the minds of the Olympic organizers, but seldom safety. There were some rules for the boxing matches, but not for the freestyle wrestling contest, called the *pankration*. As Spivey says,

> *To say that any kind of violence was permissible in this contest is not quite true: umpires were supposed to penalize biting and the gouging-out of eyes.* ★ *But to kick, strangle, smite, and otherwise beat one's opponent into submission or death was a highly esteemed art, and some statues of prize-winning pankratiasts were venerated as magical touchstones of strength and healing powers.*

---

★ Strange that rugby referees still need to look out for this.

This reminds us that the Roman national sport was gladiatorial combat. Here, the allusions to war and death were handled with a peculiarly Roman subtlety. In fact, recruits were as often as not captured in wars, and the former enemy soldiers were given more chances to display their craft. And the reference to human sacrifice was explicit, too. The earliest fights were put on by private individuals, usually to commemorate their fathers. As with the statesmen who would fund chariot-racing teams in the Olympic games, this was a way of making a political splash: When Julius Caesar was campaigning for the title of aedile in 65 B.C. he staged a show with 320 pairs of fighters. As opposed to the Greek chariot sponsors, the Roman benefactor won the crowd's applause whatever the result. It's worth thinking of gladiator fights as more forgiving than many other sports, because there was a way of coming second with some dignity: The crowds that voted with their thumbs allowed the runner-up to live much more often than they suffered him to die. Not that it was really up to them, but the president of the games would have been daft to have ignored them completely.

As the French historian and critic Paul Veyne points out, we need to stop thinking of gladiators as enslaved men fighting under compulsion: Men forced to do this business would have looked scared, and the show would have struck the audience as lame." No, they actually wanted to fight. If we can compare them to sacrificial offerings, then we know, more surely than the ancients knew about the bulls they were whacking, that these men were thoroughly prepared for death. Seneca once heard a gladiator say that he didn't get to fight often enough. Yes, they could die, but the trick was to die, as Veyne puts it, *"en beauté."* And in any case, there needed to be a few deaths. A report of a spectacle in Gaul records that in thirty-two bouts, eight men died. This would have been an expense for the man sponsoring the event, who would have had to reimburse the gladiator owner, or *lanista,* for the slain; but, given this, to allow a death here and there showed that the sponsor could afford to pick up the tab from a good day out.

As a result of the risks they took and the elegance with which they faced them, gladiators were popular as individuals; they would have their fan clubs, and people would scratch the names of their favorites on the walls. When a gladiator died, his girlfriend would erect a funeral stone to him, recording his age and counting his victories. We know they were admired and envied because citizens would enroll for the job, sometimes submitting for the job when they were in debt, and sometimes, in the case of noblemen, doing it for kicks. The emperor Commodus showed up once. The effect could sometimes be bathetic: Juvenal mocks the supernoble Gracchus, who tried to take the *retiarius* role (whose aim is to capture his opponent with a net and fix him with a trident).

Still, the bouts offered the spectators plenty of opportunities to fear for the combatants' lives, and to share a satisfied gasp in the face of slaughter. Today, still, sports offer the possibility of death, and the parting of these athletes always becomes a source of communal grieving. In his lament for the bullfighter Ignacio Sánchez Mejías, Federico García Lorca records the pounding grief felt at the moment of loss:

> *Groups of silence in the corners*
> at five in the afternoon
> *And, the bull alone is left high-hearted!*
> at five in the afternoon.

Later in the poem, Lorca writes:

> *Nobody knows you. No. But I sing of you.*
> *For posterity I sing of your profile and grace.*
> *Of the signal maturity of your understanding.*
> *Of your appetite for death and the taste of its mouth.*
> *Of the sadness of your once valiant gaiety.*

NASCAR drivers don't expect to die, but they know that it happens. It is one of the sport's attractions, not only to the fans but also, to some extent, to the drivers themselves. Dale Earnhardt, Sr., wasn't directly calling for the Daytona 500 to be more dangerous, but a year before his own death in the race, he complained about regulations that would slow cars down, saying, "They just killed the racing at Daytona. This is a joke to have to race like this." Ayrton

Senna, who died racing at Imola in 1994, confronted the risks. He once said, "If you have God on your side, everything becomes clear. I have a blessing from Him. But, of course, I can get hurt or killed, as anyone can."* The Lord gives, the Lord takes away. A recurring theme of Pindar's victory odes is that success comes not just from toil, but also from divine favor.†

So who is to blame for these deaths? The best answer comes from Bob Dylan's song about a boxer, "Who Killed Davey Moore?" The fighter whose punch killed Moore denies that it was his fault; so do the referee, the crowd, the manager, and the gambler. But each has some reason for letting the fight continue. The referee fears that the crowd will boo "at not gettin' their money's worth"; the crowd reasons, "We just meant to see some sweat, / There ain't nothing wrong in that." They remind us of the Lycians who allow Glaucus and Sarpedon to feast on fine cuts and enjoy Xanthus real estate: They want their money's worth.

Going in a blaze of glory or else disappointing us: And athletes must always disappoint. Their records are to be beaten. There's a nice irony in the sprinter Ben Johnson's remark after winning the 100 meters in the Seoul Olympics that they could take away his world record but not his medal. In fact, it took eleven years for anyone to match his time of 9.79 seconds.‡

The Olympic motto, "Citius, Altius, Fortius"—faster, higher, stronger—promises that we will never be disappointed, and that

---

* Quoted in Richard Williams, *The Death of Ayrton Senna*. The book is especially good on Brazil's national mourning. Helpfully for our argument, an online reviewer, feeling misled by the title, writes: "I don't want to read about his life. I know all about that. I know he was the greatest racing driver ever. I know he wanted to help children. I know more about Senna than is contained in this book. I want to read about his *DEATH*."

† Cf. Linford Christie, quoted by Adams: "It was always funny in the warm-up area before a race because everyone was praying. Even the atheists were crossing themselves. It's all, you know, 'Help me, God, to win.' And once you do win you begin to wonder what makes you more sincere in your prayers than the next guy. You even begin to think, damn, maybe I've done something right that I didn't realise and it has helped me. Anyway, that's the way I was brought up: in all things give praise." On Pindar, see Spivey, *The Ancient Olympics*, 141.

‡ This was Maurice Green, in Athens, 1999.

each triumph will surpass the last. The problem is that we *want* to be disappointed. The definition of cheating grows wider, harder, vaguer. This isn't limited to the regulations that decide who can be disqualified. Standards of achievement may improve, but we discount them. Is boxing as manly as it used to be? Aren't the gloves puffy? Is mixed martial arts an upgrade (it's certainly bloodier)? Formula 1 has become a procession, we hear—there's no room to overtake, and everything is decided outside the official Grand Prix, either in the practices to decide who takes pole position, or else in points deducted for some or other foul play in the pits. In the golden age of racing, the prize would go to the best driver; then it would go to the driver with the best manufacturer; now it goes to the manufacturer with the best lawyer. And what about golf, that least martial of pastimes? As pundits of all sports do, golf pundits argue that it's getting easier:

> *Callaway Golf's Big Bertha 460 Driver is longer and offers more forgiveness than its peers. Engineered with a stretched 460cc head design, a shallower face and flatter head, the Big Bertha 460 produces the highest Moment of Inertia (MOI) in any all-titanium driver of its kind. This innovation makes hitting the toughest golf club easier.*\*

There's just enough science here to reassure the buyers that something magical can happen to their game, but that last sentence gives the game away. As one player remarks of his uniquely designed club, "Since the club is a left-handed 3 iron, I had an unfair advantage and missed a dump truck by only about ten feet. Not bad since the highway is about 220 yards. We do what we can to make it fun here." This comes from the blog of an intelligence contractor who was driving balls off the roof of Abu Ghraib prison.

There are moral undertones to all of this. At the ancient Olympics, participants swore an oath to Zeus that they would do nothing to bring the games into disrepute. People accuse Bill Clinton

---

\* This is the manufacturer's promotional copy.

of cheating, not just because he is thought to miscount the number of strokes he plays, or because he had sexual relations with Monica Lewinsky, but also because he has tried to impress Greg Norman by showing off his very own Big Bertha. If sportsmen can gain rewards and glory, they can also endure pain and humiliation; so we shouldn't be so surprised if sports show up in accounts of torture. In his *L'Univers concentrationnaire*, David Rousset, an author who experienced Buchenwald and forced marches as a political prisoner, describes how Nazi punishment camps would force inmates to do sport rather than work:

> In the small rectangular concrete yard, anything can be turned to sport: making men turn round very fast, under the whip for hours on end; organizing a bunny-hop race, with the slowest to be thrown in the pond beneath the Homeric guffaws of the SS. . . .

The novelist Georges Perec draws on this world and mingles it with a fantasy island he dreamed of as a child: "a land in thrall to the Olympic ideal." It is a land that makes Spartan, nightmarish demands of its residents. By the end we know exactly where we are:

> If you just look and see the workings of this huge machine, each cog of which contributes with implacable efficiency to the systematic annihilation of men, then it should come as no great surprise that the performances put up are utterly mediocre: the 100 metres is run in 23.4", the 200 metres in 51"; the best high jumper has never exceeded 1.30 metres.

### iii. The bubble reputation / Even in the cannon's mouth

If there are moral arguments behind the ways in which mortals win glory, then war intensifies them. Achilles is the acme of heroism and valor, but not of virtue—he slaughters countless men in a torrent of unforgiving rage. Even so, his style of fighting makes him the most feared and famous warrior imaginable, and from him we can deduce what sort of war earns fame and what earns infamy.

Face-to-face, hand-to-hand combat, good; spear, less good because you're farther away, but still admirable because it takes some skill to throw it; arrows, ignoble. In the *Iliad,* we learn that Achilles will die at the hands of Paris, the puniest of the Trojans, the most effeminate man in the more feminine faction in the war. This comes in a prophecy from the dying Hector, who notes that Paris will need the help of Apollo. The legend that Achilles will be shot in the Achilles heel (and indeed the story of how that heel came to be so vulnerable) comes later, but it all makes sense—how else could you kill him?

The business of bows is a glimpse of how developments in weaponry make fighters look less manly. In the *Iliad,* a Trojan sniper named Pandarus breaks a truce and wounds Menelaus, the king of Sparta. The breach of the peace and the manner of it make for a double ignominy. And then, when Pandarus dies by having his face smashed by a javelin, which makes him as unrecognizable as possible, it's fighting with a javelin that puts him in danger. One reading of this is that he's out of his depth, and when he's using the harder weapon, he's more open to defeat. The Greeks, presenting themselves as heroes, would never use bows (like the "effeminate" Persians). And so, when the Athenians used them devastatingly during a battle in the Peloponnesian war against the Spartans, the Spartans were scornful. At the Battle of Sphacteria, the Spartans surrendered. Spartans never surrendered. From the Athenian point of view, this showed the world that the Spartans were no longer the heroes of Thermopylae and the movie *300,* who would sooner die than be captured; from the Spartan point of view, the Greeks were cheating. The arrow wasn't a manly weapon. When an Athenian jeered a captive by saying, "Did all the brave ones get killed, then?" a Spartan replied that they would have been smart spindles to kill just the brave. This put-down suggests that arrows are the kind of things women use in their looms.

But if we accuse great warriors of cheating or relying on technology too much, we're on less stable ground. It's worth bearing in mind the words of a Vietnamese general who, when asked why he rejected Chinese military advice, replied, "They were ignoring a fundamental rule of Vietnamese military science, if not the most important rule of Vietnamese military science: you must always win." And winning is never going to be pretty. True, Homer is keen to make all his many gory deaths in the *Iliad* different in some way, as if the way you go is part of the fame you win by going; but Achilles is killed by a trick, and as we learn in the *Odyssey,* Troy is captured by a Greek trick, and Odysseus is known to heaven for his many tricks.

In war, then, the methods of cheating—or, to put it more politely, of outwitting your opponent or being part of a more civilized society—can win their own sorts of fame. Seen like this, alongside the name of Odysseus there should be places for Barnes Wallis, Oppenheimer, and Kalashnikov. And yet, in the field of battle, such developments make the enemy more remote and faceless. Think of the Great War, and the desperate search for a breakthrough that would end trench warfare. The impasse led to the development of gas, and then tanks. As Hervey Allen, a veteran of the First World War, wrote in his memoir, *Toward the Flame* (1934):

> With men trained to believe that a light sniff of gas might mean death, and with nerves highly strung by being shelled for long periods and with the presence of not a few who really had been gassed, it is no wonder that a gas alarm went beyond all bounds.

And if we believe the psychologist Dave Grossman, then tanks, like airplanes, reduce the personal, wrathful, memorable aspects of killing:

> Instead of killing people up close and personal, modern navies kill ships and airplanes. Of course there are people in these ships and airplanes, but psychological and mechanical distances protect the modern sailor.

Another reason why the Great War brought these issues of death and reputation to a crisis point was because, after the failure of the Schlieffen Plan, strategists quickly realized that they were fighting a war of attrition, based on the assumption that the Allies had more men than the Germans, and that this struggle would be lost by the side that ran out of men first. The effect this had on a Tommy's sense of identity was unprecedented. The very name "Tommy," short for "Tommy Atkins"—another name that could be used by a British soldier—shows that they were already valued as a block of bodies, as Rudyard Kipling's poem of 1892 makes clear:

> *O it's Tommy this, an' Tommy that, an' "Tommy, go away";*
> *But it's "Thank you, Mister Atkins," when the band begins*
> *to play. . . .*

As faces of war dead appeared in newspapers, they would appear smaller and smaller as more room was needed for them. Unless you knew the dead, this wasn't a matter of fame but of statistics. And then there was the matter of the missing. Edwin Lutyens's monument to them at Thiepval does all it can to record them in our memories, but it was a challenge to accommodate them all.

Through a building like this, and the enshrining of the Unknown Soldier, we show that we want to grant fame to all our dead, but accept that the task is impossible. We surely want to honor the living, too, but they have a double difficulty: On the one hand, they, too, were heroes, having faced the same risks as the dead (as the Spartan's quip suggests); on the other, they are prey to the inevitability of survivor guilt. There is a troubling testimony to this on the wall of the chapel in Trinity College, Cambridge: Among the inscriptions of the dead and the missing, there is a gap. This name is said to have been erased when the man who was presumed lost reappeared.

The cruel challenge for the survivor is to achieve something else, similarly glorious, in the rest of one's life. It's impossible. If we look at the heroes of battle who try to serve their nations in peacetime, we're more likely to remember the bad things: Eisenhower's dullness, evoked in Tom Robbins's *Even Cowgirls Get the Blues*; Wellington's failure to help the people who weren't him, which Byron laments in *Don Juan;* or the utter shame of Marshal Philippe Pétain. Aeschylus knew that there was no way around it. His plays won him many victories in his lifetime and even some in his death, but he did not acknowledge these achievements on his grave at all.

What mattered to him most was that he had fought in the decisive victory against the Persian invasion of Greece. His epitaph was:

> Beneath this tomb in Gelas, rich in corn,
> lies Aeschylus of Athens, Euphorion's son:
> but Marathon's fair grove would speak of his valour
> as would the long-haired Medes, who knew about it.

# And What Became of Last Year's Snow: Are Celebrities Becoming Less Beautiful?

### i. Excellently done, if God did all

Up there with the philosophical paradoxes that have puzzled us for so long—such as, Can the hare ever overtake the tortoise? or, If a tree falls in a forest and nobody's there to hear it, does it make a noise?—is the contemporary equivalent: Does anybody know what Kate Winslet actually looks like?

And then, why does it matter to us anyway? On the one hand, we don't really know what she looks like, but we're quick to complain when we see a photograph of her that doesn't look like her. Fortunately, so is Kate Winslet. At the same time, we want a real, genuine, warm, cuddly Kate Winslet, and also someone whose looks and life somehow grace us by being in our world. Just as we've seen with athletes and warriors, we need beautiful people to do what they do, and to do it for all of us; but we don't like cheats. Magazines such as *People, OK,* and *US Weekly* play this game hard and fast. Their pap photographs will expose anyone whose nipple tape fails to adhere as she leaves a taxi, and a few pages later you can see a model make the shoes you could afford look how you could never make them look. *US Weekly* asks readers to vote on which celebrity wore the same outfit better, and even invited comparison between the tiny Suri Cruise and the tiny Violet Affleck (one correspondent complained about Violet's teeth). We want people to look glorious, but we also want them to look like roadkill; it is as if, yet again, we are working out some primal urge. It is enough to remind us of virgin sacrifices. By touching up the pictures of our victims, we make them seem untouched; and then the violence, the defilement, can begin.

But back to the homey figure of Kate Winslet. With her, there's an added twist: We end up concluding that pictures of her are a cheat, but many viewers of these pictures think that she would look more beautiful if she did look more real. We know this because of what happened when *GQ* got it wrong. The magazine ran a feature of her that included photographs she complained about. They were airbrushed without her consent, and one caption reads, "Kate Winslet looks sexier than ever—slim, elegant and self-consciously flirty." Kate Winslet certainly looks different in these photos: In her stockings and suspenders she could be somebody in *Chicago* or the love interest in a spaghetti Western. And the sexiness is in dispute even in the interview, whose subject tells us, "All I know from the men I've ever spoken to is that they like girls to have an arse on them, so why is it that women think in order to be adored they have to be thin?"

As an actor, Kate Winslet is supposed to look like other people; in *The Reader* we're even given an unlikely glimpse of how she might look when she's old. Still, as somebody we're getting to know in a magazine, we might expect to see her as those who know her see her. In a *Vogue* of January 2007, the problem becomes acute. On the cover, she has a lemony, faraway look. Her irises are given the spangle of someone eager to do well in America; her hair has an extra layer of highlights, and her face could be some hybrid of Jennifer Aniston and Courteney Cox-Arquette. As in the case of *GQ,* the article copy is all at odds with the images. Here, she is a girl from an Alma-Tadema painting, dressed in Ralph Lauren. Meanwhile, the words try to set up their own irony—that she is normal without being normal: "I know I may be the only person beating the normal drum," she says, "but I'm afraid I'm just going to carry on." But then, as it turns out, "there's nothing normal about her talent."

This is an intimate profile, and fortunately for the interviewer, Winslet cries. For a moment, this ordinary extraordinary person is ordinarily ordinary. She's talking about a recent part—Sarah in *Little Children*—that made her think of her own childhood: "I was the girl who never got the boys. I was the chubby one who never got asked to dance at the disco and would end up slow-dancing with a mate in my pink puffball skirt." It's an odd moment in the dialogue between Kate Winslet and what she looks like; she has said so much, so publicly, about her shape. For instance, she accepted a libel settlement from *Grazia* when the magazine claimed that she visited a diet doctor. In her subsequent statement, she said:

> *I feel very strongly that "curves" are natural, womanly and real. I shall continue to hope that women are able to believe in themselves for who they are inside, and not feel under such incredible pressure to be unnaturally thin. I have always been, and shall continue to be, honest when it comes to body/weight issues. I don't want people to think I was a hypocrite and had suddenly gone and lost 30 pounds, which is something I would never do, and more importantly don't want to look like that.*

Actually, we have never known what beautiful people look like. But in an age of photography, and when it is possible to prove absolutely that Jennifer Lopez sagged a little after giving birth to twins, we feel more defrauded than ever by image doctorers. As the Canadian-born model Coco Rocha put it, "It's all about the computer these days. People might look at a picture of me and say, 'Wow, I wish I had her body,' but they should realize that I often look at a picture of myself and say, 'Wow, I wish I had my body.'"

As with athletic prowess or military accomplishment, the matter soon becomes one of honor: Are beautiful people cheating or not? When Liz Hurley talked about her penchant for Photoshop, the response was gleeful: "She even retouches her holiday photos!"★ some jeered. In their eagerness to dismiss her as not for real, some readers didn't gauge the care with which she picked her words:

> *"I've always been quite particular—I don't like my face to be retouched. Often, people will want to correct one's face, and with me, they always want to change my nose"—she squishes it— "and I'm like, 'No, no, no, I can't look like that.'"*

---

★ This, from www.celebritybodygossip.com, is pretty standard. The site is beyond encyclopedic.

She passes the blame on to those nameless techies who run their mouses and cursors over women's thighs. That they trim these a little isn't her fault. And as for the holiday snaps, well:

> *"Every time I download my holiday snaps"*—she lowers her *voice for effect*—*"I always go over them. Just the red eye and colour enhancement. I don't do any slimming, because you need a silly programme, but the colour enhancing is heaven."*

Liz Hurley is in a lose-lose situation, and surely we should commiserate. Nobody really has red eyes, and as for color enhancing, people have been allowed to paint their faces for epochs. Photographs might seem a lot better at making appearances look like truth; but the truth is that any image is unreal and can be rejected as fake.

This is a new way of showing something that has always been true: When we look at a picture of somebody beautiful, it's the ideal of beauty we want to see. Athenian vase painters, who would have been acquainted with the idea of ideal beauty if they had run into Socrates during a quiet lunchtime, found a shorthand way of presenting it. They would produce images of men and women and write underneath them, "Leargos is beautiful"; "Myrte is beautiful." As the distinguished British scholar Kenneth Dover suggests, the Greeks who painted these people knew that they weren't creating real likenesses:

> *We have to consider the possibility of portraiture in vase-painting;* *not portraiture in the proper sense, for each painter adopted a standard face and figure, but in the sense that the attachment of a name to the painting of a youth could communicate 'This is the most beautiful youth I can portray, and . . . is as beautiful as that!'*

In terms of human history, it would be more extraordinary if people *didn't* fake photographs. We've always done it with pictures, which have been used to show us what something looks like when we couldn't be there to see it for ourselves. Artists might well want to represent what they see, but when someone's paying them, they see what they are paid to see.

When Henry VIII saw the political sense in marrying Anne of Cleves, he sent Hans Holbein to paint her so that he could be sure. He demanded a true portrait. Given Henry's terror and majesty, you'd think the artist would have obeyed; but the urge to flatter, to embellish and improve was stronger. So Henry never suspected about the smallpox scars, or that Anne was in fact so plain. The woman he saw in the picture was demure and dainty, with modest, pretty eyes. Whatever we make of her now, the king was eager to meet her and rushed to Greenwich in disguise. The disguise might explain why she didn't pay much attention to him when he came into the room—apparently she was looking forward to meeting somebody famous—but he was clear from the start that the union wasn't going to work.

The painting by François Boucher that is usually called *Odalisque* did a similar job, except that its subject, Louise O'Murphy, was beautiful. At least, we can assume so, since she was Louis XV's mistress, and he was in a position to be picky. And yet Boucher's art was able to represent quite different sorts of beauty. It's worth comparing his depictions of the concubine who faded away and the mistress who endured.

Boucher painted Louise O'Murphy several times, and there was even a likeness of her in the Royal Chapel at Versailles. The king's wife must have noticed it. One version of the story of how the king met the daughter of an Irish cobbler has it that Casanova commissioned a painting of her and, via a servant, snuck it under the king's nose. If this was Boucher's painting, known as *L'Odalisque blonde,* then we have some insight into its success. With her reliable timing, Nancy Mitford writes of O'Murphy, "We can still see her lovely round, angelic face in many of [Boucher's] compositions"; but however lovely her face is, it's O'Murphy's *tuchis* that sits at the center of this composition, angelic inasmuch as it faces heaven.

O'Murphy was the first resident of the Parc aux Cerfs, the house in Versailles in which the monarch would keep his concubines (some of its later inhabitants didn't always know that it was the king who visited them). The house was an index on who was in and out of favor: "Change," a doctor once told Louis, "is the greatest aphrodisiac of all." As far as his sex life was concerned, the beauty he wanted was the sort he could replace, and keep forever new.

There was one vital exception, and Boucher painted her, too. By some accounts, Madame de Pompadour ran France for twenty years. In one Boucher portrait from 1756, five years after the O'Murphy advertisement, she is lying on a bed, but she is clothed and the right way up. We know that she is a creature of the night, because there's an extinguished candle, and she holds a book. A quill indicates that she writes, too. She is robed, or rather curtained, in a vast dress with roses in neat rows about the hems. She is fragrant where O'Murphy was flagrant. She remained the king's *maitresse en titre* long after he had finished with others. Louise O'Murphy had hoped to oust her in his more lasting affections, but according to Mitford she blew it when she asked the king, "What terms are you on now with the old lady?"

This anecdote, and the images, fit a pattern in which we expect the younger girl to be trashier, more brazen. In every new age, anything goes. Here, the ancient regime reasserts itself; but in our culture of complaint, we tend to mourn what's passed. As we saw with athletes, at least there is the bonus that we can start accepting people who seemed vulgar before: As Anna Nicole Smith declined, didn't Pamela Anderson start looking more like Grace Kelly?

As with athletes, whenever we've judged beautiful people, there's always been a moral element to our deliberations. To resort to surgery is, in a sense, to cheat; and those who fall back on modern ways of looking beautiful are less likely to be considered naturally beautiful than the beauties of an earlier age. But then, to be beautiful at all can be to invite suspicion. For all their inclination to link beauty with another sort of goodness, the Greeks would keep reminding each other that the most beautiful woman ever, Helen, was an adulterer whose actions led to slaughter.

The way in which our admiration declines with each generation is especially hard on the men and women who are cherished for their beauty. Needless to say, men have a much easier time (we can agree that Simon Cowell barely needed the Botox). If men work out in the gym, it's a civic duty: Among the ancient Greeks, it made you a better athlete, a better fighter, a better looker—all in all, a better citizen. In a dialogue by Xenophon, Socrates argues that olive oil was considered the best fragrance of all, because it showed you were leisured enough to spend time in the gym, and because you were sculpting yourself into such a paragon of manhood that you could compete at Olympia or stay firm in battle. The gymnasium was also a place for manly tussles. The shady but glamorous statesman and general Alcibiades, trying to make it with Socrates, has all the thwarted tension of the volleyball scene in *Top Gun*: "I often wrestled with him, and no one else was there . . . but I didn't get any further." We should remember that Socrates was notoriously funny looking; with his plump paunch and stumpy nose, he would have been an odd catch for Alcibiades, the most head-turning figure of his age. Socrates' beauty, or lack of it, takes us back to the Platonic idea that the truly beautiful things are those we can't see with our impoverished senses. Beauty, like fame, cannot last, and Alcibiades has learned that the way to love something durable is to cut out looks altogether.

Another problem beautiful men have encountered is that they have been seen as too gorgeous to gain proper manly glory. This was true even in ancient Athens, where sex between men was standard practice. At least, Euripides has a character complain that the glory gathered by body-beautiful athletes isn't worth much, as it's no use in war:

> *What civic reward is there in one man who comes home with a crown for slippery wrestling? Or in someone with nimble feet, or who can lob a discus, or deal out a neat right hook? Will they go into battle waving a discus, or break through a barrage of shields and scatter an enemy with their fists alone?*

In a Horace ode, looks and valor are mutually exclusive:

> *Lydia, by the gods, say*
> *why you're in such a hurry to destroy*
> *Sybaris, why he disdains*
> *the training ground, when he's felt dust and sun . . .*

*Why does he hide, as legend*
*says the nymph Thetis' son did, by sad pyres,*
*who, if he wore a man's clothes,*
*would rush to slay the Lycian hordes at Troy?*

The reference here is to the legend that Thetis wanted to keep her son Achilles out of the Trojan War, and so dressed him as a woman.

To be glorious and pretty has been almost impossible to combine, although there is the odd case of Melancomas the boxer. Nigel Spivey discusses him as an example of Olympic honor, for Melancomas had a face that didn't bear all the knocks and hacks you'd expect on a fighter's face. This is because he was adept at dodging the punches and making his opponent charge about until he surrendered out of exhaustion. He would float like a butterfly without having to sting like a bee. Melancomas considered this glorious because a knock-out punch might just as well be a fluke, whereas his method relied on sheer skill. In any case, ancient amazement at his unblemished mug reminds us that men who are famous for physical achievement needn't, and indeed shouldn't, look great, as Michael Phelps so happily demonstrates.

This is tough on men, but, while their prowess in other departments can recede, they are allowed to look good as they grow old. Aristotle found a more exciting way of putting this when he divided a man's beauty into three different age groups: "In the young man, beauty consists in having a body that can endure all sorts of exertion in running or in violent force, and one that is delightful to gaze on. . . . For men in their prime, beauty belongs to those prepared for the toils of active service: such types are good-looking and awe-inspiring at the same time. As for the old man, beauty here means being physically able to deal with inevitable tasks, and not be a nuisance to others." Not for Aristotle the lingering charm of Robert Redford or Harrison Ford. Still, he leads us to strive for not looking too much like schnorring old dotards.

No, it is feminine beauty that most nearly equates to the fame-sacrifice pattern, by which we always want new blood and will replace it once it is tired. Hollywood stars are constantly complaining that, with only a few exceptions, such as Jodie Foster, studios are reluctant to cast women who are much into their thirties, regardless of how talented they are as performers. Like Louis XV, movie moguls see that constant change arouses audiences. But what do those audiences see when they enjoy and celebrate that beauty? Again, as the nineteenth-century aesthetician Walter Pater urged, they must savor those moments as they pass; and to do this, they should forget past moments. Beauty is harder to remember than an athletic achievement. With a sporting event, we are left with team lists, scores, times, batting averages, and a range of details by which a pundit or fan can summon up a swarm of impressions. But, as Proust explains, we can't capture a beautiful face in our heads:

> *That activity of all the senses at once which yet endeavours to discover with the eyes alone what lies beyond them is over-indulgent to the myriad forms, to the different savours, to the movements of the living person whom as a rule, when we are not in love, we immobilise.*

(His narrator is recalling his love for a girl of whom he says, as we must of Kate Winslet, "I no longer really knew how Gilberte's features were composed. . . .")

So we're setting today's beauty against a beauty we have little chance of remembering or preserving, even with photographs. As if this isn't tough enough for women, we still go about thinking that there *was* a golden age of female glory, even if we have no chance of holding it in our minds. If we look back at the way Hesiod presents it, then women are victims not only of each era being worse than the last, but also of time effacing their loveliness in their own lifetimes. We seem to have come a long way even from the age of iron, and when we contemplate the late Anna Nicole Smith, we are in an age of—what, exactly? Actually, let's not contemplate it. Suffice it to say that the glamorous will always be prone to accusations of false beauty, be it through retouching of images, or else surgery or Botox. In their looks and lives they offer a travesty of the Olympic slogan—higher, faster, more robust. These are ways in which the technology of the age (the age of collagen and silicon) tries to stave off age itself, when Cher ends up convincing us of her natural beauty by listing the parts of her body that haven't had any work. It is an attempt to prove Juvenal wrong when he writes:

> Young people differ lots. One's prettier
> than that, that than another, who is stronger—
> old age has one face. Trembling voice and limbs;
> a shiny head; an infant's runny nose;
> his bread is mashed, poor man, by unarmed gums. . . .

But a face *can* prove Juvenal wrong, by showing that an excess of work on it becomes its own sign of age; it's the face of Joan Rivers.

François Villon's celebrated poem "Ballade des dames du temps jadis" shows that we will always look to the past for the women we would have venerated as goddesses, and yet that past is composed of successive waves, each one of which seemed suncapped the moment it ebbed away.

> Tell me where, in what country is
> Beautiful Flora, Rome's temptress?
> Thais and Alcibiades
> Whose kinship their fine looks profess?
> Echo, at ponds and streams, who says
> Whatever you say; who could show
> A too immortal loveliness?
> And what became of last year's snow?

# 4

## Sympathy for the Devil: Have Geniuses More Often Than Not Sold Their Souls?

*I alone hold the key to this savage parade.*

—ARTHUR RIMBAUD
*Illuminations*

### i. Strange desire

If there is any debate about whether it's better to burn out or fade away, then it's a shame that we can no longer ask Michael Hutchence, who died in 1997. He had somehow managed to do both. His band, INXS, never managed to sell many records after 1991, after which time they were no longer the toast of the MTV awards, or even the BRIT Awards. But on he went, playing smaller gigs with the same ferocious energy up until his death.

That death is still being debated, too: His brother continues to dispute the verdict of suicide. Another view is that it was caused by what some have called autoerotic asphyxiation. Either he laid violent hands upon himself, or else just hands. If it was a suicide, then you can look at his lyrics as songs of despair, and find in songs such as "Original Sin" a cry for help. The "Strange Desire" of one song's title is a desire for the ultimate release, after all. "Oh my God," his fans can sigh; "he was trying to tell us all along."

But if it was the latter that was the cause of death, it still feels right. He clearly thought about death a lot; he clearly thought about sex, too. However closely these ideas might be linked, surely Hutchence had a lot to live for. He'd had romances with Kylie Minogue and Helena Christensen. It would strike most of us as odd that a fellow could get bored of this kind of thing. But bored he was. He enjoyed drugs. In one of his videos he goes about on fast bikes without wearing a helmet. The package worked. And so when he died, in a Sydney hotel room, with a belt somewhere to hand, he went in pursuit of a desire that might have been strange, or it might have been normal but risky. No matter how beautiful his lovers were, this was something he had to do on his own.

It fulfilled a demand we make of famous people. We want them for a little while, and then we let them go. Especially in the case of artists, we expect their lives to be short and glorious—temporary like Achilles. The careers of athletes, soldiers, and the beautiful—the runners, the gunners, and the stunners—are necessarily short, and some might think it far-fetched to link the bolt of the wheels of their fortune to human sacrifice, fertility rituals, and the descent of man. But those who create and perform offer themselves less ambiguously. For one thing, to be an artist is to share ideas with the rest of us. What those ideas are isn't always—or even often—clear; and often that's the point. They know things that we don't, and that is why we worship them. It's also why we try to know the things that they know—why scholars write their biographies, or why we read about them, whether it's in those biographies or in *People*.★

But does this mean their lives need to be short? I'm afraid so. It's not just in English lessons that people ask, "Why do Romantic poets die so young?" Even though this isn't always the case—Wordsworth had a good stretch, and Coleridge a respectable one, in spite of the laudanum—it's easier to think of Keats (who died at twenty-six), Shelley (not quite thirty) and Byron (thirty-six). Superstitious folk remain spooked by the list of rock musicians who died at the age of twenty-seven: Jim Morrison, Janis Joplin, Jimi Hendrix, Kurt Cobain, and the remote, famous-for-not-being-famous figure of Robert Johnson, "the King of the Delta Blues," who died of poisoning (or something) in 1938. It fits a myth: not

---

★ It's why so many interviews with writers include details, not only of relationships, but also how they write, to the smallest detail: Do they type or write? If they write, what pen do they use? What does the desk look like, and how many hours are they at it?

just a Greek myth, either, but one devised much later, and one that
Robert Johnson's story echoes. It's the myth that we can sell our
souls to the devil so that we can learn hidden truths or become
famous, or both.

Johannes Georg Faust wasn't a mythical figure. He was real
enough in sixteenth-century Germany. Although we know some
details of his life – he made horoscopes, he was denied entry into
Nürnberg—his notoriety began after his death (around 1540),
when a chapbook biography appeared of him in 1587. It tells the
story of a man who excels at his studies, and then, at Wittenberg,
begins to master spells and the dark arts. One night he conjures
the devil, and the next day a spirit comes to offer this contract:

> *Firstly, that the spirit should be subservient and obedient to him
> in all that he might request, inquire, or expect of him, through-
> out Faustus' life and death.*
>
> *Secondly, that the spirit would withhold no information which
> Faustus, in his studies, might require.*
>
> *Thirdly, that the spirit would respond nothing untruthful to any
> of his* interrogationes.

In return, Faust must pledge his soul to the devil in twenty-four
years' time. He uses these powers to ask a series of questions, to fly
to the stars, to raid the great vineyards of Europe, and to make fun
of the pope. He's not allowed to marry, because that wouldn't be
devilish enough, but he can have any woman he wants, from history
or now, and in they come, each one instantly replaced when he is
bored. It must make him feel like a member of the Rolling Stones,
except that almost all of them have managed to elude Satan for
more than the twenty-four years. One day Faust summons up Helen
of Troy to impress some students. Later she moves in with him,
and they have a son; nothing is heard of his wife and son after his
death, though. The end is lurid when it comes: "The parlour was
full of blood. Brain clave unto the walls where the Fiend had
dashed him from one to the other. Here lay his eyes, here a few
teeth. O it was a hideous *spectaculum*."

It was a cautionary tale, and one with a political point: Deep in the Reformation, Protestant authorities were eager to reject magic, not just because they were fighting witchcraft but also because they were fighting Roman Catholicism. To the Protestants, the idea that a priest could bless a wafer and turn it into the body of Christ was a con trick, made all the spookier because, like a spell, it took place in a language people couldn't understand. (Hence the phrase "hocus pocus," a corruption of *hoc est corpus*.) The Faust story was meant to be a lesson to the reader: If you mess with things you don't understand, those things could destroy you.

Sure enough, following the circulation of the *Faustbuch*, like children who are told expressly not to do something, people began messing with things they didn't understand. It backfired so superbly that the authorities in Strasbourg, Basle, and Tübingen banned it; in Tübingen a David Leipziger was arrested for writing down his own pact with the devil, in the hope that the devil would pay off his debts. Inevitably, the story immediately attracted artists. One in particular was to turn the new myth into a flawed masterpiece.

To tell the story backward: Christopher Marlowe died in 1593, at the age of twenty-nine, in a knife fight in Deptford. Earlier that year he had been arrested and charged with heresy and treason. One piece of evidence against him came from his roommate, Richard Baines, who had a file on Marlowe and listed the blasphemous things the poet was supposed to have said—that Christ was a bastard, that His mother was dishonest, and that He and Saint John the Evangelist were lovers. Among these was the accusation that Marlowe "persuades men to atheism, willing them not to be afraid of bugbears and hobgoblins." Others thought that he had flirted with Roman Catholicism. (At least this had looked true a little while before: As an undergraduate at Corpus Christi College, Cambridge, he planned a trip to Reims, a hub for Catholics fomenting against Elizabeth I. The authorities nearly denied him his degree, until it was made as clear as possible to them that he had been spying for the queen.)

Marlowe's play *The Tragical History of the Life and Death of Doctor*

*Faustus* portrays Faust as a frustrated and suggestible scholar. The pact Faust makes with the devil did nothing to allay the suspicion that Marlowe had attempted some witchcraft of his own. Even before we get to the play, we can see that Marlowe's own career was an early and extreme example of life becoming mingled with work: Already, his creations seem to come from a dark place. His accusers could plausibly make up any old thing about him; the combination of these allegations and Marlowe's writings have left people doing this ever since. The process has rendered him a more arcane and cultish figure than Shakespeare, and this has led some of his admirers to pursue the idea that he feigned his death and amused himself in retirement by writing Shakespeare's plays.*

Marlowe's play draws many details from the chapbook, except that there's more than a chance that we might feel some sympathy for Faustus. Yes, there are the same bootless tricks, such as when he becomes invisible and boxes the pope's ears, but the stakes become higher: Now an actor playing Faustus can stand in front of an audience. It's a crucial development. There is a performer who is imitating someone, which to some eyes was troubling enough—after all, actors were creating illusions and magic of their own. Even a defender of theater was able to call it "bewitching," while its detractors would call it an "idol" whose effect was "satanic."

In Marlowe's play, an actor makes Satan manifest before our eyes. Not only that, we're allowed to laugh at his jokes. The poetry that Marlowe gives Faust as he pleads for his soul is exquisitely judged, and anyone who worries that life is short can share the hero's panic. At the end of the show, the chorus tells us,

> *Faustus is gone: regard his hellish fall,*
> *Whose fiendish fortune may exhort the wise*
> *Only to wonder at unlawful things*
> *Whose deepness doth entice such forward wits*
> *To practise more than heavenly power permits.*

---

* One Marlowe acolyte, Calvin Hoffman, gave Marlowe's old school, King's Canterbury, some money to award to the author of the best essay that explores this idea.

Only to wonder at: Faust died so that the wise would confine them-selves to simply marveling at, rather than doing, the things Faust did. But the play revels in the things to be marveled at. It's this, rather than any cautionary tale, that lies at the heart of Marlowe's play. Don't try this at home, says the performer, while showing you what you shouldn't do. And these deeds to wonder at win Faust fame. When a good angel bids him choose heavenly things and a bad angel tempts him with "honor and wealth," he goes for the latter, and soon the chorus can report, "Now is his fame spread forth in every land."

There are chilling reminders of how problematic it can be to act out evil. A recent one comes from Trinity Church in Cedar Hill, Texas, where every year for Halloween, children, including quite small ones, act out some of the sins their pastor has proscribed, all in a red-bathed, infernal setting called "Hell House." In his 2001 documentary of the sessions, George Ratliff finds that the youths enjoy throwing themselves into their evil roles: Girls volunteer for the parts with the most screaming, such as abortion and rape, and boys opt for the roles of high-school killers. The church attracted national attention when it decided to stage the Columbine shoot-ings six months after the event. Even so, Reverend Tim Ferguson decided to press on with it the following year, although he drew the line at allowing a representation of same-sex couples hitting on each other, and also heterosexual couplings: "You're just together so much, I just don't want to go there," he explained to his team.

The fear that a satanic staging might become all too real hit a troupe hard shortly after *Doctor Faustus* was written. When they per-formed the play in Exeter, England, they reached the part when Faustus conjures devils who dance, and noticed that there was one devil too many in their company. They spent that night in reading and prayer, and left town the next morning. Here, at least, an en-gagement with evil seemed all the more possible, and even fruitful, because actors had dramatized it. The story was made to last.

And so the myth lurked around Europe until Faust found his big-gest fan base in the Romantic era. It was Goethe—the politician, scientist, novelist, scholar, and above all, poet—who made the figure more than sympathetic. In Goethe's two-part verse drama, Faust becomes a figure who manages to represent philosophical, artistic, or scientific enquiry. After all, between Marlowe and Goethe there had been Galileo, who had to recant his assertion that the earth moves around the sun because it conflicted with the literal truth of the scriptures. What was irreverent in the late sixteenth century had, by the early nineteenth century, become a way of making progress.

Goethe hit upon the the Faust myth after seeing a puppet-show version, and it would occupy him for the rest of his life.\* His Faust is motivated less by a desire for fame, wealth, and sex than by a desire for knowledge—but the sort of knowledge that makes people famous:

> *Ah, happy he who still can hope to rise,*
> *Emerging from this sea of fear and doubt!*
> *What no man knows, alone could make us wise;*
> *And what we know, we well could do without.*
> *But let not mortal troubles cast their shades,*
> *Before this hour of sweet content has run.*
> *Mark, now, the glimmering in the leafy glades,*
> *Of dwellings gilded by the setting sun.*
> *Now slants the fiery god towards the west,*
> *Hasting away, but seeking in his round*
> *New life afar: I long to join his quest,*
> *On tireless wings uplifted from the ground. . . .*

This idea wasn't unique to the Romantic age—there's something of it in another play by Marlowe, *Tamburlaine the Great*[†]—but

---

\* Part 1 appeared in 1808, when he was approaching sixty; he finished part 2 months before he died, at the age of eighty-two.

[†] *Our souls, whose faculties can comprehend*
*The wondrous architecture of the world*
*And measure every planet's wandering course,*
*Still climbing after knowledge infinite,*
*And always moving as the restless spheres,*
*Wills us to wear ourselves and never rest*
*Until we reach the ripest fruit of all. . . .* (*Tamburlaine the Great*, part 2, II.7.21–7; here the hero is justifying his own quest for total power.)

by the late eighteenth century, the thinkers of the Enlightenment, who were beginning to attack the religious and political establishment from all sides, established this as a creed. It was a notion that would come to transform our view of fame. The Romantic artist is the figure who knows "what no man knows."

The German philosophers whose theories lay behind the intellectual revolution of the time showed us that, in fact, we all know what no man knows, because nobody else can see the world exactly as we see it. As Immanuel Kant argued, the mind has a hard time turning abstract, intellectual ideas into images that we can put into someone else's mind; and Kant wanted us to be clear that this was down to "the limitations of the human faculties" rather than "the limits of things as they really exist." One of the things that make it so hard for our faculties is that they can't keep up with actual things: No sooner have we started to contemplate one thing than another pops up, and the mind is wearied by the hurly-burly of Romantic age life.

This is where the genius comes in—the figure who can fly over the dwellings gilded by the sunset and travel to the source of that light. It's an image that conjures up the thinking of that later man, Einstein, whose face has become the very image of genius. Goethe's idea sounds much like the thought experiment that Einstein devised: If you travel on a beam of light from the face of the clock at Berne station, will it show a different time when you look back at it? For Coleridge, a genius is someone who has "esemplastic power."★ What he meant by this (he said) was "molding into unity." The imagination, he argued, was a living and "vital" faculty that works on things that are "essentially fixed and dead." So men and women of genius, whether they're scientists or artists, will take the things of the world and transform them into their own visions. This is why, in *Faust,* scientific truth and artistic experimentation become as real as each other. In both cases, those who find out something hidden,

---

★ This kind of coinage was one of the things for which Byron would send up Coleridge: "Explaining metaphysics to the nation— / I wish he would explain his explanation"; *Don Juan,* Dedication.

who can "triumph o'er a secret wrung from nature's close reserve," become famous.

It suits us when this fame comes at a price. We have become familiar with the idea of the crazed scientist, or the mathematician whose feats of reasoning come from a brain that seems ill equipped for everyday life, such as that of John Nash, the *Beautiful Mind* man who has struggled with schizophrenia. It's a commonplace that the best mathematicians "burn themselves out" young. The truths they discover, and their equations, which are elegant or even beautiful to those who can understand them, can help us postulate the shape of the universe. For sure, many of these characters can be balanced, fully functioning beings who lead long, productive lives. But then, Einstein stopped making progress after a while, and struggled in vain to disprove that subatomic particles moved in random waves. And Isaac Newton, the calm, rational member of Parliament for Cambridge University and president of the Royal Society, attempted alchemy and was taken up with occult ideas on how bodies can attract one another—ideas that are hardly as scientific as we associate with him (though they might well have influenced the theory of gravity). The Faust story enshrines the idea that these visionary insights can't last long.

So where do these gifts and insights come from? Some place beyond the human, is the idea. The essayist and poet Clive James put it revealingly in a piece about Amy Winehouse: "When that young woman sings, it's the revelation of a divine gift—but when she behaves as if the gift were hers to destroy if she feels like it, you can't help thinking of divine wrath." The argument here is that Amy Winehouse's gift doesn't belong to her, and the idea of divine wrath suggests that she has gone over to the other side. James adds, "Can't the force that made her so brilliant give her strength?" It's a moving hope, but it's one that goes against the convention. If anything, Amy Winehouse's career fits the Faust pattern of allowing us to "wonder at unlawful things." Like Billie Holiday before her, she articulates a pain that goes far enough beyond ordinary experience to offer a kind of consolation to anyone who shares any measure of it. When she sings, "Tears dry on their own," it's such a neat line that it seems found rather than planned, as though she has been given a unique understanding of tears; and it's an understanding we can now share whenever we cry.

The problem here is the same as it has been since the early nineteenth century at least: When we admire our favorite artists, are we rejoicing in the inspiration that comes to them from beyond, or are we fascinated by what those artists do with the inspiration? The question goes to the heart of modern celebrity: When we concede that certain people are gifted, we come to expect them to live a life replete with hedonism. To follow the Faust myth again, we allow them their twenty-four years of fame, so long as it is tinged throughout by the knowledge, imparted presumably by the agents of darkness, that it will all end horribly.

For a moment, though, let's work with the assumption that fans look up to artists because of those artists' own abilities to give their wild feelings some kind of expression. You don't need the devil to be an artist; you just need to make sense of your own crazy life. Like Amy Winehouse singing about rehab in our own time, the Romantic composer Hector Berlioz is supposed to have been writing his *Damnation of Faust* from firsthand experience. This isn't to say that he met the devil and had a great time; but, as his biographer, David Cairns, explains, he was himself Faust-like:

> *The sufferings of the central character echoed his own: he had been there, he knew it all: the disillusioned idealism, the attachment to an idea of love that never found fulfilment, the wanderings, the thirst, like Byron's, for sensation, the pantheistic worship of nature, the longing to be united with all existence, the terrible sense of alienation, the self-questioning that turned beauty to ashes, the black depressions which precipitated from the depths of the psyche the demon of eternal denial.*

Certainly Berlioz's life was crazy, and he wrote superbly about it, for anyone to read, in his *Memoirs*. But he was more of a misunderstood genius than a hugely famous one. There were others who met the public halfway, so that their artistry could seem at once remote and wickedly impressive.

The nineteenth century was the age of the virtuoso, when musicians such as Liszt and Paganini would strive to do impossible things on their instruments. Paganini in particular was thought to have sold his soul to the devil, because he played the violin at unsurpassable speeds; he could play chords and still have a few fingers spare to pluck some strings in accompaniment; and he could do all this in fiendish keys. That last part wasn't always true; he would sometimes retune his fiddle so that it sounded as though he was playing in a harder key than he really was. Those punters who still thought that the Faust story was more than a myth were happy to believe that Paganini's powers came from somewhere else.

He didn't do much to discourage the idea, which was terrific box office, and he was the prototype of musicians who leave as much as possible to the imagination. Several have tried to conceal what their fleet fingers do: The jazz trumpeter Frank Keppard would play with a handkerchief over the valves; both Robert Johnson and Naftule Brandwein, the "King of Klezmer Clarinet," who flourished in 1920s New York, would play with their backs to the audience. Like the priests in the Orthodox Church who sing from behind a screen, they, too, offered the possibility that these sounds really did come from another place, but not a holy one. With Paganini (as with Robert Johnson), audiences developed a clear idea. As Liszt wrote of him,

> *The excitement he created was so unusual, the magic that he practised upon the imagination of his hearers so powerful, that they would not be satisfied with a natural explanation. Old tales of witches and ghost stories came into their minds; they attempted to explain the miracle of his playing by delving into his past, to interpret the wonder of his genius in a supernatural way; they even hinted that he had devoted his spirit to the Evil One, and that the fourth string of his violin was made from his wife's intestines, which he himself had cut out.*

It would seem odd for Paganini to have used his wife's intestine for just the one string, since his tone would have sounded uneven, but then, this "delving into the past" involved a fair amount of fantasy. Paganini's fans were less inclined to speculate on his esemplastic faculties and more on his friendship with the devil. There was a handful of reasons for this. One is that there was already a tradition that linked the devil with fiddlers: the eighteenth-century violinist and composer Giuseppe Tartini was supposed to have written his *Devil's Trill* Sonata after a dream in which the devil shared some crafty double-stopping techniques. Yiddish storytelling has an impressive repertoire of devilish fiddlers. One, in "The Dead Fiddler" by Isaac Bashevis Singer, comes back as a spirit (a dybbuk) to inhabit a virtuous girl, and he makes her swear her head off. Another, Stempeniu, the hero of a novella of the same name by Sholem Aleichem, has that Faust/Jagger knack with women that is supernatural:

> *They say he was acquainted with all the witches and warlocks, and that if he even felt like stealing a girl away from her intended he could. He knew a kind of spell, and all he had to do was look at her, just a direct look at a young woman, and she would be his—heaven protect us!*

(It's true that in many cultures, musicians, though vital figures, are marginal ones, much like actors, and certainly in the Jewish storytelling tradition they're the very last people you'd want to marry your daughter.)

Paganini was a useful Faust figure not only because of the violin's devilish place but also because he looked scary. Berlioz said he had "long hair, a keen eye, a strange and ravaged face." The face had been ravaged by jaw operations. The conductor Charles Hallé described him as ghostlike. But if there's another reason why people were more interested in Paganini's past than in his ability to make sense of the universe, it's because of the music he came up with. Apart from the twiddles and leaps, it's not all that interesting. Like other violin stars after him, such as Fritz Kreisler, he wrote pieces with a view to showing off his own skills. This was the artistic genius as sellout celebrity, as his old friend Liszt observed after Paganini's death:

> *May the artist of the future gladly and readily decline to play the*
> *conceited and egotistical role which we hope in Paganini has had*
> *its last brilliant representative; may he set his goal within, and*
> *not outside, himself, and be the means of virtuosity and not its*
> *end. May he constantly keep in mind that though the saying*
> *is* Noblesse oblige, *in a far higher degree than nobility:* Génie
> oblige!

This was a big problem for Liszt, too, because he struggled all his life with an addiction to showing off. Sometimes he would play Beethoven and introduce schmancy passages of his own; at other times he would play Handel straight. His piano concertos were barnstorming showdowns between soloist and orchestra; but then there's his B Minor Piano Sonata— unthinkably difficult, but with a properly searching exploration of ideas. His words on Paganini should be read as a note to self.

As was true with Paganini, Liszt's virtuosity led people to want to know more—much more—about him. At one concert, two Hungarian countesses fought over his snuffbox. He set the benchmark for stalked celebrities, although he did at least attract a better class of stalker. One was the exotic dancer Lola Montez (who was Irish but pretended to be Spanish); although the couple had met before, she showed up uninvited during a tour with a Beethoven theme that was going really badly, burst into a private dinner, and danced on the table. Then, toward the end of his life, there was Olga Janina, a nineteen-year-old pretend countess who had married already at fifteen (she drove her husband away on their wedding night after horse-whipping him) and had a daughter at sixteen. He accepted her into his piano classes, and she managed to seduce him. This was bad news for Liszt, since he had by this point taken holy orders in the Roman Catholic Church, and when he repented of his lapse, she arrived at his apartment with a pistol threatening to kill them both. She didn't, but she did take some fake poison and roll around the floor for a bit.

The speculators and the stalkers show us how desirable these artists became, and how intimately their admirers wanted to know them. And Liszt's trail of high-profile lovers gave people lots to speculate about. It helped that Liszt broke new ground in composing music that listeners could consider autobiographical, and so there was material to work with. But the tribe that has always had the trickiest relationship with a public trying to learn everything about them has always been the tribe of poets.

This relationship, too, shifted in the nineteenth century. In the eighteenth century, Samuel Johnson offered the readers of *Lives of the Poets* almost nothing of the poets' actual lives, since he preferred to criticize and expatiate (although he did feel free to provide a character analysis of Alexander Pope). Once we're into the age of Byron, though, the situation is completely different. Why? There was the age itself, as we have seen, but then there was Byron. Byron was titled—penniless, but titled—and then his private life attracted some attention. It wasn't long before his marriage to Annabella Milbanke fell apart, and soon after the two were separated, she discovered that Byron was conducting a relationship with his half sister, Augusta Leigh. He was already renowned: When the first two cantos of *Childe Harold's Pilgrimage* were published in 1812, he "woke up and found [himself] famous."★ This was even without his name on the text.

He woke up to a new type of fame, not least because of the growing insistence that a poet revealed his or her inner torments through poetry. It's a sentiment that is strongly with us today, and explains why Ted Hughes's *Birthday Letters* (1998)—his poems about Sylvia Plath, written throughout their relationship and afterward—made the bestseller lists. (This almost never happens with poetry.) In Byron's case, he was keen to distance himself from his hero, a dissipated member of the nobility who turned his back on his homeland in favor of the strange and beautiful, even though he was a dissipated member of the etc. Although the poem stands in its own right and can be read with pleasure by anyone who doesn't have an

---

★ The first print run, of five hundred copies, went on sale at a thumping fifty shillings a copy, which one commentator has calculated to be half a gentleman's weekly income. (See Fiona MacCarthy, *Byron: Life and Legend* [John Murray, 2002], 159.)

intimate knowledge of Byron's private life or who hasn't seen his Russell Brand–like portrait, he still knew how to draw his readers in with a little self-packaging. Before the hero was called Harold, he was called Burun; and most thought Byron protested too much when he wrote in the poem's preface:

> *It has been suggested to me by friends, on whose opinions I set a high value, that in this fictitious character, "Childe Harold," I may incur the suspicion of having intended some real personage: this I beg leave, once for all, to disclaim—Harold is the child of imagination, for the purpose I have stated. In some very trivial particulars, and those merely local, there might be grounds for such a notion; but in the main points, I should hope, none whatever.*

As with Liszt, Paganini, and Berlioz, it mattered to readers that they were in touch with the real Lord. For them, it was better still when the narrative of *Childe Harold* became all the more like life. In the poem's opening, Byron wrote that his hero "loved but one, / And that loved one, alas! could ne'er be his"; that "loathed he in his native land to dwell"; that he would "visit scorching climes beyond the sea; / With pleasure drugged, he almost longed for woe." That was in 1812; in 1816 he had to leave England again, this time, as it turned out, for good. The scandal of the affair with Augusta meant that all but a few friends abandoned him; he really did spend the last eight years of his life in scorching climes.

By that point he had a reputation for disaffected brooding and reckless womanizing. (Fortunately for him, his homosexual dalliances remained fairly secret.) In his next big narrative poem, *Don Juan,* the reckless womanizing remained, and the backdrops were still in sultry climates, but this time, it's a romp. Its energy comes from its digressions, from its More-ish rhyme scheme, and, most important, from the string of women who offer themselves up to the hero. In working with the Don Juan legend, Byron was taking on a Faustian theme. Others who had tackled it—Molière and Mozart—ended the story with the devil inviting the hero to dine with him in hell. Byron's version doesn't end. He kept on adding to it, putting Juan into ever jammier situations, and having him meet consistently obliging beauties.

Six years after he had begun the work, Byron was dead. The doctor who examined his body found that the heart and cranium resembled the organs of a much older man. Byron's life, his work, and now his corpse were telling the Faust story: There is a sort of sensual indulgence for which people envy you, and so long as you suffer for it, that's fine. As we have seen, these kinds of artistic revelations rely on an inner pain, and as Aeschylus wrote, "Suffering teaches."

But the pact with the devil has to work both ways. If a Faust or a Liszt or a Byron is going to sign on the line and offer up his soul, then there has to be something in it for him. If there weren't, then the myth wouldn't keep going; what would be the percentage? If Michael Hutchence had a wish list, then the spirits kept their part of the bargain. Just as it was with Romantic poets, not all rock stars die young, and some—Iggy Pop, Mick Jagger—have managed to combine endurance with indiscretions. The myth doesn't always hold up. Still, it's prevalent enough to enable stars to cash in on their rights to luxury. These days stars have "riders," clauses in their contracts specifying the goodies that must be ready for them in their dressing rooms if a gig is to take place. Jennifer Lopez and Mariah Carey have some riders that are notorious for their exacting demands. Mariah Carey has denied that she ever asked for puppies and kittens for an MTV performance, but her riders are elaborate. When you see the specifications for lunch and dinner, then you realize that such orders as "tea service for 8 – must use Poland Springs water" and "plastic bottles of Evian are the only acceptable bottles of water for the dressing rooms" are the least of her caterers' worries.*

Yes, these conditions sound sad, but it's hard sometimes not to

---

\* For a compendious assembly of stars' riders, see the indispensable thesmokinggun .com/backstagetour. I confess not to understand why you need mineral water for tea, if you're going to boil it in any case.

see them as nutty attempts to win some pampering within a short time span, because even if life can sometimes be long, fame and success seldom are, as the dips and peaks in Mariah Carey's popularity have shown. Indeed, there is even medical evidence to suggest that famous people should expect to live for a briefer spell than the rest of us. A study by Mark Bellis and others, conducted at Liverpool John Moores University, looked at North American and European musicians who had performed in any album on a list of All-Time Top 1000 albums, and found that they were 1.7 times more likely to die at an early age than the rest of us. (The study also found that after twenty-five years of fame, European musicians become less likely to die at an early age, although Americans remain at risk.) One consolation is that it was riskier to be famous before 1980—yet more proof that celebrities just aren't what they used to be.

The Liverpool survey suggests that one reason for this statistic is "high levels of stress in environments where alcohol and drugs are widely available," and it urges that "collaborations between health and music industries should focus on improving both pop star health and their image as role models to wider populations." Germaine Greer, the Australian writer, reflecting on the death of her acquaintance Heath Ledger, is in sympathy. After explaining that celebrities on tour have to deal with doctors who know nothing of case histories, and who merely "guess and prescribe," she concludes:

> *An actor such as Ledger, who seems to tear his best work out from somewhere deep inside him, is as highly tuned and fragile as an athlete. Yet the fitness of footballers and tennis players is guarded by armies of retainers, who watch over their diet, their exercise, their levels of hydration—and their sleep patterns. Ledger was left to take care of himself, with the occasional help of a motley crew of expensive showbiz doctors, who, scattered as they are across the globe, will never be called to account.*

The Faust myth is maintained. Observers can think that famous people are having the time of their lives, while the famous know that their lives have less time to run. It is hard to gauge which comes first in this chicken-egg cycle: Does the lifestyle come as a bonus to people who win fame, or do people seek that fame because they want the lifestyle? Either way, the link between earthly fulfillment and heavenly comeuppance holds firm.

Here, too, there's a strong element of sacrifice. James Frazer tracked down a ritual that took place among Roman soldiers stationed by the Danube as it flowed through what is now Bulgaria. This ritual was attached to the Saturnalia, when, as Frazer says, "the customary restraints of law and morality are thrown aside . . . and when the darker passions find a vent which would never be allowed them in the more staid and sober course of ordinary life." It was a time when the statue of Saturn in the temple was freed of the rope that hung about him; slaves could command their masters. The soldiers on the Danube developed the practice of selecting one of their number, a pretty fellow, necessarily, who would become the lord of misrule. He could do whatever he wanted for the thirty days leading up to the Saturnalia, and force his peers to be his accomplices. And when the thirty days were up, he would have to kill himself on the altar of Saturn. We know about this custom through the life of Saint Dasius, a Christian who was martyred for refusing to take part.

It's one of the ironies of fame that Dasius avoided the celebrity cycle but still became famous; or at least, he's the one whose name is written down. Just as the publication of the *Faustbuch* made people want to do what Faust did, even though the text tried to make selling your soul to the devil seem unattractive, so many still have the strange desire to live the revealing, potent but dangerous life of fame. And the more there are, the less likely we are to hear of them.

### ii. Lonely hearts club

O! It requires deeper feeling and a stronger imagination than belong to most of those to whom reasoning and fluent expression have been as a trade learnt in boyhood to conceive with what might, with what inward strivings and commotion, the conception of a new and vital truth takes possession of an uneducated man of genius. His meditations are almost inevitably employed on the eternal or the everlasting; for "the world is not his friend, nor the world's law."

—COLERIDGE,
*Biographia Literaria*

So the Faustian pact is a mixed blessing. But the Romantic age—the age of the individual genius—brought one big consolation to those of us who want to achieve renown: You no longer need to be posh or educated to do it. In fact, if we believe what Coleridge says above, then reasoning and fluent expression are disadvantages.

As if the political revolution in France of 1789 wasn't enough, along with the parallel, more peaceful transformations in British society, the intellectual revolution was also changing the nature of who became famous. Take the examples of Mozart and Beethoven. Mozart kept trying to become a freelance musician and composer, even though it was safer for him to stay with his regular employer, the archbishop of Salzburg. But he risked losing his job once when he went absent without leave. When the archbishop was in Vienna, he summoned Mozart; but rather than deal with the composer directly, he put a courtier, Count Arco, on the case. These discussions are notable not least because, on June 9, 1781, the count not only made Mozart sit at the servants' table, along with the people whose job it was to light candles, but he also kicked Mozart's arse. We know this because Mozart wrote to his father:

> *If he was really so well disposed towards me, he ought to have reasoned quietly with me—or have let things take their course, rather than throw such words about as "clown" and "knave" and hoof a fellow out of the room with a kick on his arse. . . .*

By the time Beethoven was dealing with his patrons, the situation was completely different. One evening he called on Prince Lichnowsky, carrying the manuscript of his *Appassionata* Sonata. The prince was entertaining some of Napoléon's troops. This was

already enough to anger Beethoven: He was depressed that Napoléon's wars, which had seemed to be in the name of liberty and the
values of the Revolution, were in fact in the name of Napoléon's
glory. (Beethoven was so dejected when Napoléon crowned himself emperor that he scratched out the original dedication to the
*Eroica* Symphony.) But worse still, the composer was expected to
play for these troops. He stomped out into a rainstorm, which
spattered his manuscript, and on returning home is supposed to have
written the widely quoted lines, "Prince, you are what you are by
accident of birth. There is, and always will be, only one Beethoven."

Mozart would have loved the spectacle of genius trumping nobility, but it would have staggered him. Still, Wordsworth had already been trying to write poetry in "the plain language of men,"
with results that ranged from the moving to the painful.* Now it
was the time for people to come from anywhere and dazzle the
world, just as Beethoven had.†

One striking example of this was John Clare (1793–1864), a poet
who showed that there's no such thing as a plain man or plain language. He was a farm laborer from Northamptonshire at whom
people marveled, baffled, when he arrived in London as a published
poet. He could see sharply through the inanity of it:

> *Surely the vanity would have kill'd me 4 years ago if I had
> known then how I should have been hunted up—and extolld
> by personal flattery—but let me wait another year or two and
> the peep show will be over—and my vanity if I have any will
> end in its proper mortification to know that obscurity is happi-
> ness and that John Clare the thresher in the onset and neglected
> ryhmer [sic] in the end are the only two comfortable periods of
> his life.*

---

* Some poems—"Tintern Abbey," the "Intimations on Immortality" ode —really are
sublime, but for examples of Wordsworth at his worst, it's hard to beat "Ellen Irwin, or,
The Braes of Kirtle."
† Beethoven did end up being much more famous than Mozart in his lifetime. Although
Mozart wasn't exactly thrown into a pit and there was a funeral for him, the turnout
was jolly low; like Mozart, Beethoven was buried in Vienna and had a cortège of
twenty thousand.

But then, it's the part about the threshing that accounts for the fame, just as contestants on *American Idol* get surges of sympathy if they're plumbers and/or sing only in their bathrooms (or bathrooms they might be working on). Even before the Romantic age, this kind of thing was appealing, and we can see Giorgio Vasari paving the way for it in his *Lives of the Artists*. His account of the young Giotto is pleasingly quaint, combining as it does a Renaissance excitement about innate talent with a more ancient pastoral scene. Giotto's father lets the lad look after sheep, and who should pass by the field but the great painter Cimabue:

> *He came across Giotto who, while the sheep were grazing near by, was drawing one of them by scratching with a slightly pointed stone on a smooth clean piece of rock. And this was before he had received any instruction except for what he saw in nature itself.*

The story is satisfyingly similar to the tale of the teenage Alfie Boe, an apprentice mechanic from Fleetwood, Lancashire, who was cleaning a car in the garage when someone from a recording company heard him sing. Boe has since performed at Glyndebourne and in the English National Opera. Stories like this hearten many of us because they teach us that, with our own special gift, we too should be famous. Never mind the dictum of the 1980s television show that "fame costs, and right here's where you start paying—in sweat." Never mind that, for all the excitement about Leona Lewis working as a waitress/receptionist when she won *The X-Factor,* she had been in stage schools since she was five. Similarly, Kelly Clarkson's lawyers had to point out that some songs she had already recorded before she won *American Idol* were just demos and involved no contract. It's the innate talent that turns the heads of the crowd; understandably, the training is of less interest to us than the miracle.

Still, pop music takes the idea of the untrained genius to a new level. It's something inherent to the blues and also to punk: the notion that raw feeling should take precedence over complexity. The idea of a BRIT School, where people can go and learn to be pop stars, seems inimical to the whole art form. But then, every-thing a musician does is learning. In his book *Outliers: The Story of Success*, Malcolm Gladwell calculates that between 1960 and 1964, the Beatles had performed twelve hundred times together. In in-terviews Paul McCartney, for one, has sometimes been low-key about the impulse that led him and John Lennon to write their own songs—they were simply running out of material to cover.

Whatever it was that made them great, the Beatles took this cre-ative kind of fame to a new level. They were prolific, and the more they produced, the more sophisticated their work became. By the time of *Sgt. Pepper's Lonely Hearts Club Band,* there was a meeting of many minds: The adoring fans were at one with a growing band of academics such as George Steiner, who once remarked that the ascendancy of the Beatles was the last time England as a country was producing anything in English that made a difference to the English-speaking world.* In addition, their songs won the admi-ration of musical scholars such as William J. Mann of *The Times* and Wilfrid Mellers. Mellers was at once capable of pointing out the plagal cadence at the end of "She's Leaving Home" and of praising the music as if it was naive:

> The essence of [the Beatles] was this guileless honesty, the spirit of Beatle genius is what we call its adolescence, this pristine ver-bal consciousness.

The Beatles enjoyed global mastery; John Lennon bragged that they were more famous than Jesus. They were clear that drugs were among their influences; the work of Dr. Timothy Leary and others had led to the belief that these were mind-enhancing or mind-expanding (which assumes that there is a mind to expand in the first place). This all seems at first to sate Faust's ambitions for power and glory, with some chemical magic thrown in. But if that's the case, how do we explain the innocence that Wilfrid Mellers celebrates? Perhaps the clue is in his word "adolescence"; perhaps

---

* Surely Monty Python and *The Office* can be appended to this.

the clue is in the nature of the 1960s. But then, in the 1960s, much of the world was adolescent, with an adolescent's belief that pretty much anything was possible. For a moment, there was a break-through that built on the success of the Romantic Age. To be worth listening to, you didn't need to sell your soul to the devil; you just needed a soul.

# 5

## Divas and Divinities: Are
## Celebrities (Anything) Like Gods?

### i. Intimacy

Angelina Jolie went into a pub. The pub was on Sauchiehall Street in Glasgow; it was called The Gate and isn't there anymore. She was paying a visit to the set of *Trainspotting* and, as Saul Metzstein, at the time a production assistant, recalls, "We had to take her out for a drink in Glasgow":

> *I remember every guy's head literally turning as she walked in. One particular individual walked into a pillar with his pint because he was staring at her so transfixedly. Importantly, it wasn't recognition that captivated them—she wasn't yet a star. It was just that here was this ridiculously beautiful girl in a very average Glasgow boozer—she shouldn't have existed in that universe.*

This kind of beauty can happen, but after a certain point, it strikes us as just wrong. The twentieth-century Greek poet Yannis Ritsos puts it so well when he writes that beauty stares at us "as though we were the ones who'd made the mistake."

Why isn't a Sauchiehall Street pub the place for such visions? Metzstein is right; it just isn't. The clichéd but likely answer is that things we see that appear to come from movies don't belong in our ordinary lives; we go to see films knowing full well that they're not real, and the occurrence of such glamour really is a blurring of worlds. But it's possible to suggest a religious answer as well, and to consider the idea that some sights and sounds come from a place beyond us.

Just as our source says, the important thing is that, at the time, Angelina Jolie wasn't recognizable, but everyone knew that she was not of their welkin. There is something about our response to the famous that reveals the difference between them and us in a way that becomes spiritual. As we have already seen, over the ages, famous people are marked out as chosen offerings, are consecrated and sacrificed; we're drawn to the idea of "killing the god." But what visions do they vouchsafe us now, and do celebrities somehow fit in with ideas of religious belief over the ages? Were gods ever celebrities, and can celebrities be gods now?

People do say that they can feel the presence of God. But most of us doubt that we will ever see Him or Her. Plenty believe that Christ was born in human form, moved among us, and will appear to the world in the flesh once more. But as we go about our lives, we don't expect to see apparitions from an eternal, untarnishable world outside of our experience. And you would have thought the same would be true for the ancient Greeks, who had the same sorts of eyes in their heads, roughly, as we do, and ought to have had the same sort of relationship with their senses.

And it's true that, for the most part, they didn't see the gods. But, like many among us, people really wanted to see them. To do so, you had to have a god's favor, and nobody could be reliably sure of that. Stalkers today must feel a similar excitement when they sight their prey: He's appearing to me! And, like celebrities with restraining orders, gods hated being seen when they weren't ready to be seen. One version we have for why Teiresias went blind is because he saw Athene in her bath. Actaeon was chewed up by his own hounds because he saw Artemis, the goddess of chastity, naked. But these were people from an earlier age—the age about which the Greeks devised myths. Then gods could appear in as many forms as they pleased, and Zeus, when he went courting, could be a swan, or a bull, or a golden shower, or a bolt of lightning. This last disguise shows the problem with seeing gods, especially one as potent as Zeus.

Ancient peoples went about thinking that, although they didn't see gods these days, their ancestors did. A poem by Catullus links this fall from grace to the slaughter of the Trojan War, and in particular the carnage Achilles caused. In his *Histories,* Herodotus tries to work out how long ago Egyptians could see gods, and calculates that it was 11,340 years earlier. And it surprises Herodotus when the Athenians, of all people, think they have seen a god. He describes how the tyrant Pisistratus found a tall, statuesque woman, dressed her in a suit of armor, put her on a chariot, and claimed that she was Athene. This was taken to be a sign of the great honor in which the goddess held the mortal. The Athenians fell for this and "spread this nonsense all around town." Herodotus's tone here tells us how impossible it was that the goddess really did arrive. Even so, people were prepared to believe that Athene would make this unique appearance just for Pisistratus. It suggests that the Athenians really wanted to see a god among them, just as we might want to see Angelina Jolie, even though their reason told them how unlikely this would be.

All this is a reminder of the gulf that separates us from deities. But we do see the lines as blurrier further back, in the age of heroes, and the age of Homer's characters that followed—in fact, some of their divinity becomes transferred to humans early on. In the *Iliad,* Achilles is regularly referred to as *dios,* godlike, and so is Odysseus in the *Odyssey.* Achilles is the son of a goddess, the sea nymph Thetis, but he is mortal. His mortality is one of the most heroic things about him. In the *Odyssey,* Odysseus is godlike in different ways; often he is godlike because Athene, goddess of wisdom, has made him so.

Not only are these heroes godlike; they are also blessed enough to have fairly regular commerce with the gods. For a moment, we have a vision of what it would be like if we really could try to take on our latter-day gods. At one point in the *Iliad,* Achilles yells at Apollo, but recognizes the limits of his own power to sway or harm the god. At an earlier point, gods become involved in a fight with humans, and Diomedes injures Aphrodite, which feels less than gallant. Often the drama dictates that the gods arrive at moments of crisis—when Achilles is about to stab his king, Agamemnon, for example, or when Priam evades certain death by going into Achilles' compound to retrieve his son's body from the man who slew him in such a frenzy of rage and vengeance; the Trojan king is accompanied by Hermes, disguised as a beautiful young prince.

As it turns out, unusual beauty, like Jolie's in the pub, is one of the signs that you are in the presence of a god. Gods are real enough to Odysseus—they are his constant companions or obstacles on his long journey home to Ithaca—and so when he arrives at a new island, he's wise to be cautious. When he is washed up on the Phaeacian shore, he is stark naked and hides in the bushes because he hears girls playing with a ball. Out he steps and they flee in terror, except for Nausicaa, who is emboldened by Athene to stay. As Odysseus starts to talk his way out of this delicate situation, he addresses Nausicaa as if she were a goddess, and suggests to her that she is Artemis. Later, Odysseus has a bath, and then it becomes his turn to assume divine beauty: Athene pours grace on him and gilds his good looks. As a result, the king of Phaeacia, Alcinoos, assumes that Odysseus, too, is a god. The quality Athene adds to the bathwater is *charis*, grace—she completes her grace-giving work—a word the Greeks gave to a goddess in her own right, and then to the three Graces. *Charis* in this context is the divine favor we see in a person that accounts for his or her outer beauty. It helps us understand why he or she is different from the rest of us.

This is just one way in which humans can seem to be divine. In the Greek world, men and women would be more on the lookout for gods among them at times of unease or anxiety, such as when the suitors who have squatted on Odysseus's island while he is away sense that something is amiss, and one refers to the gods as "spies in disguise"—figures who are possibly always there, and watching over our transgressions. In later times, this theme has recurred in the tales of kings who dress as paupers to see how their kingdoms are doing. The idea that anyone could turn out to be a god is more ancient than the Greeks, and forms a self-interested motive for that crucial virtue, hospitality: In Hindu culture, if a guest enters your house, you must offer something to eat or drink, in case you are in fact entertaining a god. In Ovid's *Metamorphoses,* Zeus and Hermes do just this—they go among mortals, asking for food and shelter, and find to their dismay that the only people willing to provide them are Baucis and Philemon, an elderly couple who appear to make the most of nothing. The gods reward this pair and punish the rest of the world, making the moral clear—you will never know the hour of our coming.

As a result, people in the ancient Mediterranean were on the lookout for gods the whole time, which could be socially awkward. The apostle Paul was caught up in it on his travels. He traveled to Lystra with Barnabas, and there he told a man to stand up who had never walked. When the man stood, the crowd exclaimed, "The gods have come down to us in human form!" They called Barnabas Zeus, and Paul Hermes. The crowd nearly offered them a sacrifice, too, but Paul stopped them, saying, "We are mortals just like you, and we bring you good news."

As the historian of antiquity Robin Lane Fox points out, later Christians were less scrupulous and became quick to manipulate pagan ideas of divine power. The inventor Hero of Alexandria had worked on ways of making statues appear to move, and craftsmen worked on ways of giving them amplified talking heads. Rather than rejecting these potent icons, Christians explained to those who believed in them that actually it was Christ working miracles through the statues.

To many Christians, this kind of thing would count as blasphemy, and explains Paul's shocked rending of his clothes in Lystra. Christ does what Christ does, and would surely not make Himself manifest through pagan toys. The most noticeable difference between the ancient gods and the Christ who took their place is that there were so many of them and they acted as the worst sorts of humans—jealous and vindictive. On the other hand, there was just the one Christ, and He appeared to show how humanity could become perfect by being like Him. In either case, divine beings were there to set us an example, just as famous people always have done. But there is another way of looking at ancient religious experience that links it much more intuitively to Christianity: It is the way followed by philosophers such as Pythagoras, who believed that there is a divine soul that moves through all of us. As Joni Mitchell reminds us, we are stardust.

Even this idea, called Orphism, had its roots in the polytheistic universe of Greek mythology—giving it a cause, however fantastical, made it more believable. To cut a long story short, people who followed the cult of Orpheus believed that mankind is composed of the dust left over from the remains of the Titans, who were defeated by the gods, and the god Dionysus. As a result, humans are part god and part not god. The faith that resulted from this contested that everything in creation had some portion of the divine spark in it, from humans through flocks and birds down to plant life. Virgil gives the idea some of his most prophetic poetry, in the *Georgics*. Toward the end of his poem about farming and how to live in harmony with the earth, he contemplates bees, and what they teach us about the universe:

> *These signs and instances make people say*
> *that bees share in the godly mind, and drink*
> *heavenly draughts, because the god pervades*
> *all earth and tracts of sea and depths of sky;*
> *herds, flocks, men, all wild species come from this,*
> *whatever nascent thing summons sweet life:*
> *then all things, once released, return to it,*
> *and death has no place, but they live, to spin*
> *at star's level, to reach high in the sky.*

For this reason Pythagoras was fastidiously careful about what he ate. Some aspects of these ideas appealed to Plato, who preferred to see divine activity as something beyond human comprehension, and didn't like the idea of gods behaving badly. But then, without the idea of gods mucking around and scheming against each other, we would be less likely to call celebrities gods or goddesses now. It's almost never a moral judgment these days. But the Orphic view of the divine does have moral implications: For example, in this view you can be punished for your bad actions in the afterlife. A sense of this all-permeating godhead is picked up in Virgil, and chimes with the Christian notion of the Holy Ghost.

This is relevant to us because, according to this belief, everybody really is divine. No need for guessing; no need to go to the oracle at Delphi to see if a god's about or not; you can safely assume that anybody you meet is special in some way, and that you should love your neighbor as you would love yourself. What's more, you don't have to be a Homeric hero to feel the workings and presence of a deity; you could just as well be a slave to feel this inner kind of *charis*. By this line of thought, the balance of fame swings away from the gods, and toward mortals. Souls could progress into the next life in bigger and better forms; the possibilities of you becoming a god begin to open up. Now, this doesn't mean that everybody believed it. In fact, the ancient Greeks could dismiss it outright. In Euripides' play *Hippolytus,* Theseus talks of it abusively as cultish nonsense. And it was cultish, just as the worship of other gods could be. But it was there, somehow, among the earliest stirrings of Greek philosophy, and it existed alongside the stories about jock gods and catty goddesses.

Either way, the ancient Greek mind was well set to have intense and individual experiences of divinity. As Lane Fox points out, there was a mixture of awe and intimacy in these encounters. On the one hand, according to the philosopher Iamblichus, "No mortal eye or mind could ever contain the size or beauty of a pure divinity's arrival." But then, they did not always put on such productions. They weren't just to be seen; their votaries could hear gods or feel them. The gods could appear in dreams, as Pan often did, giving out advice, such as telling a man that his wife was cheating on him. Pan would preside over orgies, too, particularly where a woman would take multiple partners. In a piece of fiction from about the second century A.D., perhaps reflecting a local custom, a man who had doubts about his wife's virginity could take her to a cave where Pan played his pipes. If she was chaste, he knew, Pan would make the sound of a sigh on his instrument. If she wasn't, he would hear a scream.

You could invite gods to dinner. Tickets have survived from Palmyra, so that you, too, could come to the banquet; the god Serapis would hold parties at which he was at once "host and guest." To the Romans, gods of the home and the hearth—the *lares* and *penates*—were just as vital as any. In Virgil's *Aeneid,* it is Aeneas's mission to find a new home for them. This can be compared to the companionable ease the Babylonians felt with their representations of gods: "Not only were they rendered by artisans in the most life-like manner, they were literally treated as such, with their daily meals and outings borne by the temple priests." Jews celebrating Pesach are surely doing something similar when they leave a space at the table in case Elijah should be passing by. In 2007 a judge in India summoned the gods Ram and Hanuman to a court. They had become involved in a property dispute with a priest, who claimed that some land belonged to him because a local king had given it to his grandfather. But his neighbors disagreed, saying that it be-longed to the gods. When Judge Sunil Kumar Singh sent out his summonses, they were returned because they had incomplete addresses; so he took to placing advertisements addressed to them in newspapers.

If these supreme beings can flit among us and make the occasional public appearance, what about the Christian God? Glimpses of Christ and of Mary have been intimate and intense, and those who have seen them have considered themselves blessed. As we'll see, the unexpected nature of the encounters can have something in common with the celebrity dream. Perhaps the best known is the experience of Saint Teresa of Ávila:

> *I saw in [a seraph's] hands a long golden spear, and at the point of the iron there seemed to be a little fire. This I thought that he thrust several times into my heart, and that it penetrated to my entrails. When he drew out the spear he seemed to be drawing them with it, leaving me all on fire with a wondrous love for God. The pain was so great that it caused me to utter several moans; and yet so exceeding sweet is this greatest of pains that it is impossible to desire to be rid of it, or for the soul to be content with less than God.*

Teresa here has the awe and intimacy simultaneously. It's a striking example of a human being having a direct experience of God Himself; striking because even this didn't happen so much to Christian mortals. As Christianity spread around the Mediterranean, it was less likely that humans would have a hotline to God, and more likely that they would go through an intermediary, such as a saint.

These saints were a strange mix of the patron—in Roman tradition a big and powerful man would bestow favors on lesser ones, in exchange for his own prestige—and of the imaginary friend. So a saint would be someone outside of you—whom you would praise, perpetuating his or her memory after death—and also inside of you. People would call this figure their daimon; it's the Greek word for spirit or genius that is now a more familiar idea thanks to Philip Pullman's His Dark Materials trilogy. The relationship becomes so cozy that there are moments when the saint becomes you. If, as Plutarch argued, the soul has a supersoul of its own, that is as superior to the rest of the soul as the rest of the soul is to the body, then in the Christian world, this higher part would be given over to the special companion and protector. It meant that people could sign off letters as "Your Angel," because a better part of them was involved in the correspondence. Your connection with a deceased (though eternal) saint can in turn make you more famous, too.

This shows us how a special kind of mortal can give us the feeling of something divine and bestow on us at least a hint of heavenly grace. The Christian development is that this favor is available to everyone, rather than just those Homeric heroes who would outstrip the rest of us in valor and beauty, thanks to their divine favor, or those Olympic athletes who were never to forget that their victory belonged as much to the gods as to them.

There have always been ways for humans to be gods by representing them, either falsely, as Pisistratus's tall look-alike did in Athens, or as proxies, as the human victims did in Aztec sacrifices. In ancient Greece, you could even have sex with a goddess. Phryne was simultaneously a courtesan and also a priestess of Aphrodite. She would take on the role of the goddess in a reenactment of her birth, emerging from the water. As the ancient historian James Davidson writes of her, "A statue of the courtesan (as herself) was placed beside that of Aphrodite in Thespiae in the Temple of Eros, the city's most important cult, a cult that many think Phryne founded."

Human beings can seal their fame by becoming gods in battle, too, such as the slain Vikings who would go and dine with Thor and Odin in Valhalla. The Spartans would carry the mortal remains of the hero Orestes into battle with them, and this was as effective a standard as a god would have been. If we project from the kinds of spiritual presences felt by soldiers in all conflicts, up to and beyond the "Angel of Mons" in the First World War, it doesn't seem too idle to add to them the names of the army pinups, and the characters such as Betty Grable, Jane Russell, and Rita Hayworth, who would be painted on the sides of airplanes, or Jean Hay, who hosted the radio show *Reveille with Beverly* and assured her U.S. Air Force listeners that "the turntables are loaded and they're bustin' with bounce."

But celebrities? Now? Can we have an experience of them that is at once intimate and awesome? Well, they do awe all the time—on the catwalk, on the red carpet, on the screen, on the gridiron. Intimacy, you would think, would be much harder. Once we have intimacy with somebody we see as coming from another realm, then, perhaps, we are feeling something that could be compared to a religious feeling. After all, when receiving a prayer in older English, God expects worshippers to address Him as "Thou," which might sound formal to us but is really the more familiar form of "you"; so in French "He" is *tu,* not *vous.* In Yiddish, the Hebrew G-d is called by the term of endearment *Gotteniu.* If we are truly to believe, then we need to feel that closeness is at least possible, even if we don't feel that closeness for ourselves.

Evidence of this kind—of ordinary folk feeling close to celebrities—is hard to collect. Sharing knowledge of our dreams is helping us to understand how people can either feel intimate with the famous or project their own concerns onto these suddenly less remote figures. In his book about Jacqueline Kennedy-Onassis, Wayne Koestenbaum shares details of his own two dozen nightly visits from the former first lady, and also wonders (playfully) if different celebrities can symbolize different things. The blog I Dream of Both has invited people to submit their own dreams about the contenders for the presidency in 2008.★ (In one, a gay man imagines making out with Barack Obama, only to be thrown out of the house by John McCain's mother.)

In 1993 Kay Turner published a collection of dreams women had told her they'd had about Madonna. At the time when she was gathering the material, she was researching into folklore, and the idea of Madonna as divine had already struck her powerfully. In the introduction she wrote:

> Like a (virgin) goddess, she gleefully released the contents of her own Pandora's Box, which among other things contained Aphrodite's love girdle refigured as a golden bustier, Artemis' bow transformed into a microphone, Athena's Gorgon shield revealed to be a Boy Toy belt, and the Virgin Mary's blue mantle translated into a black slip.

Now, even by the comparison-happy standards of the present book, Kay Turner takes the analogies a bit far—any further and Madonna could end up as Demeter, goddess of corn. But she is right, I think, to see her as a numinous presence for those to whom she appears, but also as familiar, in the two senses of recognizable and comfortable:

> Interestingly, women don't seem to dream of Madonna as an unapproachable superstar. . . . In fact, the theme that most widely characterizes the dreams in this collection is that of friendship with Madonna. The dreamer realizes that Madonna wants to get to know her or that the two are really friends.

Even when this chumminess is taking place, the dreamers are aware that although she is theirs by night, her day job is still being a public and famous person. Chris, aged thirty-five, says that in her dream that Madonna "was really friendly, and it was almost as

---

★ I have had a dream about Barack Obama, in which we were leaning on a radiator and having a beer at one of those parties where there aren't real glasses. He was glad he could sit and talk to a friend for once. That's about it.

though she wasn't even a celebrity." Denise, aged fourteen, dreamed she was onstage at her school air band contest, and she was joined by "Madonna—I really mean *Madonna*." A bunch of contributors dreamed of having sex with her. One appeared in her own dream as a man, and gave Madonna a sheep s/he fetched out of a lake.

In other dreams, Madonna helped the dreamers overcome some trauma from the past, or made them feel more confident about their fantasies or the future. She filled that role the gods once occupied, of being present in trouble or arriving at times of anxiety. This explains why the god who would appear to the ancients most often would be Asclepius, the god of healing. It helps us understand, too, why so many have turned to the late Diana, Princess of Wales, especially since her death.* There is at least one seer who does a number in relaying Diana's advice to us from beyond the grave. At Diana's funeral, her brother referred to her "constituency of the dejected." From that moment, her life was perceived to have been one of constant mortification, as though she couldn't enjoy mortal love like the rest of us, suffered from bulimia, had no privacy, and struck up a rapport with anyone in difficulty. It doesn't matter if any of this is true or not. The point is that many of her mourners felt that they had a private relationship with her, as though they were following her on some kind of journey.

As in other religious experiences, people who have such visions can see that there is good that they can do for their visitor. Just as the Bacchant women not only delight in their god Dionysus, but also serve him by honoring his rites, and as Christians will go out to do good works in the name of Jesus, so dreamers want to help the famous. In the Madonna dreams, one ends up rescuing her from an encounter with a creepy guy. Those whom Diana has helped must wish that they could help her in return. And Gloria Steinem has identified that many men's experiences of Marilyn Monroe amount to what she calls "rescue fantasies."

It's easy to throw around the epithet "goddess" or "god," but the

---

* A book of dreams about Diana appeared as early as January 1998 (ed. Rita Frances, Robson Books). Its 130 pages could doubtless be expanded now.

more we do so, the less divine our own celebrity gods and goddesses become: We lower the wall that separates our realm from the one Angelina Jolie inhabits. Like sportsmen, warriors, and the beautiful, even the gods are becoming trashier these days. A splendid recent book plays with this idea: in *Gods Behaving Badly* (2007), by Marie Phillips, the ancient Greek deities are living in a tatty house in Hampstead: Artemis takes dogs for walks, Dionysus is a DJ, Apollo does spells on daytime television, Eros is becoming Christian, and Zeus is dying. One of the poignant things about the satire is the way in which the gods are losing their power, and they must try hard to preserve their energy.

But if we are allowed to find the divine among mortals, then surely Marilyn Monroe is the acme. This became true because we allowed it to become true. It wasn't that she was beautiful or a great singer or a fine actor (although she was all of these); it was that somehow she came to look like somebody who came from a better world. She married a man better at sports than other men, and then she married a man who was cleverer than most other men. In the excellent play *Insignificance,* Terry Johnson has her explaining the 1905 theory of relativity to Einstein and then seducing him. It feels right.

The career as deity reaches its peak when she sings "Happy Birthday" to JFK. This performance isn't Marilyn Monroe; it's Marilyn Monroe doing Marilyn Monroe, just as Phryne took off Aphrodite in ceremonies. The breathy voice is breathier still; the torchsong singer slows it right down for her man, and Kennedy laughs. He, too, can get away with this kind of thing; so long as we don't know about the prescription drugs and the desperate, indiscriminate sex, they both lead charmed lives.

She'd done a similar self-impersonation in the 1955 film *The Seven-Year Itch,* in which she played a character called "The Girl." When Tom Ewell's character hides her in the bath and a neighbor asks who's in there, he says it could be anyone—"for all you know, it could be Marilyn Monroe." So in her own lifetime, she had accepted roles that told her audience, "I'm not a real person." The otherworldly person, the Marilyn Monroe who was beyond

Marilyn Monroe, belonged on a sphere with the president of the United States.

They would both be dead soon, but this makes them less, rather than more, mortal. They appeared among us briefly, and didn't grow old. They fulfilled their divine roles just as they were supposed to, and left a range of myths behind them.

### ii. Awe

In A.D. 54 Nero became emperor. People loved him. They were even relaxed about his singing. He was the adopted son of the previous emperor, Claudius. Nero went to some trouble to have his predecessor deified. This, surely, would have given Nero the stamp of divinity he needed to command the Roman people. And yet, not long into his reign, a book appeared called *The Pumpkinification of the Divine Claudius.* The title suggests that Claudius went up to heaven but ended up as a pumpkin.

The book is probably by Seneca, a stern moralist who was one of Nero's closest advisers. Seneca bore a grudge against Claudius, who had banished him to Corsica (there are worse fates). So he wrote a satire that travesties the notion that Claudius could become a god. In his version, Claudius appears at Mount Olympus as a stammering, murderous gambler, and when he tries to explain who he is, none of the gods can understand a word he's saying. Once one of them has recognized him, they debate whether he should stay or go. In the end they send him to Hades, and decide that, just as Tantalus will always reach for fruit, only to have it withdrawn from him, so Claudius will be condemned to play with dice with a bottomless box, so that he has to spend eternity fumbling about for the things when they fall out. He wasn't just a loser; he was banned from the roulette table. So Claudius's hell was a bit like Vegas, only without the bright lights and the dancing girls.

One interpretation of Seneca's lampoon is that Claudius became a god too easily. The senate was sending too many of them to Mount Olympus, and it was time be more selective. One of the gods who speaks out against Claudius's admission is Augustus, who had been emperor himself and didn't want the honor of becoming a god to be abused. In any case, if there were so many gods, why should anyone believe in them? So Nero seems to have sanctioned Claudius's loss of sanctity. But he paid for it in the end. Although most citizens continued to love Nero until his death, he was disposable. He was hounded out of power and was killed himself. He didn't become a god. In the following year, A.D. 69, the throne changed bottoms three times.

We saw earlier how our relationship with gods and/or celebrities can be a private affair. The late Princess of Wales's acolytes can find some aspect of her that makes her just like them, and feel that she shares their pain. The opposite is true with these imperial gods, who have enjoyed a controlling power over the masses. Even when Roman emperors were changing rapidly, as if there were a revolving door at the imperial palace, they still sent images of themselves around the Roman world, to sit above shrines and to receive sacrifices. These weren't so much "spies in disguise" as the constant face of Big Brother, watching the citizens of the empire. It reveals a different sort of fame—the sort that's insecure about how long it lasts. As a result, it takes the form of control-freakery, and takes self-promotion to the highest level possible. The only way from this bad eminence is down, so that today our irreverence feels healthy, and something we can wear like the cap of a freed slave.

In spite of all this, Roman emperors made themselves seem more glorious as time went by. It was a sure sign that they were more worried that their fame would pass. This was legally true: If they didn't deliver, then there was every chance that the senate would pass their harshest judgment on their rulers—the *damnatio memoriae,* by which it was decreed that they had never existed. It was the opposite of being promoted to heaven. This anxiety meant that imperial cults would become more and more dominant throughout the history of the Roman empire. In the Ara Pacis, the Altar of Peace that became a key part of the iconography surrounding the emperor Augustus, the ruler appears among his family, and is on a level with the priests and celebrants of the sacrifice. Even Nero, whom we associate with public cruelty and delusions of grandeur, allowed himself to be seen doing his own thing. In his *History of the Decline and Fall of the Roman Empire*, Edward Gibbon suggested that the reason people were prepared to believe such extraordinary things about Nero was not only because he had killed his wife and mother, but also because he was too freely visible: "Nor could the prince who prostituted his person and dignity on the theater be deemed incapable of the most extravagant folly." No, for much of the Roman empire, emperors had to be men of the people, and they relied not only on the support of the senate but also, more important, on the goodwill of their former companions in arms from the officers' mess.

But the empire became big—so big that it eventually needed splitting into two—and in the early fourth century, an emperor converted to Christianity. Constantine secured his own control of the empire and the Battle of the Milvian Bridge in 312. The night before he did so, he looked at the sky. People had often done this as a way of seeing gods; often gods appeared to mortals as shapes in the clouds, or as constellations. Now Constantine saw the Greek letters *chi* and *rho* combined, standing for Christ, and the words *"In hoc signo vinces"*—in this sign you will conquer. Along with God's appearance to Saul of Tarsus on the road to Damascus, this is the manifestation of a god that has done the most to change the history of the world.

The results for the history of fame were that some human beings could somehow become even more divine, more special, more remote from the rest of us. The emperor now became more than somebody who may or may not be elected as a god on the say-so of the senate after he had died; he became a representative of a single, unchanging, eternal God. At around the same time, the representation of emperors became more otherworldly, too: The Colossus of Constantine in Rome was about forty feet high. Before long, the appearances of emperors were rigorously controlled. Not long after the death of Constantine came Constantius II, whom the writer Ammianus Marcellinus praises because he "maintained in every way the prestige of the imperial majesty, and his great and lofty spirit disdained popularity." Here is Ammianus's account of Constantius's entry into Rome in 357:

*Saluted as Augustus, he never stirred when the roar thundered
back from the hills and shores . . . as if his neck were fastened,
he kept his gaze straight ahead and did not turn his face to right
or left; and—as if he were a sculpted figure—he was never seen
to droop his head when his carriage-wheel jolted, or to spit, or to
wipe or rub his face or nose or move his hand. Although this was
a studied attitude on his part, yet these and certain other features
of his inner life were indications of no ordinary endurance, or so
it was given out, granted to him alone.*

The comment about the statue is revealing: It recognizes that
by now, even when representations of emperors were becoming
further removed from what people actually look like, they still
had to look as much as possible like the media through which they
were seen. Ammianus notes, by the way, that Constantius II was
small in real life.

The historian Geoffrey de Ste Croix says that "from the mid-
third century onwards . . . barbarian irruptions began to threaten
the very fabric of the empire, and the social evils the regime bred
within itself became more apparent and more evidently harmful."
So the Goths were coming, and the office of emperor had begun to
look too humanly fallible. In addition, a faith was gaining domi-
nance that saw this world as transitory. The late Roman empire becomes a time of fear—an age when leaders traded on awe, and those
associated with them did everything they could to emphasize even
the subtlest nuances of superiority. As de Ste Croix tells us: "There
were now more grades within the senatorial order: the lowest were
*clarissimi,* then came *spectabiles* and finally *illustres;* by the mid-fifth
century the most illustrious were *magnificentissimi* and even *gloriosis-
simi.*" By this point they were exhausting words that mean "the most
famous"; you could use those words to translate even the humblest
rank on this hierarchy.

And who were these cronies? Ryszard Kapuściński witnessed
the last days of Haile Selassie, emperor of Abyssinia, and offers an
answer. Selassie may well have discouraged the kind of reverence

that led Rastafarians to proclaim him as the messiah, but as he reigned, he maintained his profile zealously:

> *The condition for remaining in the Emperor's circle was practis-ing the cult of the Emperor, and whoever grew weak and lost eagerness in the practice of this cult lost his place, dropped out, disappeared. Haile Selassie lived among the shadows of himself, for what was the Imperial suite if not a multiplication of the Emperor's shadow? Who were gentlemen like Akliku, Gebre-Egzy, Admassu Retta, aside from being H.S.'s ministers? No-bodies. But it was precisely such people the Emperor wanted around him. Only they could satisfy his vanity, his self-love, his passion for the stage and the mirror, for gestures and the pedestal.*

Power systems establish their own groupies and entourages— their own hints that we, too, could get intimate with the awesome. But the luster this gives us is fleeting, and not even our own. The horror of this situation is that our sense of who we are depends on others. It is as though we live in a "Total Perspective Vortex"—the name Douglas Adams gives to a machine that shows us how insig-nificant we are in relation to the rest of the universe. In Adams's *The Hitchhiker's Guide to the Galaxy,* one character discovers that in fact he is quite significant in comparison to creation. His name is Zaphod Beeblebrox, and he has two heads. Even in the system Ad-ams devises, there is the possibility of mattering to others beyond the time and space allotted to us. In his *Symposium,* Plato shows how all humans do this, and, as Plato tends to, he puts us on a lad-der. Most of us, he says, leave something to posterity in the form of children. Others go a step further by writing things that will sur-vive us. But the very best sort of fame, Plato tells us, is to be earned by making laws. The problem is that this last category of fame be-comes warped in the hands of the most immortality-seeking rulers, for whom the best sort of monument is evidence that their subjects damn well did what they were told.

Most of the time, our treatment of famous people is a systematic cycle of celebration, consecration, and sacrifice; and the sacrifice can take the form of humiliation or neglect. But the allure of fame leads some to think they can buck this. They are the emperors; the kings who built the Louvre and Versailles; the monarchs who believed they wielded a divine right; the president of Turkmenistan, Saparmurat Nyazov, who sought to have months of the year named after members of his family. They are all like the unnamed leader in Ngũgĩ wa Thiong'o's satire, *Wizard of the Crow,* who proposes to build a Tower of Babel so that he can climb up it and talk to God. And fame is all the more alluring because the effort is in vain. The fear this sense of futility instills is precisely what makes the quest as desperate as it is.

As it turns out, not even gods are immortal. After all, even the gods can grow old, too, and need replacing, so that springs and harvests and life itself can be replaced and refreshed. James Frazer explains that "at an early stage of his intellectual development man deems himself naturally immortal, and imagines that were it not for the baleful arts of sorcerers, who cut the vital thread prematurely, he would live for ever." But then we realized that we were doomed to die, and that humans did not perish out of individual instances of magic, but because of "mysteries in the universe which [man's] feeble intellect can never fathom, and forces which his puny hands can never control":

> But if he reluctantly acknowledged the existence of beings at once superhuman and supernatural, he was as yet far from suspecting the width and the depth of the gulf which divided him from them. The gods with whom his imagination now peopled the darkness of the unknown were indeed admitted by him to be his superiors in knowledge and in power, in the joyous splendour of their life and in the length of its duration. But, though he knew it not, these glorious and awful beings were merely . . . the reflections of his own diminutive personality exaggerated into gigantic proportions by distance and by the mists and clouds of ignorance upon which they were cast.

If we believe this, and take Frazer's deductions from it seriously, then our need to kill gods becomes a matter of our own survival. We need our gods to be eternally potent, but if they're too much like us, then they won't be; so they need to be dispatched along the same lines as the rest of us. Christianity doesn't alter the picture much, because Christ Himself becomes another god whom humanity killed, in order to make Him stronger, and Christians now can replenish this strength in themselves every Sunday, by sharing His flesh and His blood.

We can see in the scribblings of Nero's apparatchik the germ of the same mortal insecurity. Nero wants to be divine, but does what he can to undo or subvert the divinity of his predecessor, Claudius. But Nero suffers the same fate: When he dies, the senate does not declare him to be a god.

So can we be gods and goddesses? Can we make people dream about us? Can we, too, wow the people we like, granting them our grace by appearing to them in unexpected places? Maybe we can. Maybe we can inspire a cult, along ancient classical lines. Maybe people will remember us after we've gone. But even if our devotees think we're divine, that's no guarantee that we'll live forever. For that kind of reassurance, we need a whole new definition of fame—one that the Christian martyrs will provide.

# 6

## Eternal Flame: Did the Early Christians Find a Way to Be Immortal?

Perpetua had been expecting her martyrdom. The emperor, Septimius Severus, was upholding the law that Christians who failed to renounce Christ should be executed. She'd been given every opportunity to recant her Christianity, and her father had begged her to choose this life, but she insisted on the next. When it was time to kill her and her maid, the slave Felicity, the organizers (or in the Christian account, the devil) sent out a cow. It was a joke that mocked their sex. Bulls were the animals reserved for women who had been taken in adultery; the cow was a gibe at their innocence. Innocence, but not virginity. The custom was that the victims be naked, but when these two appeared, the audience saw something that disturbed them: Perpetua was a mother whose son was still suckling; Felicity had given birth in the cells and was lactating. The cry went up that they should dress. There are odd moments in the history of fame when people shrink from their own ghoulishness, like readers of weekly magazines who no longer want to see Farah Fawcett or Amy Winehouse suffer. Even though the crowd in Carthage had paid to see slaughter, this was too much.

When the two reappeared, the cow rushed in and knocked them down, but it didn't kill them. Perhaps Perpetua was concussed: When she rose up again and saw the cow, she thought it hadn't attacked her yet. The faithful took this as a sign that she wasn't feeling the pain. But then, she was ready for pain. The man who had to put her to the sword was a novice: He pierced her between the bones, before she guided the blade to her own neck. "Perhaps so great a woman could not have been slain otherwise . . . had she not willed it herself."

The details of this martyrdom, which took place in 202 or 203 in Carthage, come from *The Passion of Saints Perpetua and Felicity*. The bulk of the document is Perpetua's own account of her trial and imprisonment, and of the visions she had during that time. (It is often said to be one of the first texts written by a Christian woman.) The denouement is recorded faithfully, and the afterword of the text is clear about why:

> *O blessed and valiant martyrs! O truly called and elected unto the glory of Our Lord Jesus Christ! Those who praise him who magnifies, honours and adores, should read these witnesses . . . so that these new wonders may testify that the same Holy Spirit works even now, and with Him God the Father Almighty, and His Son Jesus Christ Our Lord, to whom be glory and unend-·ing power for ever and ever. Amen.*

Today we remember the early Christians, and we remember them because of their deaths. Retrospectively, the day was about them becoming famous. After all, they were dying to eternal life, and were seeking to inspire others on earth in a full range of ways. But the man who paid for the show, provided the beasts, and took care of the arena thought that he was the one gaining the fame. Enter-taining the public with shows was a way of gaining political ad-vantage. Just as earlier, when Caesar was running for political office, the point of putting on spectacles with animals and gladiators was to make people admire you for your wealth and thank you for your generosity. The motive for this was "love of honor"—the sort of thing to which a Christian could aspire.

In the Roman world, public games were funded by private in-dividuals. They had to be done lavishly, and they had to be done right. They had to sort out which Christians would face the ani-mals, and which would fight the gladiators. It mattered to the bill-ing. Animals first, gladiators later. Then there were the executions. We're accustomed to think of public executions, at Tyburn or the Place de la Concorde, as entertaining days out, and so they were, full of music, markets, pickpocketing opportunities, and com-munal bloodletting. But for Romans, that was the boring part.

They had much better deaths to sit through. Gladiators executing people coincided with the lunch break, and was a tepid sort of
warm-up for the denouement—gladiators versus gladiators. When
Polycarp, the eighty-six-year-old bishop of Smyrna, was martyred,
the crowd urged the event's organizer, Philip the Asiarch, to let
loose a lion on him. But Philip wasn't going to change the program.
The slot for the wild beasts was over, perhaps for health and safety
reasons.★

It's worth remembering Paul Veyne's observation, mentioned
earlier, that fights between people who were forced to fight would
be no fun at all: The conscripts would look scared and perform
badly. The twist is that the martyrs thought that they were fighting, and fighting willingly. It's just that they had a different definition of victory. When Perpetua and Felicity survived the cow, the
crowd called them back to the Porta Sanavivaria, the Gate of the
Healthy and Alive, by which victorious gladiators would leave.
But they went back to receive their martyrdom.

This misunderstanding shows a meeting of two views of fame.
The crowd felt moved by the performance and wanted the two to
live; but the women hadn't yet won. Again, it suggests that although
the audience in Carthage wasn't full of Christians and wouldn't
be for maybe a century, for them, watching Christians dying for
their faith was an extraordinary phenomenon in itself. It raised the
tone of the whole games; even the lunchtime executions were worth
staying for.

And then there was the Christian view of fame. When we meet
Saint Augustine (in chapter 11) we will see that a Christian shouldn't
seek fame for his or her own account, but for the greater glory of
God. Nearly two centuries earlier, though, if a lawyer was trying
to persuade a Christian to convert, he could bring the charge of

---

★ The proconsul decided to execute Polycarp with fire instead. The symbolism in the
narrative of this martyrdom shows how early Christians would press their arguments by
using earthly images: "As soon as he had uttered the word 'Amen,' the officers lighted
the fire. The flame, forming the appearance of an arch, as the sail of a vessel filled with
wind, surrounded, as with a wall, the body of the martyr; which was in the midst, not as
burning flesh, but as gold and silver refining in the furnace."

vanity. In his book *Pagans and Christians*, Lane Fox devotes a lot of time to the martyrdom of Pionius, a man who refused to renounce his Christianity in 250. (You could do this by eating meat of an animal that had been sacrificed to a Roman god or, for that matter, to the Roman emperor.) When the orator and widely admired sophist Rufinus came to prosecute this Pionius in the agora at Smyrna, he said to him, "Do not strive for vainglory." As Lane Fox explains:

> *[Rufinus's] ideal of true value lay in public service, acclamations in the theatre and wild-beast shows, magistracies beyond the call of duty and civic buildings at personal expense. To die out of obstinacy, denying the gods in public, was a negation of such values, a theatrical self-indulgence.*

It strikes us as peculiar now that Christian martyrs should be seen as egotists. As Augustine argued, the glory should belong to God, and we have come to think of Christianity as the faith of the humble and meek. But if their detractors were right, and Christians were seeking fame, then they can be seen as a point at which two sorts of glory meet: Jewish ideas of martyrdom, chronicled faithfully by the rabbis; and the Greco-Roman tradition of winning crowns. The link with the Middle East, and with the faith the West was rejecting, seems strange to us, but it was real enough, and it presents the modern world with urgent problems. Lane Fox suggests that Islam picked up "the ideal of martyrdom" from Christians, rather than Jews, even if it had been the Jews whose uprisings against the Romans sparked the impulse for self-sacrifice and perpetual glory. In 1986 he was already able to write, "In the war against Iraq, the Iranian dead are publicized as martyrs, whose instant reward is granted in Paradise. Dreams of a martyr's glory impel boys to volunteer, as Christians once volunteered for trial." The parallel has become all too neat of late, as young men record themselves in the moments before they undertake missions in which death is certain and fame promised.

Saint Paul, with his genius for capturing the Zeitgeist, was quick to make the connection between martyrs and athletes. He knew his audience when he wrote to the Corinthians. He went for the sporting image:

> Know ye not that they which run in a race run all, but one re-
> ceiveth the prize? So run, that ye may obtain. And every man
> that striveth for the mastery is temperate in all things. Now they
> do it to obtain a corruptible crown, but we an incorruptible.

Saints are traditionally depicted with crowns. One reason for this might be a visual pun: The Greek for crown is *stephanos*, and Saint Stephen was the first Christian martyr. But crowns were for athletes. When Perpetua had a dream in prison, she saw herself in the arena, facing a stand-in for Satan:

> And an ill-favoured Egyptian came out with his helpers, to fight
> against me. Some comely young men came to me, too—my help-
> ers and aiders. And I was stripped naked, and I became a man.
> And my helpers began to rub me with oil as their custom is for a
> contest. . . . He tried to trip up my feet, but I smote him on the
> face with my heels.

She wins and goes with glory to the Porta Sanavivaria; then she wakes up. Her own part of her passion narrative ends there.

If one way for an antique Roman to impress those around him was circuses, the other was bread. It was a way of securing popular support, just as Silvio Berlusconi has contrived to do, by owning television stations and a football club. Christians, too, had their uses for both bread and circuses. Admittedly, Christians wouldn't have put on the bloody shows; it's just that they were an attraction—people found them compelling, not just because of the blood but because the audience could witness a faith whose otherworldliness was a feat in itself. But feeding people, as distinguished Romans did, fitted the Christian brief immediately. Indeed, it was one of the ways in which you could be Roman and Christian at once. When the senator, and later saint, Pammachius wanted to mark the year that had passed since the death of his wife, Paulina, he gave a feast for the poor in the Basilica of Saint Peter. Not all Roman dignitaries felt this way. One Lampadius, the prefect of Rome,

seeing the way in which things were changing, made a joke of it:
If the well-off were supposed to feed the people, he would parody
the process by feeding only the very poorest, not with the inten-
tion of being generous, but to stretch, as if comically, the idea of
what a person is. Ammianus Marcellinus tells the story:

> [Lampadius was] a man who took it very ill if even his manner
> of spitting was not praised, on the grounds that he did so with
> greater skill than anyone else. . . .* When this man, in his
> praetorship, gave magnificent games and made very rich distribu-
> tions of largesse, being unable to endure the blustering of the
> commons, who often urged that many things should be given to
> those who were unworthy of them, in order to show his generos-
> ity and contempt for the mob, he summoned some beggars from
> the Vatican and presented them with valuable gifts.

Using the language of the traditional Roman society, which was
based on the patron-client relationship, with reference to the culture of giving alms, Lampadius managed to show his contempt for
pretty much everybody. He decided he wouldn't give treats to the
*Volk,* and bestowed them instead on the *Untermenschen.* Another
motivation for this could have been that to mingle with the lowest
of the low would have done all the more to foreground his own
illustriousness.

Still, at least when the empire became increasingly Christian, a
network arose in which there was now the possibility for fairly
ordinary people to achieve wide fame. Before, cults of different
gods would prevail in different areas. Even if the cults of the saints
reproduced this kind of diversity, worshipping any one of them led
to the same God. This absolutely didn't lead to cohesion within
the emerging church—if anything, the vision of a City of God led
people to disagree about how to reach it. But its boundaries could
extend anywhere. For instance, Demetrias was a noblewoman who
had been expected to make some good marriage to revive her
family's fortunes. When she took the veil, Saint Jerome wrote to

---

* Surely this is the Latin equivalent of "He acts like his shit don't stink."

her saying that if she had married, she would have been known in one region only; now she would be acclaimed throughout the Christian world. Just as exists today, there was a kind of globalization that meant that people could be stars anywhere. Then, however, the forces that leaped borders were spiritual rather than economic.

As if running in parallel to actual Roman practice, the saints themselves would become patrons, and bishops would do their best to be associated with particular saints—not just in the intimate way mentioned in the previous chapter, whereby believers would have their own invisible friends or daimons, but also in very public ways. This kind of *charis* might begin at home, but it doesn't end there. Why not have a shrine built for your patron saint in your diocese? Why not build a basilica for him or her? Come to think of it, why not get some relics of the saint? These will turn out to be a terrific tourist attraction. A shrine to a saint is a great venue for annual processions, where boys can meet girls in ways they can't within the city walls. (The jokes about these fruitful meetings have lots in common with the ancient Greek lines about going as a maid to sacrifice and returning as a maid no more.)

To a believer, the presence of a relic can deliver that mixture of intimacy and awe—you are in the presence of the real person. The advantages of being in the presence of a real saint are that heavenly grace will have preserved them and, with God's help, they will exude the odor of sanctity. If you're ill, the saint might even work a miracle on you. At the very least, the relic can impress you with some aspect of the saint's story. If you go to Assisi, you can see a relic of Saint Francis's counterpart, Saint Clare of Assisi. The whole body is there, in the crypt. It isn't quite as pristine as the church expects a saint's body to be; but then, there's a reliquary through whose glass you can see her perfect hair. This is the very hair that the very Saint Francis of Assisi cut off; we can witness the object of a significant moment in the lives of two great people. There is also the very sackcloth shirt Francis made for her. The hair is a troubling sight. It combines the idea that the saint should be beautiful with the idea that she must give something up. Clare has it both ways: She loses the hair during her lifetime, but we remember her by it forever.

Hair, the crowning glory of a head, was often the part that could become immortal. In Greek tragedy, characters are able to identify other characters by a lock of hair alone. Catullus wrote a poem in which Berenice's hair goes to heaven and becomes a constellation; it's a translation of an earlier Greek poem by Callimachus. Its influence is in the climax of Pope's *The Rape of the Lock,* in which a young woman's hair is pinched and then, when liberated, becomes stars. Pope's poem was a way of placating one Arabella Fermor, who really had had a lock cut without authorizing it; but if this hadn't happened, she wouldn't have achieved her enduring fame.

So hair makes for a great relic. As we saw, it connects us with a living person because traditionally, even if not biologically, hair contains life. And in keeping with the theory that things get worse and worse, especially our famous people, relics today seem so much worse than they were. Yes, Britney's own hair was on eBay for a moment, but you were more likely to get her chewing gum from the auction site. In Liszt's time, women would fight over his cigar butts when he left the concert platform. Still, the more we can accept increasingly lame relics, the more we can feel a celebrity's presence among us. The more Bubblicious Britney chews, the more keepsakes to go around.

For some, though, it's not just that relics are unimpressive—it's that they don't work at all. They no longer give us that direct feeling of something spiritual, or of that otherworldliness to which the saints were so willing to ascend. It's something that occurs to Proust's narrator in *Swann's Way,* when he's thinking that the women walking about the Bois de Boulogne aren't a patch on the ones he used to see. He can no longer look upon them as queens, and complains that they are now in "accentuated Liberty chiffons sprinkled with flowers like wallpaper." (Is that all he's complaining about? He should see the place now.) Such disappointment:

> *They were just women, in whose elegance I had no faith, and whose clothes seemed to me unimportant. But when a belief van-*

*ishes, there survives it—more and more vigorously so as to cloak the absence of the power, now lost to us, of imparting reality to new things—a fetishistic attachment to the old things which it did once animate, as if it was in them and not in ourselves that the divine spark resided, and as if our present incredulity had a contingent cause—the death of the gods.*

The divine spark within us—that is what makes us believe; and it's what makes us look for something divine in the famous. Mortals mostly want to be immortal, and fame offers the hope that this is possible. We see this idea in a new way with the Christian martyrs: The spectators could watch people who believed with a phenomenal intensity that this immortality was real. The crowds didn't show up for the blood alone, but because faith in action was astonishing to behold. And in showing such faith, the Christians were establishing a new sort of divinity and a new sort of fame—one that would last forever. Has it lasted? Maybe not. As Proust argues when discussing the women on Boi de Boulogne, not even the relics move us anymore. If anything, they're relics of how powerful relics used to be. But we still want them to be real—for these objects to be potent, and extensions of fame.

# I Want to Be Like You-hoo-hoo:
## Why Do Famous People Influence Us?

Madonna's book *Sex* isn't the first source we'd consult as a guide to good or responsible behavior. After all, the singer spends a lot of time in bondage gear waiting for people to show up and do her. And yet this turns out to be the very moment for a health warning:

> *THIS BOOK DOES NOT CONDONE UNSAFE SEX. LIKE MOST HUMAN BEINGS, WHEN I LET MY MIND WANDER, WHEN I LET MYSELF GO, I RARELY THINK OF CONDOMS. MY FANTASIES TAKE PLACE IN A PERFECT WORLD, A WORLD WITHOUT AIDS. . . . SAFE SEX SAVES LIVES. PASS IT ON.*

There's not a lot in the book to link us to the world of the saints or heaven. It could present a glimpse of the Garden of Earthly Delights, except that she and her friends dress more for the Damnation part of Bosch's triptych. So we're left with the puzzle of these well-meaning words at the beginning. Of course people having freer sorts of sex should wear condoms. We would like to think we had got that far now, and people can be grateful to those, including Madonna, who have made us more aware of how to protect themselves against HIV and AIDS. (Madonna was writing in 1993.) But the words leave us wondering, Should we do as Madonna does in this book, or shouldn't we? Should we believe Madonna as much as we believe in her? And if we should meet Ice-T or Naomi Campbell, should we or shouldn't we bump and/or grind with them (provided that we have a condom)?

To be frank, many of us would be flattering ourselves to think that the question would ever arise. When are we ever going to meet these people in a situation from which one thing could lead to another? It turns out that Madonna's fantasies do not take place in a world that's merely perfect; they're better than that. They take place in the celebrity world. And the celebrity world is beyond perfect.

I don't say this with much irony. Yes, there is a lot to mock in a world in which the famous work and play: We see Tom Cruise jumping on a sofa, learn about Star Jones's wedding, or hear anything at all about Michael Jackson, and can thank the Lord that our world is different. But somehow, some celebrities want to welcome us into their world, however crazy that world might seem to outsiders. These characters appear to be good eggs. Like Jennifer Lopez, who is, after all, still Jenny from the block, they know where they came from, no matter where they're going.

It's impossible to say how they see us as individuals. The evidence tends to be anecdotal, and not all celebrities are known to be all that nice; but word is that David Beckham is a decent sort, and that Samùel L. Jackson gave Jade Goody the time of day on an airplane (she saw him in his pajamas, and he laughed). Still, there are plenty of famous people who see us collectively in the most divine way: They see us as God would see us. That is to say, to some of them, the best-meaning ones, we are perfectible. Life itself could be perfect, and not just for celebrities.

Clearly, "[We're] beautiful, no matter what they say," as Christina Aguilera reminds us; not only that, but beautiful "in every single way."

This is why celebrities are keen to give something back to us. It's possible to see these characters as genuinely surprised, and probably pleased, that they have attributes to which others aspire, and to help us to attain those attributes or qualities for ourselves. They help us make the most of our most precious natural resource—our very selves.

They do this by offering us advice; by letting us see their homes on *MTV Cribs;* by designing clothing lines, with the collaboration of fashion designers; by showing us, or telling us, what to wear; by deploying more than their usual charisma on advertisements; by divulging their skin-care secrets and workout regimens. The phenomenon is an ancient one (they tend to be, as should be clear by now), but it has its modern side effects; one is that someone who tells us how to live can become a celebrity in his or her own right.

In 1993 it was a rare celebrity who was prepared to talk about his or her sexual fantasies, let alone reenact them on camera. But here Madonna was, in her perfect world, introducing readers and viewers to a range of new possibilities. That might not have been the primary purpose of the book. Critics at the time had a hard time establishing what that purpose was, and it's still hard to know if she was, as she suggested, letting her mind wander, or else promoting an album, whose lyrics happen to have been scribbled throughout the book. And she clearly had a lot to tell us. The business about contraception was sincere and had been part of her act for a while. At moments in her Blond Ambition tour of 1990, promoting safe sex seemed as important as promoting sex per se. At one point she and her dancers interrupted the music sequence to chant, "Don't be stupid, don't be silly, / Put a condom on your willy." She was aware that people the public like are going to be more influential than authority figures.

By being so open with her sexuality, Madonna did a lot to create a culture in which the famous felt happier telling us what they were up to. The question becomes somehow even more complicated when we consider the case of Kim Cattrall. Here is somebody who became famous by playing a woman who makes love enthusiastically and experimentally. In 2002 she collaborated with her husband, Mark Levinson, on a book titled *Satisfaction: The Art of the Female Orgasm*. At first, the book seems to appeal to our instinctive association of Kim Cattrall with Samantha from *Sex and the City,* which is transparent but at least puts out a clear message of the sort of tip we can expect. Except that, once the reader opens the book, he or she meets the Kim Cattrall who never really thought of herself much as a sexual being before the age of forty. Unlocking this secret earns Mark Levinson his joint-author credit. The key, it turns out, is more to do with love than sex.

Giving out this kind of advice leaves hostages to fortune. It helps our confidence to know, for example, that Dr. Atkins wasn't unhealthy while he lived by his own diet. So what are we to make of Cattrall and Levinson's divorce in 2004? Artists that they are, did they forfeit their own happiness for that of others? Or is the world still in the long process of becoming as perfect as it could be? In any case, if people buy the book now (and they do—it has run into subsequent editions), before they approach the counter, or click the Go-to-Checkout icon, they must ask, Who will be helping me to satisfaction today—Samantha from *Sex and the City,* or Kim Cattrall, or Mark, who was so good for Kim back then?

Either source can be discredited in this way, but it doesn't really matter. Sex tips are sex tips, and have come from unlikely sources for so long that a celebrity can hardly do worse. In the Renaissance, guides on how to conceive and how to please or control your wife appeared in a flurry. "If she should climb on top of you during intercourse, bounce her off," says one, urging the kind of husbandry you'd associate more with livestock. The problem with many of these sex tips is that they came from monks, and these monks didn't much resemble Shakespeare's Friar Laurence. They, in turn, took their cues from Aristotle and Galen, who could be quite helpful but who thought that ovaries were much like testicles, only on the inside. In the Dutch enlightenment of the seventeenth century, doctors began to command more respect than churchmen as sources of advice; Simon Schama deduces from the advice available that many in the United Provinces had an advanced understanding of reproductive science.

Seen this way, sex is an area in which expertise belongs to more and more of us; and yet the more information is available, the more need there is for guides. The result, for celebrities, is that they, too, can be sexperts if they want; and for the rest of us, those who want sexual advice can have a kind of brand recognition for the type of guidance they want. Given that the confused can choose between experts as far apart on the spectrum as Dr. Ruth Westheimer and Dan Savage to learn quite different things, then the more famous your syndicated sex counselor, the better people will know what to expect.

When people complain that celebrities have a bad influence on us, and particularly on our children, it's true at least that they have an influence; but the proliferation of famous people, celebrated for so many things, means that we have a choice of influences, some bad, some good. Sometimes which is which can be confusing, much as in the movie *Heathers,* in which an alternative rock band is booked to perform their song "Teenage Suicide—Don't Do It."

It's inevitable that the world into which children grow shapes them; when we set up rituals or practices to control this process, anthropologists call it "imprinting." It's the way in which customs, routines, and familiar objects become embedded as much in the subconscious as in the conscious mind. The idea of exposing children to what some call the "celebrity culture" might not be immediately appealing, since there's all that explaining to do, with drugs and dalliances to omit, and upsetting notions of hamsters; but it does happen, through a child-friendly approach to fame.

The rise of Miley Cyrus is unlikely to upset the sorts of parents who had read about Donny Osmond in *Tiger Beat.* Some might draw the line at Bratz, the dolls that look a bit like Naomi Campbell or Courteney Cox-Arquette and who live expensive lifestyles, not least because this crosses the line between fact and fantasy (the dolls themselves are proportionately expensive). Or the Barbie magazines, in which spot-the-difference exercises lie beside photo stories about shopping trips in Rome. Childish things and growing concerns mix intriguingly in the back pages of French *Elle,* where there are celebrity puzzles and quizzes. If you happen to be stuck with your child and a copy of French *Elle,* he or she could perhaps work through a color-by-numbers that turns out to be Amy Winehouse, or help Kate Moss through a maze, leading her to a designer bag but *avoiding* the healthy food on the way. Another example of celebrity influence on children is the debate about sex education, and who should deliver it – parents or schools? The British government has now decided that celebrities should do their bit. (In the United States, the debate takes a different direction:

Should children learn about how to have safe sex or how to have no sex?*)

Fame and education have always been linked, and people have always worried about it. Plato did, anyway. In *The Republic* he was seeking to define the best kind of education for philosopher kings, and he had a special problem with Homer. The Greeks read and recited Homer not just for the poetry but because the deeds and sayings of the gods and heroes in the *Iliad* and the *Odyssey* contained what they took to be good advice. So if a hero took a corner in his chariot, and Homer was assiduous enough to mention how the warrior held the reins, then the Greeks would make a mental note and bear it in mind for their next chariot outing. It's this kind of clout that Plato has in mind as he sets about debunking poets:

> *We are told that they are masters of all forms of skill, and know all about morality and religion; for, the argument runs, a good poet must, if he's to write well, know all about his subject, otherwise he can't write about it. . . . But we have a right to cross-question Homer when he tries to deal with matters of such supreme importance as military strategy, political administration and education.*

Earlier in the book, he blames Homer for offering feeble-minded heroes and feckless gods. He sounds harsh even now, and must have sounded outrageous to readers who had looked to these characters as guides and beacons. He blames Achilles for weeping too much: "We can give [these lines] to the less reputable women characters or the bad men"; he is cross with him for addressing Agamemnon, his king, as "a drunken sot, with the eyes of a dog and the courage of a doe"; nor does he enjoy the passages in which gods couple. The passage in which the cuckolded Hephaestus makes a trap for his wife, Aphrodite, and her lover Ares raises no smirks from Plato. All these high-profile expressions of feeling and snippets of divine gossip were worth banning for the good of children.

---

* It's a rare reminder that Britain is a part of Europe after all.

The Athenians did what they could to promote civic valor: They would award crowns at their drama ceremonies and would educate your children for you if you fell in battle. You could be an Olympic victor, which would have entitled you to free meals for the rest of your life; but soon somebody would be better than you, and you would be pudgy. Being famous was such a slippery business that the only characters who could no longer disappoint were either deities or dead.

Still, all ages have had their influences, in spite of moralizers. Infectious behavior has prevailed, sanctioned or not, and sometimes flourished all the more for being subversive. A clue about how is in the work of the French sociologist Émile Durkheim, whose view that societies act collectively we encountered earlier. In his book *Le Suicide,* he looked at that most individual of actions and tried to see if society can account for that, too. He concluded that a range of social circumstances could make people more or less likely to kill themselves, and one of the factors he looked at was imitation. He examined imitation in its own right, and divided it into three sorts. The first he called "mutual transformation," by which there is a kind of "leveling" among a social group; the second accounts for how we follow fashions and customs, so that we can harmonize with society; and the third is the murkier idea of copying for its own sake.

On the face of it, it's the second category, the "fashions and customs" sort of imitation, that has the most to do with famous people. It's into this category that Durkheim puts the kind of behavior that a leader can inspire in a crowd. He's careful to say that this doesn't count as reciprocal imitation, but as unilateral imitation. From this we can assume that celebrities don't imitate us. It's why Naomi Campbell and George Michael dress up when they do community service.

So we dress like celebrities; that is our misfortune. Celebrities don't dress like us; that is theirs. (Or at least, when they try to disguise themselves as us, it tends to go wrong. After all, who among us wears baseball caps and oversize glasses to visit the local bodega?) There are often moral consequences for dressing like the famous, especially for women. When the early Roman empire grew a little more decadent, so did the hairdos. Valeria Messalina, the wife of the emperor Claudius, would sport a coiffure that crested like a wave emerging from her crown and at its peak broke into ringlets. It was widely copied; as women followed her, they departed from her predecessors, Livia Drusilla and Octavia the Younger (Augustus's wife and sister respectively), with their simpler chignons and center partings, and departed, too, from Augustus's idea of Roman morals with his back-to-basics family values. Moralists would quickly identify this as the wrong sort of influence. It anticipated the kind of detail W. H. Auden would play with in his poem "The Fall of Rome": "Fantastic grow the evening gowns." Ovid would make the link between hair and morality earlier, in his *The Art of Love*, which he says shouldn't be read by women who wear chaste vittae on their heads:

> *No Alice bands. No signs of modesty.*
> *No skirts with hems much lower than the knee.*
> *Discreet seduction—safe sex—is my song,*
> *and in it, nothing is considered wrong.*

Historians were not kind about Messalina. Juvenal has her in the brothel so long the pimp sends the prostitutes home; Pliny has her competing with a prostitute, and managing twenty-five partners in twenty-four hours.* All this made her a useful cultural reference point for the French *libellistes* as they scribbled their pornography about Marie Antoinette. Like Messalina, she went for beehives and extra bits of architecture, but took these to new extremes. She was the queen of the pouf, the elaborate hair ornament built on wire scaffolding. These silhouette-altering contrivances would involve hair extensions and figurative sculpture. The first time she wore one in France, at her coronation, noblemen told her to her face that she looked ridiculous, and one spectator complained

---

* Pliny was a philosopher with a strong interest in natural history, so he managed to write this up without sounding too prurient: He was comparing monogamy among birds to humans, who can sometimes turn out to be less picky.

that her headgear blocked the view of the king. Soon, though, people came to love them. Her hairdresser, M. Leonard, wrote of one of his creations, when it appeared at the Opéra, that "people in the pit crushed one another in their endeavors to see this master-piece of cunning audacity: Three arms were dislocated, two ribs broken, three feet crushed. . . . In short, my triumph was com-plete." Concerned that this wasn't quite enough exposure for her poufs, the queen asked the designers, M. Leonard and Rose Bertin, to keep newspapers updated of the latest pouf developments. What made this worth doing was the fact that she would make them topical, with references to popular contemporary opera, or a scene that included the snake of Asclepius, god of healing, to celebrate the fact that she had persuaded Louis XVI to take a smallpox vac-cine (a bigger feat than it might sound to us).

The fashion historian Caroline Weber argues that this "revival of royal splendor at first held great appeal for the French public, especially after Louis XV's well-publicized debaucheries with Ma-dame du Barry, a former prostitute," and that women would pay their tributes to her by imitating the style. And yet it was the kind of thing that would sour as the Revolution drew near. The tale chimes with the murky world of the diamond-necklace affair (of which more later), but here, the criticism came because debutantes were "squandering their dowries" in the effort to imitate the queen. The craze peaked early in Marie Antoinette's time as consort, but, as Weber tells us, "By the end of 1776, journalists were complain-ing that that, by making the pouf such a coveted accessory, the queen 'had done irreparable injury' to her subjects' finances and morals alike." As with Messalina before her, the satirists were mer-ciless; and, in the case of Suetonius and the *libellistes,* the lack of mercy, as likely as not, came from an economical sort of misogyny: If you attack the trendsetter, then you can attack womanhood in general, for being fickle and female enough to follow her.

In fact, if the moralists had anything to do with it, the sheer fact of a woman being famous should have been enough to discourage other women from seeking glory. For a long time women were supposed to be famous for not being famous. Montaigne ends his essay "On Glory" by arguing that women have no need to worry about honor, because it tells us nothing about their intentions and desires, which should be as well regulated as their actions. The few women who make it into John Aubrey's *Brief Lives* provide striking examples of either extreme. One, the Countess of Warwick, receives an elegiac entry, listing the things that made her great, concluding that she was:

> *Great in a thousand things beside, which the world admires as such: but she despised them all, and counted them but loss and dung in comparison of the feare of God, and the excellency of the Knowledge of Christ Jesus.*

Another, the Countess of Sussex, is given a short paragraph beginning, "Countess of Sussex, a great and sad example of the power of Lust and Slavery of it," and ending, "About 1666 this Countesse died of the Pox." The few words in between are just as effective, but the crucial one here is "example." Whereas the men in the book are given their fame for their achievements, the women are presented as patterns, or cautionary tales.

This kind of thing has taken an age to shake off, but in Britain, we can see the very beginnings of the change after the Second World War. The years after the war were harsh in Europe. Rationing prevailed, and peer pressure did what it could to keep glamour in check. In Paris, Christian Dior launched the New Look, although it took a brave woman to wear it—one photograph shows an elegant woman having her dress ripped from her back. In Britain we can document this gradual slink back toward color and style by going through episodes of a radio program called *Woman's Hour.*

The program now regularly approaches sexual health with a bracing frankness, but when *Woman's Hour* began in 1946, it clearly owed its place to a sense of noblesse oblige at the BBC. The clue is that men hosted it. But look more closely at 1940s Britain, and you begin to see a tolerance toward women who pushed the envelope. In the program's first year, there was even a whiff of a celebrity:

*The Rt. Hon. Margaret Bondfield, J.P., LL.D,\* Deborah Kerr,
film actress, and Mrs. Elsie May Crump, housewife of Chorlton-
cum-Hardy, give their reactions to yesterday's programmes.*

Here Mrs. Crump appears to be joining Deborah Kerr out of a
sense of public duty, but gains her own exposure in the process.
And anyway, Deborah Kerr was the safe end of Hollywood. Still,
it was no longer inexcusable for ordinary women to be glamorous.
It's hard to gauge how the social control is working in this advertisement from 1947, when there was still rationing, but it is:

> *EVEN A FILM STAR CAN BAKE BEAUTIFULLY
> NOW! FEATHERY CAKE every time − when you use
> Miller's, the sure-action baking powder . . . Miller's means suc-
> cess! See the marvellous difference Miller's makes in all your
> baking! Get a tin today.*

A recipe for Hollywood Cake follows. On one level, housewives
are to believe that this powder is so fail-safe that even a ditzy
famous person can use it; but the ensuing recipe suggests that
movie-style glamour can be yours. The last sentence of it is simply,
"Decorate."

But then, *Woman's Hour* and the world of rationing wasn't *Vogue*.
*Vogue* became the guide to a truly international style: It was the
medium that would convey Hollywood glamour to anyone who
could copy it. In her book on the magazine's history, Georgina
Howell turns to the trends of the thirties, the age of the Depression,
and quotes James Laver, who, in the magazine, called the camera
the first "engine for imposing types of beauty." As she describes
them, the types are instantly recognizable:

> *Every important film star appeared in* Vogue *and contributed
> some new look or fashion:*
> *Garbo—hollowed eye sockets and plucked eyebrows*
> *Dietrich—plucked eyebrows and sucked-in cheeks*
> *Joan Crawford—the bow-tie mouth*

---

\* Justice of the peace, doctor of law.

*Tallulah Bankhead—a sullen expression*
*Mae West—the hourglass figure and an attractive bawdiness*
*Constance Bennett—a glazed, bandbox smartness*
*Jean Harlow—platinum hair*
*Katharine Hepburn—red curls and freckles*
*Vivien Leigh—gypsy colouring, a glittering combination of*
*  white skin, green eyes and dark red hair*

Howell reports that *Vogue* would find models to copy these looks. And if they could copy them, why couldn't you?

By the 1980s, famous women were seen by some as positive influences *because of* their freedoms and power, rather than in spite of it; and there was less and less worry about how this power had been achieved. Madonna arrived as the standard-bearer for what would later become the tricky idea of "third-wave" feminism—the movement that has led some women to seek equality with men by being what men want them to be. Here's how Madonna's music worked on fifteen-year-old girls in northern England during the early nineties:

> *It's like after you've watched her on telly or something, you walk, no you flaunt out of the room, thinking, well if she can, why can't I . . .*
>
> *We always put her on before we go out on a Friday night. It makes you feel good. It makes us feel stroppy, like we could take on anything. Yeah, it makes you feel, like, good in yourself.*

Here people really are harmonizing with each other, and gaining a kind of confidence, because they are following a trendsetter. Durkheim is clear that it doesn't work the other way around, and we can be pretty sure of it, too: Kate Winslet attempts to be normal, but she isn't now, because she's famous, and looks it. As she observed at the 2009 Academy Awards, an Oscar is not a shampoo bottle. Victoria Beckham's book *That Extra Half an Inch* strikes a delicate balance here: Its author, Hadley Freeman, relays to its readers some genuinely helpful tips on how to wear what.

Still, the famous can try to fit awkwardly into the first type of imitation that Durkheim talks about—the sort that explains how a cause or "bundle of causes" makes us all rub along together and somehow affect each other so that we do the same sorts of straight-forward things, such as gossiping at a watercooler, saying "like" a lot, or eating less red meat. It doesn't account for the way in which celebrities influence us, but it does tell us something about those impossible moments when they try to pretend that they haven't been removed from the rest of us. For example, why do interviewers report what women order in the restaurant where they meet? One effect it has is to make the subject look at once more like us, for liking profiteroles, and more fabulous, too, because the profiteroles make so little difference. But there is much joy in the heaven of tabloids and PR offices when a celebrity repents of extreme behavior and, among us all at last, finds that it's better to be human after all. Danniella Westbrook's words are sobering:

> My week's stay in rehab may not have cured my drug addiction but it paid off in other ways. Back in February of that year the press had got wind of the fact that I was addicted to cocaine, and the Sunday Mirror had rung my agent to say that they were going to run an exposé on me. . . . And so back in February I had agreed to do my first "cocaine shame" story. . . .
>
> Now I had been to rehab—even though it had done nothing for me—it was time for a follow-up piece. . . . In this one, which was accompanied by photographs of me playing tennis, to prove I was "100% fit," I talked about how I had successfully overcome my battle with cocaine addiction and vowed never to touch the stuff again. "Cocaine ruined my life," I told the paper. "I'd look in the mirror and see this horrible gaunt face. I hardly recognised myself." It was, of course, just one big lie. Not only was I still using the drug, but I remember taking it just minutes before I did the interview.

We do slip into a different world when we try to emulate the famous. It's like Jean Cocteau's film about Orpheus, *Orphée*, in which a French poet slips into the underworld by putting on black rubber gloves and walking through a mirror that melts into water at his touch. We think we can see ourselves in there somewhere, but find ourselves surrounded by different people entirely. It's a mysterious world evoked by Durkheim's third sort of imitation:

> *Finally, it can happen that we reproduce an action that has occurred in front of us or to our knowledge, uniquely because it did occur in front of us, or because we heard talk of it. In itself, it has no intrinsic character that would give us any reason to perform it again. We copy it, not because we find it useful, nor to be in agreement with our model, but simply to copy it. The representation that we make of it for ourselves automatically determines the movements which make it real again. This is why we yawn, we laugh, we cry—because we see someone yawning, laughing, crying. And this is how the idea of homicide passes from one conscience into another. It is the ape-house for its own sake.*

We must remember that Durkheim's study was about influences on suicide, and he was considering imitation as one of them. Celebrity suicides were not in his brief. Others have studied this area since, and some have concluded that celebrity suicides don't make all that much difference to overall suicide statistics. Graham Martin and Lisa Koo looked at the total rate of suicide in Australia for young people (aged fifteen to nineteen and twenty to twenty-four years) for the thirty-day period after the announcement of Kurt Cobain's suicide in 1994, and compared it with the same period for each of the previous five years. Like Durkheim, they found there was little or no change, nor a change to the number of those suicides that were the result of gunshot.

In a paper published the following year, Martin looked at media reports of suicides and found that they gave the suicides high prominence and even ended up glorifying them. This is nothing new. In 1772 an aspiring poet, philosopher, and painter, Karl Wilhelm Jerusalem, shot himself, having fallen in love with a married woman. He became the celebrity suicide of his age, and gave Goethe's book *The Sorrows of Young Werther* its denouement. The book was enormously popular until the beginning of the nineteenth century—Napoléon told Goethe in 1808 that he had read it seven times, and he wished he had written it himself. Jerusalem's grave became a cult shrine: torch-lit processions would lead toward it; other people would drink toasts; the site appeared in John Murray's *Handbook for Travellers on the Continent*. (At Père Lachaise cemetery in Paris, you can still see the same fuss made of Jim Morrison's grave, with arrows painted over other graves, and graffiti reading, "This way to the king.") And then there were suicides.

One in particular is easy to link with the novel: When Christine von Lassberg drowned herself in the River Ilm in 1778, she did so behind Goethe's garden with a copy in her pocket. But was this just because of the book? As Durkheim does, we could find that a bundle of factors contributed to this death. She had been deserted by her lover, and the novel would certainly have suggested to her a way of expressing her grief. But then, Brahms felt the same thing about his love for Clara Schumann, the wife of his friend and mentor. "You may as well put my picture on the cover," he remarked of his dejection. Here the book seems to be doing everything a work of art should do: to offer compassion to the suffering, and to show the extremes of behaviour the rest of us should avoid.

Other things in Durkheim's third definition of imitation give us pause, though. One is the imitator's need to make something real again. It's troubling when we look at the world of celebrities, because so little was ever real in the first place. Ideas of what is real end up in the heads of those who really are capable of homicide. When John Hinckley, Jr., was looking for ways to impress Jodie Foster, he took as his guide the part she played in *Taxi Driver*—he modeled himself after Travis Bickle, a man who thinks up ways of assassinating a senator. Jodie Foster was appalled when Hinckley fired on Ronald Reagan and wounded him just two months after his first inauguration in 1981. Others have killed strangers, and then themselves, and let it be known that they did so with fame in mind.

No, the world of celebrities is not real. It is like the world of the movies, and the narratives about them are to be read with the same level of personal investment. Like Madonna's fantasies, they take place in a world that may or not be perfect, but at least makes sense on its own terms. It has its own ironies, its own suspense, and its own surprises; but like any story, with a beginning and an end, it has its limits. The only way to enter it is to become a celebrity—to use the phrase of Chantelle Houghton, who pretended to be a celebrity and then ended up as one for a bit, then you can be "living the dream." And how dreamlike it is: Here is Jade Goody again, on the plane trip during which she saw Samuel L. Jackson in his pajamas.

> *Orlando Bloom was sitting there in a black jumper. He didn't say very much, just seemed to want to keep himself to himself, but he did smile at me. . . . Then I got up to go to the toilet and found myself stood in the queue with Kate Moss. She started chatting to me, asking how my boys were and stuff. I couldn't believe it—it was like I was in a parallel universe.*

It is the privilege of the rest of us to dream it. On the airplane, Jade Goody becomes our emissary into that dreamland; as she flies with the stars, she represents ordinary people everywhere.

That was her then, but as people in the UK readily know, her story took an incredible turn when she was diagnosed with cervical cancer. She hired a publicist and resolved to die in public. It was a kind of sacrifice, as she acknowledged, so that her children could have some of the advantages in life that she had lacked in southeast London. The sacrifice had another impact on the public good: Her famous illness led to a 20 percent increase in cancer screening. Even this had dreamlike, if surreal, elements to it—in particular, her fairy-tale wedding in a sumptuous hotel to the sleek but violent Jack Tweed, an electrician who became a model. Since he was in prison at the time of the wedding, he appeared, tagged, by permission of the secretary of state for justice.*

---

* Tweed was serving an eighteen-month prison sentence for assaulting a teenage boy with a golf club.

For all that, the day was moving, and even Gordon Brown wished Jane Goody all the best. (In later attempts to show his understanding of celebrities, he would at least get their names right—he expressed his touching concern for Susan Boyle after her breakdown, heedless of what this would do to his popularity ratings.) Afterward Jade said, "Now I'm ready to go to heaven," and the day seemed like a last glimpse of heaven on earth: Things were luxurious, such as Jade's fun eyelashes and the dress, a present from the owner of Harrods himself. There were celebrity guests, such as the daytime television hosts Richard and Judy.★ Here was a real person with a real illness, creating a world around her that went beyond our reality.

The illusion relied on us knowing that reality—two sons facing the loss of their mother, wheelchairs, chemotherapy—and then accepting the pageant as deliberately unreal, to the point of burlesque. The French philosopher Jean Baudrillard felt it necessary to make something like this point when he was writing about Hollywood: "The screen idols are immanent in the unfolding of life as a series of images. They are a system of luxury prefabrication, brilliant syntheses of the stereotypes of life and love. *They embody one single passion only: the passion for images.* . . . They are not something to dream about; they are the dream. . . . Fetishes, fetish objects, that have nothing to do with the world of the imagination, but everything to do with *the material fiction of the image.*"

So we know the celebrity world isn't real; but it's nice for us to know where celebrities shop and where these fetish objects come from, even if we don't go out and get those items for ourselves. They go to their shops, or get their stylists and personal shoppers to help them bypass the shops altogether, while we can choose between theirs and ours. Victoria Beckham can tell you that she buys baby clothes from Petit Bateau, but also helpfully mentions the more affordable Gap and H&M; meanwhile, children are introduced to a world of shopping and handbags that is as viable as the world of

---

★ They have a daytime television show and a book club, just like Oprah.

princesses and spinning wheels. Kim Cattrall can tell you how to enjoy sex, but you might not enjoy it as much as Samantha does; Madonna can picture herself in a perfect world, but if you want to join it, wear a condom.

# 8

## If You Want to Evict Jade, Vote Now: How Democracy Has Given Us Ways of Saying Whom We Like, or Dislike, or Both at Once

Big Brother is a British invention, along with Parliament. I don't mean *Big Brother* the television show, which began life in the Netherlands (although *Big Brother* has always been bigger in Britain than in the United States). Big Brother, as he appears in *Nineteen Eighty-four,* is the brooding, omniscient presence with a friendly, familiar name. He becomes a metaphor for the sort of control a government can have over us, without us ever having to know who or what is exercising that control. The analogy is to Comrade Stalin: His title suggests that he's one of us, looking after us just as we look after each other. But we're terrified because somehow he's looking *at* us.

With the television program, the metaphor changes. We control the fate of the housemates. We look at them. We control them with our votes; or is it the network that's controlling them? In both cases, Big Brother is there to enforce things that are for the common good. We may not always think they're for the common good, but if we subject our impulses to his will, then we should be all right.

In Britain *Big Brother* was more or less absorbing for its first couple of seasons. It was only in the third that we met Jade Goody. She came in fourth place. Still, she was the real winner, from the moment she left the house. It was like a rally. There was a lot of cheering from a large crowd, many of whom had turned out to catch a glimpse of the trainee dental nurse from Bermondsey. There was a fringe of protesters, but otherwise, for a host of different reasons, and for now, they wanted her.

They didn't want her enough to make her win, you notice. She had done all right in a negative vote. This meant that not enough people had cast a vote saying that they *didn't* like her, and so spared her banishment from the *Big Brother* house. To make the matter more complicated, plenty of voters didn't vote for her eviction precisely *because* they didn't like her and yet enjoyed watching her.

Still, to Jade, it was a victory. As she says in her memoirs, "I wasn't gutted that I hadn't won. I was really happy that I'd got that far: I was one of the last four in the *Big Brother* house!" Her leaving of it became her. There is a tradition in *Big Brother* that contestants set aside one special outfit for emerging from the house. Jade's coming-out dress was a revealing pink satin number with sequins around the top. It was accompanied by a satin glove (just the one), with its sparkling buttons left expansively open. She had regrets about the ensemble, but it was made by her friend Tina, and Jade didn't want to cause offense.

This was in the late summer of 2002. At the beginning of the season, the flamboyant Irish talk-show host Graham Norton branded her a pig. At the end of the first week, her fellow housemates nominated her for the public vote that would evict her. She survived that, and subsequent attempts to oust her. Before long, Graham Norton changed his tactics (as Jade would call them, tictactics), and campaigned to keep her in the house. After all, what would be the sense in removing someone from the public eye when she would ask what asparagus was, or, "Rio de Janeiro, ain't that a person?" Rio de Janeiro is in fact a place, and its language is Portuguese.

It goes some way toward explaining the nature of her reception. Spectators held up placards saying BURN THE PIG, while they yelled "Burn the pig" (as if their message might prove hard to read); and Jade detected other notes of disapproval. She recalled later, when the vote results were read: "I just heard loads of cheers. I think there were a couple of boos but the cheers gave me such a boost. The thing is, two people booing is much louder than a million people cheering."*

---

*Jade: My Autobiography,* 138. Kate Lawler, who won *Big Brother* that year, proves the truth of this remark. Although she won by being pretty and charming, she was mortified by remarks about her complexion, such as "You've got more orange peel than an orange."

The story of how Jade Goody stayed famous is an extraordinary one. At first it was some alliance between the people who thought she was ridiculous and the people who thought she represented the constituency of the demotic and the mocked. We tried to forget about her after a later *Big Brother* exposed that she could be a racist bully. And then she died.

All along, she was right to listen out for the boos. The principle of making people famous while booing them is now enshrined in the American way of life. The vibrant Web site www.vote fortheworst.com plausibly trumpets its success in galvanizing support for the lamest contestants in *American Idol*. Stars are only just learning to be grateful: Sandra Bullock showed the way in her speech accepting a Razzie for her performance in *All About Steve:* "When I said I would show up, I miraculously won." She brought along DVDs of the film for jurors who hadn't seen it.

These seem like examples of democracy for fun, but they help us understand things about how democracy works. For one thing, it's assumed that the more playful versions of voting involve us more instinctively. It's sometimes used to shame us: If voter turnout in Iraq can remain strong in spite of the perilous walk to a polling booth, what does it say about the eagerness to vote in elections between yodelers and break-dancing cows in *America's Got Talent?*★

So the complaint goes. In this chapter, we shall see that these worlds—the worlds of celebrity and of power—are not so much contrasting as complementary. The combination tells us two important things about democracy. One is that voting might seem like a way of choosing our leaders, and our leaders would perhaps prefer to see it like that; but really it's our guarantee that we can get rid of them. In doing so, we have institutionalized the killing of our gods. Second, in establishing our rights to exercise this power over our leaders, we often have celebrities to thank. Here, too,

---

★ In Afghanistan, an estimated one-third of the country watched the final of *Afghan Star* on television, and three hundred thousand voted for the two finalists. Figures for the real election are harder to determine.

famous people have served us by showing us how we can reject them.

The amazing thing about Jade's emergence that night is that it was a democratic event. People could cast a vote simply to say what they felt about her. Should she stay in your face or get out of it? You decide. Throughout much of human history, we have had only limited ways of deciding who is in our faces, and getting them out has been a bigger problem still. They have often been rich, either by good luck, work, or accident of birth; they have often been beautiful, by the same means. Jade Goody was neither. Democracy, an invention of the Athenians in the late sixth century B.C., which reappeared fitfully in Britain before becoming an ideal in eighteenth-century America and France, has given us a system whereby people go about seeking popularity, and from time to time we can tell those people that we don't like them anymore. So then we nail them. One of the most topsy-turvy consequences of this is that, bit by bit, everyone is eligible for fame. Even you, the voter; even Jade.

Politicians want as many people to like them and dislike them—that is, to be interested in them—as possible. So they look at reality voting programs and wonder if "real" elections can learn from them. As a result, voters in some local elections in England have been able to send their choice of candidate by mobile telephone, using a PIN. Nick Raynsford, who was minister for local government, said of the trials in 2002, "This marks an important first step towards e-voting across the country. .... We are particularly keen to engage younger voters and feel these innovations will help." But Jade's story is altogether more complicated. For a while, she was adored not least because, to many, she was ignorant and ugly. What electoral reformers need to remember about Jade is that she won votes from people who couldn't stand her as well as from people who could sympathize with her; like the contributors to www.voteforetheworst.com, they were seeking entertainment for as long as she could be entertaining. When she became unacceptable, they stopped.

This reminds us that, when we vote, we treat politicians just as

we treat celebrities; and the closer we come to rejecting them, the more we rely on gossip, innuendo, and slander. We see it in the origins of Greek democracy; we see it in the pornography circulated by *libellistes* in the French Revolution; we see it in different ways in America and Britain.* The more a politician trades on personality, the more intense our feelings are either way. It might make us want them, but in the end, as it is with lovers who in time find the causes of attraction repellent, it's what makes us dump them.†
Game shows, then, aren't just a by-product of voting and a fun thing we do with mobile telephone text messages. They show us the reasons why we invented voting at all.

In 513 B.C, an Athenian aristocrat called Cleisthenes, whose family claimed descent from Heracles, reorganized Attic Greece. The most important of his reforms was democracy. It was a system by which every citizen could speak in an assembly and have a say in the state's decisions. In this system, it was the right of every citizen to take part in a vote that could ultimately lead to an eviction. In fact, this was the very first component of Cleisthenes' reforms. The idea was to prevent violent factions from emerging or individuals from becoming too important. The process involved all the vote-rigging, multiple voting, and attempts to fix nominations that characterize *Big Brother*. It could happen once a year, and it required crowds. An assembly of citizens would meet in the *agora,* the marketplace. To qualify as a citizen, you had to be male and free—that is, not a slave. Living close by was a help, too.

The process was called ostracism because *ostrakon* was the word for a bit of broken pottery. If six thousand people each produced a bit of broken pot with somebody's name on it, then an ostracism could take place. The citizen whose name came up most

---

* During the recent British election campaign, much depended on the temper of the prime minister, Gordon Brown. Did he really push past people? Did he really shove a trolley at someone? Was he disagreeable to secretaries? He and the leader of the opposition relied heavily on their wives, who were on hand to point out that these candidates were messy and rose at antisocial hours, but were doing it for us.
† For example, the British might have applauded Churchill's defeat of the Nazis, but voters were alarmed when he claimed that the Labour Party would need to fall back on some form of gestapo if they were to turn the country to socialism.

often on the sherds would have to go. This would mean leaving Athens for ten years. You would remain a citizen and could keep your property; but the eviction would do your political career serious damage. And yet, for enough people to evict you, enough people needed to have heard of you. There was a real kudos in being famous enough to face this vote. It explains why Aristotle referred to politicians as *gnorimoi*—people you'd recognize. And it also explains how come, when the people accidentally evicted a nebbish, the system broke down and ostracism ended.

In theory, you could evict anybody. If you had a grudge against your neighbor, then you could write his name on a sherd. But not everyone would have the same grudge, so it was pointless, if satisfying, to try. More satisfying by far was the eviction of famous people. People did a lot to make themselves famous and popular in Athens, and the lists of the ostracized tended to show up the people who did the most to please.

Plutarch's brief biography of Aristides the Just is clear-eyed about this. The account begins with Plutarch trying to work out how rich Aristides was. Plutarch concludes that Aristides was wealthy, and one of the reasons is the very fact that he was ostracized, a sanction "which was not usually inflicted on the poorer citizens, but on those of great houses, whose station exposed them to envy." Now, this can be seen politically as a kind of class war, which would be true to some extent.* After all, Cleisthenes meant the practice to help the people get rid of a select few, feuding aristocrats poised to fight civil wars against each other. (Cleisthenes so embodied the kind of noble soul who, throughout history, has given away his own powers that we shouldn't be surprised that he himself was ostracized.) But Plutarch offers another reason for Aristides' banishment:

> It is reported that an illiterate clownish fellow, giving Aristides his sherd, supposing him a common citizen, begged him to write Aristides upon it; and he being surprised and asking if Aristides

---

*G. E. M. de Ste. Croix's formidable *The Class Struggle in the Ancient Greek World* (1981) sees everything like this.

*had ever done him any injury, "None at all," said he, "neither*
*know I the man; but I am tired of hearing him everywhere called*
*the just." Aristides, hearing this, is said to have made no reply,*
*but returned the sherd with his own name inscribed.*

So why did the Athenians want so much to evict their best
men? Did they see through their politicians' attempts to be liked?
Maybe. But they were helped by a range of tactics, including smears
and multiple voting. The case of Cimon offers a useful insight into
the system. He was known for his generosity. He had an orchard
with no fence around it, so that passersby could pick fruit from its
trees; he was pleasant to look at (tall, with thick, curly hair, as the
poet Ion recorded); he was supremely good at gesture politics; he
won stylish victories against the Persians, from which he was able
to fund large dinners, and also provide the cash needed to pay jurors (which was expensive when a jury had 501 men in it) and
build a wall for the city. How did Athenians respond to all this
kindness? They weren't as grateful as you'd think. They ostracized
him in about 461 B.C. The political reasons for this were complicated: He was a natural aristocrat and a prominent admirer of the
Spartans; but for many voters, what sealed it for him was the notion that he was sleeping with his sister. The poet Eupolis wrote:

> *He was all right—except for his boozing, his irresponsibility,*
> *And his occasional trips abroad to Sparta,*
> *Leaving Elpinice [his sister] alone in her bed at night.*

This kind of thing was clearly on the minds of the people ostraciz-
ing him. One of the best things about voting by writing on a
sherd, rather than ticking a ballot form, is that you can write a
little note explaining your reasons. "Get out, Cimon," says one
piece of pot, "and take Elpinice with you." It's worth noting, as
Plutarch does, that the Athenians were fine about Cimon's domestic arrangements while there was no political crisis (and, presumably, while he was giving them free groceries); but to oust him, it
took a proper campaign.

This suggests a conspiracy theory, which in turn reminds us that Greek democracy could be as murky a business as any skulduggery Michael Moore could wish to find. In the way votes are rigged, we really can detect forces mobilizing the masses, without the masses knowing. The very name "democracy," so sacred to our ears, has more than a tang of snobbery about it when used in Athens. It becomes a collective word for "the mob," and conservatives used the term to dismiss the system altogether. Even when we look at the birth of democracy in the United States, we find, not snobbery exactly, but caution; and when we look at how democracy emerged in France, we can see how that caution was justified.

In ancient Rome, meanwhile, people were under few illusions that the system was rigged. Votes for the republic's highest office, along with decisions to go to war, were taken by the *comitia centuriata*—the Gathering of the Centuries. Men who were associated with the army would vote in their centuries, in a block vote: Each century would have one vote. The cavalry voted first, then the infantry, then the rest. This slanting meant that, generally, the oldest and richest soldiers voted first, and when the majority was declared, the vote was over. This meant that the nebbishy centuries never got around to voting at all. Their best chance of being heard was to see the *tribunus plebis*, the tribune who had a holy duty to reflect the will of the plebs. And failing that, they would take to the streets.

To put it briefly: The story of the Roman constitution, and the eventual change from republic to empire, is the story of how people courted fame for power, and how backroom boys struggled to control the situation. It is revealing to look at the careers of prominent Romans through the cult of celebrity: Tiberius Gracchus, the charismatic tribune of the people, who tried to implement land distribution in a way that favored the poor, and ended up murdered. Julius Caesar, who, on his way toward ultimate power, staged such vast gladiatorial combats that their scale had to be capped; who would time (and even cancel) his triumphant parades to gain maximum political advantage; who published his memoirs in the third person and who tried to have himself elected as a god; and who ended up murdered. Mark Antony, the playboy tribune who melded into Antopatra (or is that Clantony?). And Augustus Caesar, who preferred modest titles; who, as we shall see in chapter 9, would appear in his Altar of the Peace as one of the crowd; who pooh-poohed gossip, and died old, in the arms of his wife. For a moment, it looked as though the Romans had learned that you held power by avoiding celebrity. Subsequent emperors' attempts to control access and imagery remind us that this was always a matter of trial and error.

Through it all, there was a pretense that the people were in power. In practice, people could riot and fight or seek to disrupt the constitution, but it's impossible to escape the evidence that they were gangs that statesmen could manipulate—just as Cleisthenes had sought to avoid in Athens. Nowadays, we masses can operate in our own murky ways. In 2007 there was a bitter feud in the *Big Brother* house between a faction that centered on Jade Goody and Shilpa Shetty, a Bollywood actor who arrived on set seeming pleased with herself and left looking glorious. During the spat, Jade Goody and her new friends emerged as petty and racist. Channel 4 received more complaints for *Big Brother* than any other program or advertisement had attracted before. It was a strange moment. It was as though people demanded an eviction immediately; the idea that we could make the rules was unthinkable as the rules were then constituted by the founding brainstormers. The existing *Big Brother* constitution wasn't good enough for the electorate, who took an alternative form of action. The result was that an advertiser withdrew its sponsorship, the voice of Big Brother had to be seen to take control of events in the house, and politicians cheerfully became involved. Viewers took more control over the program than they had before. It was a revolution of sorts: Not quite a mob bursting into the Tuileries, but, within the laboratory conditions of a game show, it was a spontaneous demonstration of resentments nonetheless.

With such a large number of complaints, it was tempting to

conclude that the chorus of disapproval had been organized.* The historian of ancient Greece can be more confident about his or her conspiracy theories. For a start, as was the case with Cimon, voters would sometimes use the sherds to share their feelings, often including doodles and ditties. Even though he had been a victor at the Olympics, Megacles was clearly unpopular for many reasons: He was adulterous, rich, had a family curse, and bred horses. Any one of these could have swayed an individual voter, especially those who didn't like horses.

And then, the more formal *ostraka* can be just as suggestive. Themistocles was a man who, among other things, had saved not only Athens but also the Greek world from the Persians, and changed history in a way that ought to have pleased his compatriots; and yet he was ostracized in about 471 B.C. Archaeologists have found handfuls of the sherds from that eviction, and they all appear to be in the same handwriting.

This has led historians to explore two possibilities (or a combination of both). One is that not enough people could write his name (and it is tricky—is the first *e* long or short? And what about the second *e*?). The voter who asked Aristides to write "Aristides" on his sherd falls into this category. The other possibility is that these *ostraka* were already inscribed. Are you having a problem deciding whom to vote for? Confused by all those rumors about incest and treason? Then leave it to the experts. Give this to the official over there, and all your ostracism worries are taken care of. And maybe both options could be true at once—that voters queued up for some kind of inscription service, where they might have received a little friendly advice along the way, perhaps like accepting a lift to the polling station from a GOP campaigner. One wonders if the process was entirely honest:

---

* The Internet has made this process quite straightforward. Once when I was working on a newspaper letters desk and a journalist had rubbished Russell Crowe, waves of e-mails lapped into our system, all of them making the same comments, often in the same words.

> Voter: *Hello. I'd like to vote for an eviction, please. Could you make it out for Thucydides, son of Melesias? And I don't mean Thucydides the historian.*
>
> Scribe [producing a bit of broken pot with the name 'Cimon' written on it]: *There you go.*
>
> Voter: *Thank you very much. Hang on. This looks a bit short for Thucydides, son of Melesias.*
>
> Scribe: *No one's voting for him these days.*\* *Trust me, it'll be fine.*

In these evictions—in the stories of Aristides, Cimon, and the peculiar case of Hyperbolus—we see a process in which the people, the *demos,* appear to have controlled the *gnorimoi.* But did they? The history of popular participation in politics sometimes seems as if it's a complicated narrative that at least goes in one direction: Bit by bit, humanity is liberated so that we have a greater say in who represents us, and hey, we can even have a pop at representing ourselves. It becomes a wrangle between us and the sinister controllers of the establishment or of celebrity, those nameless types we call "gatekeepers." But the history is really more nuanced—indeed, it shows its own blips and spurts, or, as the framers of the Constitution would have it, checks and balances.

Once we have been given a feeling that we control things, we are all the more likely to be upset when it appears that we don't. When television was invented, things that happened on it were beyond our reach—they happened in another world, and very few viewers could ever be a part of that world. Now that votes can make things happen on it immediately, and anyone can be on it if, say, they can't decide how to decorate their home, or if they think someone should come and clean it, we are all the more alive to anything that is awry. That distant world has become ours. It's almost as though we have re-created Athens—small enough to be what one historian, Moses Finley, could call a "face-to-face society"—but now on a global scale.†

---

\* This much would have been true: Thucydides, son of Melesias, was ostracised about seventeen years after Cimon was.

† Finley's idea is often cited and much disputed; as the business of ostracism rigging

Enshrined in the constitution of *Big Brother* is the illegality of conferring about eviction nominations. Housemates were not allowed to coordinate their votes. There are many reasons for this. It was supposed to stop secret sorts of bullying (and anyway, the overt forms proved so much better for ratings). Another perceived advantage of the system was that it stopped housemates from trying to get out of the house by having themselves evicted. (An irony of this was that the penalty for doing this kind of thing became a nomination for eviction.) But best of all, it meant that the members of the house had to nominate one another as individuals. There could be no block voting, no unionized power behind their decisions. They were to have as little power as possible so that we could have more.

Again, fifth-century Greece shows us how this works. In 417 B.C., the Athenians delivered their final ostracism. It turned out to be the final one because it was rigged. At the time, the two principle candidates for eviction were Alcibiades, the young, lovely playboy who wanted an armed expedition to Sicily, and Nicias, the less sociable, older man who advised against it. The prospect delighted a man called Hyperbolus, whom Plutarch dismisses with rhetorical brilliance: "He was a man with bravado which had no basis in power, but who came to power on the basis of bravado, and who brought the city into disrespect because of the respect he received in the city." Hyperbolus, we are told, began to brag about the imminent clash, thinking that he would become the rival of the man who survived. This led Alcibiades and Nicias to hold secret talks, and together they arranged for Hyperbolus to be exiled rather than them. It worked, in the short term, at least. There must have been many times in their subsequent clashes when both wished the other had gone, but for the result was that they could both stay.

This debacle shocked the Athenians so much that they abandoned the whole process from then on. It must have shocked them for many

---

shows, it's hard to know if people really recognized the faces with whom they came face-to-face, although the architecture was full, not only of public meeting spaces, but also of cliquey hangouts, as even the names of philosophical movements tell us.

reasons. The first, and perhaps the most important to them, was that ostracism, though a punishment, should be administered only to people worthy of it. If the Athenians were *really* worried about a citizen, they would have come up with something worse. As Plutarch reminds us, it was "designed to placate their envy rather than any possible fear." The consequence of the Hyperbolus case was that it gave him a dignity that they felt he didn't deserve. We can see a parallel in *Big Brother* evictions. As we've seen, you get to dress up for the occasion; a crowd greets you; you become a celebrity. In the case of Jade Goody's second eviction (as a result of the Shilpa Shetty affair) there was no crowd. Jade no longer deserved the dignity of fame. She had received the punishment that the Roman senate would mete out to their rubbish emperors after their deaths: the *damnatio memoriae*—for a time, her memory was condemned.

But perhaps even more disturbing to the Athenians was the idea that Alcibiades and Nicias could have conspired. The audience of this drama had come to rely on the conflict, and for a moment it looked as though there was none.* They knew that ostracism could be a good-natured, honorable affair, but they didn't think it should have been a game. As soon as they saw that it *was* a game, which involved gamesmanship, they stopped it.

So the *demos* didn't control their rulers, then, or at least, not on that occasion. But we see that their disappointment came because they thought they did. And now, we make a fuss about "gatekeepers" because the right to select and reject our celebrities is something we guard assiduously. The idea of a media machine that does it on our behalf is abhorrent to us. This, by the way, is why the argument "the media are to blame" is so attractive. It's a relief not to have to take responsibility for our crueler decisions, and it's fine to delegate the job to journalists; and yet previous societies show us plenty of examples in which we, the people, have longed to do it ourselves.

---

* Actually, the rivalry between Nicias and Alcibiades was about to become vital to a story that has it all: the invasion of Sicily, the execution of Socrates, and, lurking behind these things, a plot to lop the penises off statues of Hermes. Another time.

### i. The people's people

A democracy ought to be the vehicle that brings to prominence people who are quite like us; and you know, they really could *be* us. These days, politicians do well to proclaim their humble origins. When Abraham Lincoln was on campaign, he summarized his background to a biographer by saying, "It can all be condensed into a single sentence and that sentence you will find in Gray's "Elegy Written in a Country Churchyard"—'The short and simple annals of the poor.'" Bill Clinton's memoirs expand on those annals, with a mother who left Bill in the care of her parents, and a stepfather who beat the mother, all set against the backdrop of a little place called Hope. John Edwards would remind his audiences that he is the son of a millworker, and that during high school he would clean soot from the mill ceiling. His former aide, Andrew Young, describes his boss's car, a dirty, dark blue, dented, beat-up Buick, but adds, "Much later I would learn that the car was a bit of a ruse. A multimillionaire, Edwards started driving the Buick and put away his BMW and Lexus coupe to effect an 'everyman' image." Myth or no myth, few phrases can sell the American dream as evocatively as "son of a Kenyan goatherd."

The reality isn't quite like that, and in practice not even Arnold Schwarzenegger can blast through the obstacles that stand between him and the presidency. But what gifts these examples are to our aspirations. They remind us that Mr. Smith, or Dave, can go to Washington. But could he really?

He'd have had a hard time in Athens, at any rate. Not even the ancient ordinary Athenians could have stood up, seduced the assembly, and achieved greatness. The oligarchic writer Xenophon attributed the following to Socrates, as good advice on how a nervous aristocrat should regard the riffraff waiting to hear him:

> You [Charmides] are neither overawed by the cleverest people, nor are you afraid of the most powerful; and yet you claim to be afraid to speak in front of the most stupid and ineffectual. Of whom are you afraid? It's surely not the fullers, or shoemakers, or carpenters, or smiths, or merchants, or shopkeepers—whose

*business it is to buy at a cheaper rate and sell at a dearer one?*
*Because all these go to make up the assembly.*

It sounds so snobbish now. Today it seems as a given that a statesman's job is to improve the lot of workers and traders; to the ancient Athenian they provided a harmless but sometimes distracting backdrop to a stage that only the good and the beautiful could tread.* An implication of Xenophon's pep talk is that for a cobbler to address and sway the assembly would be absurd. The very idea is what would have made Aristophanes' play *The Acharnians* so funny to an Athenian audience: In it, a nebbish stands up and urges the assembly to make peace with Sparta, and when the assembly doesn't go his way, he makes his own peace.

Aristophanes, like Xenophon, was another writer who suggested that the idea of democracy is absurd. But then, he was a satirist, and democracy gave him many excellent targets, especially those politicians who courted popularity by pandering to the people. Watching the early phases of American democracy in action shows how carefully sages were considering these issues, and also the extent to which the fame of politicians characterized the system that emerged.

In his ingenious book *Making the American Self* (1997), Daniel Walker Howe shows how late-eighteenth-century thinking about the individual connected directly with the planning of an ideal society. He offers some sketches of the characters who personify the delicate balance between the individual and the state. It's fair to say that fame turns out to be a vital part of this negotiation. When he discusses Abraham Lincoln and Frederick Douglass, we are introduced to the idea of the "representative man," someone whose way of life becomes an example of how a human being, and also a state, should be.

The discussion of individual and society looks like a metaphor, the comparison being between a human being's ability to use reason

---

* In Athens, if you were beautiful, you were, by implication, good. In Greek such people were called *kaloi k'agathoi*—the words were run together because they were as inseparable as fish 'n' chips. The superlative of *agathos* is *aristos*.

as a way of governing passion and a government's ability to use reason to control spontaneous social urges. And yet, because a society is made up of those individuals, and because, as Howe points out, those individuals were becoming all the more individual throughout the eighteenth and nineteenth centuries, it matters more and more that a society consists of well-adjusted people, and those who best represent this kind of balance are especially valuable.

If you're going to be representative, then you'll need to do some work on yourself. Howe's studies of individuals show just how carefully figures such as Benjamin Franklin and Abraham Lincoln constructed their identities, with Franklin crafting his memoirs, and including his mistakes, into what Howe calls "one of the classic 'how-to' books," and with Lincoln cutting his family completely out of his own self-construction: He didn't invite any of them to his wedding, for example.

Benjamin Franklin's legacy goes further than the fostering of American democracy, in which he manages to be both the commonsensical author of *Poor Richard's Almanac* and the waggish Renaissance man who can run rings around the Englishmen in their coffeehouses. The French, too, idolized him during their own more chaotic lurch toward representation, when he was the American ambassador to the court in Paris. As Simon Schama writes of him, "Franklin was, of course, the designer of his own particular celebrity. . . . Aware that the French idealized America as a place of natural innocence, candor and freedom, he milked that stereotype for all it was worth." Hence the beaver cap. It was immediately recognizable: "He was probably better known by sight than the King, and his likeness could be found on engraved glass, painted porcelain, printed cottons, snuffboxes and inkwells."

His significance in the story of the French Revolution, and popular sentiment against King Louis XVI, becomes clearer in his dealings with the Marquis de Lafayette. It fell to Franklin to present Lafayette with a sword from Congress, in gratitude for the valor with which the marquis had conducted himself during the War of Independence. From this war, Lafayette, too, had emerged as a celebrity, but his éclat was ambiguous. On the one hand, he had showed himself to be a true patriot by thumping the Brits; on the other, he was involved in a struggle against a divinely appointed monarch. On his return from America, he put Louis XVI in a difficult position: Was he a hero or a threat? The king put him under house arrest briefly while he mulled this over. Lafayette had to come out.

But the love of Franklin was just as problematic for an aristocracy eager to stifle the spontaneous overflow of powerful feelings. Like Lafayette, he had thumped the Brits. One minister of Louis's had compressed Franklin's electrical antics and his revolutionary adventures into a pithy epigram: "He ripped lightning from the sky, and the sceptre from kings."* The king had to bear all this calmly, even when members of his own family idolized the man, although he found ways of expressing his own view in private. He added to the household objects bearing Franklin's likeness by sending his Franklin-smitten niece a portrait of Franklin on the bottom of a chamber pot.

Franklin was lucky: His most direct influence was in America, that gloriously blank canvas on which an ideal society was waiting to be etched. He could start from scratch and, with Thomas Jefferson, draft a constitution. Back in Britain, there was no such luck. "No taxation without representation" was a great slogan, but the British who stayed at home had almost no representation themselves. Their own story owes much to celebrities attracting attention to the popular cause. In the two examples we'll look at, one did this on purpose, the other by chance.

First, let's look at a British election—or at least, William Hogarth's images of one. In 1754 he captured a moment of change. This was a time when few seats were contested. Even in the early nineteenth century, only about 50 of the 658 seats in the House of Commons were allocated by an actual ballot. Not many people

---

*Not so pithy in English, but dynamite in Latin: *Eripuit coelo fulmen, sceptrumque tyrannis.* The author, Baron Turgot, didn't go for the singular, *tyranno,* surely because it would have made for an irritating internal rhyme; but that plural, tyrants, is menacing: Who's next?

could vote in those, either. Those who could were offered bribes, more or less openly. Candidates could always check that voters ticked the right box—secret voting didn't begin until 1872. Most constituencies were pocket boroughs, in which a local lord could name his MP, or rotten boroughs, where there were no electors. Others went to the highest bidder. So at least the practice of holding banquets meant that politicians met people who might have been electors. Hogarth's *Humours of an Election* is a series of paintings, of which the crammed canvas *An Election Entertainment* is the first. It shows the lengths to which politicians had to go to win a seat in Parliament. The bitter humor of it comes from the clash that arises when grandees suddenly have to make themselves agreeable to hoi polloi, and it depicts the kind of snafu that was the election banquet.

We meet two Whig candidates surrounded by constituents. One of the hopefuls, Sir Commodity Taxem, has a large crone on his lap, and he can't see around her to catch the little girl who is stealing his ring. His wig is about to catch fire, thanks to a careless man with a pipe behind him. Another punter has his arm around the second candidate. Tobacco fumes come from his mouth as he looks with upturned, drunken gaze toward the gentleman. His wig is slipping off. From the boot polish on his face, he seems to be a shoemaker.*

The scene resembles a carnival—a ribald, Mardi Gras kind of occasion—and it portrays the role reversal we can associate with such feasts. Suddenly, the politicians are at the mercy of their subjects, rather than the other way around. From the crowd outside comes a brick through the window; another brick has already grazed the election agent's head. A flag flutters in the street saying, MARRY AND MULTIPLY IN SPITE OF THE DEVIL (in reference to a Whig policy to emancipate the Jews). Things are not as they should be. If this *is* the only time the powerful meet their public, they're seeing them at their most fearsome. In the last of this

---

* The discussion of the *Election* series in Mark Hallett and Christine Riding's catalog of the Tate's 2007 Hogarth exhibition is helpful.

sequence of four paintings, the successful candidate, a Tory, is borne aloft on a chair, and ends up facing a pair of black boys who position a skull and crossbones before him. This glimpse of a *vanitas* motif makes the whole parade seem as pointless as possible: Just as all in life is vanity, so is all in a political career, or any quest for fame, because the end is always approaching.

The level of license the crowd is enjoying, with its rapid release of riotous energy, shows how contained and controlled they've been when there was no campaign on. So how could anybody give them the power they wanted, without unleashing proper terror over the land? It took a figure such as John Wilkes, the parliamentarian, pug-faced playboy, and purveyor of pornographic poetry. He defied contempt of Parliament for, among other things, criticizing the king as directly as possible; by the end of his life, he was daring to propose not only that Parliament's procedures should be public, but also that more people could have a say in who sat there. The philosopher-politician Edmund Burke accused him of loving the mob.★ The popularity he earned by doing it made him a celebrity. He didn't live to see the reforms he proposed come into effect; but after him, lawmakers had to take public demands for more control over their affairs with a new seriousness.

It is one of the many ironies in John Wilkes's life that, however honorable his ambitions for his fellow citizens, he was a notorious letch and seducer. It's one of many instances in history when a garish private life can do much to endear the public, who are, after all, the ultimate court of what is and isn't scandalous. As his biographer, Peter D. G. Thomas, points out, "To the mob, if not polite society, Wilkes was to be fireproof against rumour and innuendo."

John Wilkes was born in 1725 to a father who was a malt distiller and a mother who was the daughter of a tanner; he grew up at the prosperous end of the mercantile class. Wilkes advanced by a number of shrewd steps: by networking with Whiggish types at

---

★ Edmund Burke hadn't thought so, and said of Wilkes's election to the seat of Middlesex in 1768: "The crowd always want to draw themselves, from abstract principles to personal attachments, and since the fall of Lord Chatham, there has been no hero of the mob but Wilkes." Thomas, *John Wilkes: A Friend to Liberty*, 13.

the University of Leiden; by marrying a Puritan with a large manor in Aylesbury; and by attending raucous orgies in the ruins of a Buckinghamshire monastery.

The members of this coterie called themselves the "monks of Medmenham," or sometimes the monks of Saint Francis. One would have thought the complicity of free sex in monastic cells might have had a bonding effect on the participants, among them many ministers of state. In fact, throughout his career, Wilkes was often stitched up by the club's habitués. In 1754 Wilkes wrote *The Essay on Woman*, which he had elegantly printed in 1764—precisely the wrong time, because it appeared while he was engaged in his biggest political fight. Whatever one thinks of this piece of porn, it is a pitch-perfect parody of Alexander Pope. During the campaign to expel Wilkes, parts of the poem were read in the House of Lords, which must have been a livelier place then than now.

These antics, which made him such an affront to his peers, did much to endear him to the people, who seldom failed to show him intense support from the first moment he landed in trouble. The trouble was a tangled story involving Wilkes's journalism. Briefly, the circumstances were that George III had ascended to the throne, eager to show that he could wield some power over the government, and to end the Seven Years' War. To satirize the new age, Wilkes founded a popular paper called the *North Briton*, which purported to be an organ read and written by a cabal of Scots bent on world domination. (One of the new king's first moves was to install his former tutor, a Scot, the Earl of Bute, as his prime minister.) In its forty-fifth issue, he wrote of the King's speech that concluded Parliament in 1763:

> *Every friend of his country must lament that a prince of so many great and amiable qualities, whom England truly revere, can be brought to give the sanction of his sacred name to the most odious measures, and to the most unjustifiable, public declarations, from a throne ever renowned for truth, honour, and unsullied virtue.*

The ensuing row over this apparently fawning prose shows just how touchy the king was about his royal dignity; and also how the virtue of the monarchy had become so sullied over the years that by now it was fair game. In addition, George III was eager to make it seem as though the policies in question were not only his, but also good. The idea that he was in control would later be dismissed completely in America; but for now he had to quash Wilkes. His government did manage to do it, in the short term, but only by straining the constitution to its limits, and ultimately by cheating: redefining the notion of parliamentary immunity, for example, or by assuming that he'd written the (irrelevant) *Essay on Woman* without actually proving it. So in the long term, Wilkes became a hero.

The affair led to his exile. When he returned in 1768, an outlaw and in debt, he was obliged to serve time at the King's Bench Prison, even though he kept winning parliamentary elections in Middlesex, one of those rare constituencies in which people could actually vote. Middlesex was then the seat that represented Greater London, and so Wilkes could call on the support of the capital's many radicals. As one of them, Sir Joseph Mawbey, pointed out, "It was not the refuse of the people, it was not the mob, who had elected Wilkes." During the hearings in the courts, and the debates in the Commons, there were cries of "Wilkes and Liberty" outside Parliament and in the galleries of Drury Lane; there were riots in the City, too, where the authorities refused to condemn the violence. In Limehouse, five hundred sawyers destroyed a windmill in protest. The demonstrators made it clear that they weren't going to stop: "No justice, no peace," they shouted as they threw stones at the troops who hounded them, bent on killing. In one confrontation, seven were left dead, and fifteen wounded.

For all this, the business of John Wilkes and his reelection to Parliament doesn't look much like an English revolution. But it was a vital lesson that the people wanted a direct say in who represented them, and that the government couldn't debar candidates simply because they had written artful satire or pervy verse. If anything, these things were positive qualifications to voters, especially in London, just as Bill Clinton's approval ratings remained high throughout the Monica Lewinsky business.* Throughout Wilkes's later career, he did things still more directly relevant to the relationship between politicians and their public. Having done so much for the freedom of the press already—making fair comment about public figures both a joy and a right—he went on to ensure that the press could report on parliamentary debates. To us today, it might seem staggering that these details couldn't be published: After all, Parliament now has its own television channel, à la C-SPAN, so that even as obscure a figure as the leader of the Liberal Democrats can achieve a kind of fame. But then, it must have led eighteenth-century Britons to suspect what the Athenians of 417 B.C. knew: Things that were presented as having been done in their name were anything but.

Wilkes wanted to change that, too. He was in the privileged position of knowing not only what the people wanted but also how little of it they were getting. He wanted people to be better represented than they were, and with this in mind, on March 21, 1776, he proposed the first ever motion on parliamentary reform. He wanted to scrap the rotten boroughs, the ones where no one voted, and to reallocate those constituencies to the rapidly growing urban areas, which had no seats at all in the Commons. It would be fifty-six years before anything like this became law, with the Great Reform Act of 1832; but Wilkes started it.

Still, people couldn't rely on being heard merely through well-meaning politicians, and they needed other celebrities to assert control over public affairs. At a time when the royal family seemed remote from the people, the wronged, neglected Princess of Wales, conducting her own dalliances abroad, was the ideal figure to attract those who began talking of a republic. This was the case with Caroline, Princess of Brunswick-Wolfenbüttel, who married the future George IV in 1795. As a later Princess of Wales would say, there were three people in this marriage, although in 1795, this was a legal

---

* Andrew Young writes of John Edwards that he was elected to be a senator in North Carolina "with a big majority among blacks and women and that he benefited from a national backlash against the Republican moralizers who had hounded President Clinton."

fact: George had already been through a marriage ceremony with a Mrs. Fitzherbert, but she was a Roman Catholic and the union, if allowed to stand, would have deprived him of the crown. (Caroline later said that her one faux pas was her affair with Mr. Fitzherbert. By the standards of both prince and princess, wife swapping must have seemed tiresomely straightforward.) When Caroline arrived in Britain, George declined to meet her. He had already been told by his staff that she was loose living, foul mouthed, and smelly, and he sent his then mistress, Lady Jersey, to pick her up at the port. When he did finally set eyes on her, he quickly looked away and asked for a brandy.

Her popularity was inversely proportional to that of the prince. The people hated him, so they loved her. He had affairs, as everyone knew, and they vilified him; in her case, they sympathized. George did nothing to help his image by banishing her from court, allowing her only occasional encounters with their daughter. (It's a miracle that this daughter was ever born; by George's reckoning there were only three occasions when she could have been conceived, and these were all in the first two days of their marriage.) She went to live in Blackheath, where she was the hostess of a fruity salon, and where she was surrounded by children, at least one of whom was likely to be hers—by an unknown father, possibly someone she met at the docks. She managed all this with an insouciance that showed how precarious the prince's position was. If people could tolerate her flagrant misconduct in their midst, what other inversions of the social order might they contemplate?

George made repeated attempts to divorce her, but looked sillier each time. In 1806 he was overruled by his father (who was in fact Caroline's uncle); in 1813 he sent spies to Italy, to gather evidence of her promiscuity for a later trial. In 1820, when George became king, Caroline was offered £50,000 a year so long as she dropped her claim to be the queen. When she refused this, George managed to have Tories in the Commons bring the case before the Lords.

The case nearly cost him his crown. In her trial, she was advised by the radical former lord mayor of London, Matthew Wood, and represented by Henry Brougham, who would later do much to have the Reform Bill passed. These causes didn't mean much to her, but she meant a lot to the champions of the causes. Cartoonists engraved obscene images of the king with his mistresses; *The Times* supported Caroline; women in particular rallied to her. As with Wilkes, and as, indeed, with Cimon, people were prepared to ignore gossip about their leaders, so long as those leaders were prepared to act in their interests.

And yet this support was never assured. After its third reading, Parliament voted against the "Pains and Penalties" Bill—whose purpose was to dissolve the prince's marriage to Caroline—to widespread jubilation, not least because those few constituents who were able to vote made the national feeling clear to their representatives. It is true that when Caroline showed up to take her throne at the king's coronation on July 19, 1821, the door was shut on her and the congregation jeered. But those gathered within the Abbey on this occasion weren't a typical slice of the population. There would be no jeering three weeks later: Caroline died on August 7.

In her last days, she told those around her that she had been poisoned. There was no autopsy. She had declared her wish to be buried in Brunswick, and troops tried to slip her body out of the country as discreetly as possible, but crowds attacked them and forced the cortège to parade through the city.

The whole affair stirred up the kind of revolutionary feeling that Shelley's poetry espoused so openly, particularly throughout the year before. In 1819 troops had moved in to disband a peaceful meeting in St Peter's Field in Manchester, killing eleven people and injuring five hundred. Seven years before, a prime minister had been assassinated.* It was a time when weavers were smashing up their frames in Nottingham, and the Lords were debating whether the death penalty was an appropriate punishment.† In short, it was

---

* John Bellingham shot Spencer Perceval as the latter entered the lobby of the House of Commons. The motive turned out to be personal rather than political.
† Byron spoke in this debate. He was against.

as close as Britain has come to a revolution of its own; and throughout the period, facts, myths, and propaganda concerning celebrities became vital. As E. A. Smith writes of the Caroline case, "The adoption of her cause by radical and whig politicians gave the private lives and morals of the royal family a public and political significance." Elsewhere, it was the kind of gossip that could foment a revolution for real.

Although the British didn't have a violent, French-style uprising, in Britain we have ended up with a similar situation: Our politicians need to deploy the common touch, and to stay as our leaders, they pretend they really are like us. And although the processes by which they and the French got there—the ballot box and the guillotine—seem to represent the instincts of two hugely different cultures, still, the result is the same: The noble, the glorious, and the rich can no longer demand our love. Nor can the merely popular; so every five years or so we can punish them, these days without beheading them.

## ii. *Égalité*

> *Qu'un sang impur abreuve nos sillons!*
> (Let impure blood water our furrows!)

> — From *La Marseillaise*

When a crowd came to the Place de la Révolution to see a guillotine blade fall upon Marie Antoinette's neck, a lot of the hatred they expressed toward her came from a diamond necklace she never wore. But stories about it, garbled fantasies deriving from an already complicated truth, led people to believe their queen to be *capable de tout*. Throughout her time as queen, her image made her first attractive, and later loathed.

We shouldn't underestimate the extent to which image and boudoir speculation led to the upheaval that followed. Clearly, to many Frenchmen and Frenchwomen, Marie Antoinette couldn't put a foot right; one moment she was too remote from the people, and the next, she heinously inspired them to imitate her. The way in which the slightest sign she gave them could be twisted and travestied reveals an urgent need to destroy someone who had stood for everything that was once à la mode. It was a time when these details were no longer irksome or risible; they were lethal.

One way of reading the change in the way the public felt is by looking at the pornography they produced. In the early days, it had a kind of classical elegance about it. Orgiasts would hide in bushes, and lovers would be praised for beauty and brawn in mythological terms: "Prince, lord, or simple gentleman, you're Hercules in the form of Adonis." It was what readers expected of the genre. These vignettes appeared in little books—*libelles,* from the Latin *libelli.* Lies were so inevitable that the genre gave us the word "libel." But then came the affair of the diamond necklace. By 1791 the pamphleteers described Marie Antoinette as having gang bangs with guardsmen.* In 1792 those involved in tricking her were listed as her lovers, regardless of their gender. (The queen was regularly portrayed as an insatiable lesbian.) Finally, at her trial in 1793, prosecutors were accusing her of abusing her eight-year-old son.

The French Revolution shows democracy in its most brutal form: Indeed, it's the "rule of the mob" that Xenophon and Aristophanes found so uncomfortable, although the events of 1789–1793 showed that they should have considered themselves lucky. Here we see again how people would rally around the famous to lead their causes, or else would turn those who sympathized with them into celebrities. It happened all the time during these years. For example, when the king sacked his finance minister, Jacques Necker, a crowd flocked to a waxwork seller so that they could parade his image through the streets.† The waxwork maker, Peter

---

* The inspiration here was still classical, but the comparisons were with Messalina, the insatiable wife of Claudius, rather than any Olympian.
† The king sacked Necker on a Sunday, hoping that it would receive less attention. As it happened, more people were milling around Paris then than at any other time during the week.

Creutz, made a rousing pro-Necker speech himself. This was on July 12, 1789. In October that year, during the stampede to the Palace of Versailles, the figure of Théroigne de Méricourt became the darling of the mob. She was a former courtesan and singer who became a full-time revolutionary, especially visible and rousing with her riding gear, plumed hat, and pistol. Her downfall, too, came to symbolize the decline of the Revolution: She was stripped naked and flogged, and lived on in an asylum until 1817. Even then, she was often visited as a spectacle.

In its way, her fate was as spectacular as Marie Antoinette's; but Marie Antoinette is a reminder of the other kind of crowd instinct that democracy tries to tame. She shows clearest of all that phenomenon that Cimon has revealed already—that the more gossip adheres to you, the sooner your time is up. Pornography was one thing; more credible, somehow, was a long story involving a necklace that was made for the late Louis XV's mistress, and which was worth 1.5 percent of France's national debt in 1786. This necklace had become so famous that it became the object of a sting operation, in which a fake noblewoman who had wheedled her way into the court wangled it out of a cardinal.

Marie Antoinette had never wanted the necklace, but it became a byword for her profligacy—a bauble she happened to have lying around. And then the con woman, Jeanne de la Motte, added to the fund of pornography written about the queen with allegations that she had enjoyed lesbian romps with Marie Antoinette, whom she gave lustful lines that read like a pagan travesty of Saint Teresa's effusions: "What rapture! I thought that I saw Olympus open and that I entered, for my ecstasies were not of a mortal kind."

Jeanne de la Motte's *Justificatory Memoirs* appeared in 1788. Mirabeau, a revolutionary who did as much as he could to retain the monarchy, said about the events of the following year, "Madame de la Motte's voice alone brought on the horrors of July 14 and of October 5." He was referring not only to the storming of the Bastille but also to the moment when fishwives charged from Paris to Versailles, intending to slaughter the royal family. The necklace even came up at Marie Antoinette's trial. By this point people were prepared to believe anything about her. Some thought that the whole thing was a plot conceived by the queen herself to destroy the cardinal in question; and how useful that it should have involved diamonds. Many more were prepared to believe a simpler version: that the cardinal used the necklace to seduce the queen behind a bush.

Jeanne de la Motte, who came to style herself more aristocratically as Jeanne de Valois, was nothing like John Wilkes. Civil liberties didn't interest her. She wanted money and status, and thought of herself as an aristocrat. The pretension did her no favors. When she was punished, she was branded with the letter *v* for *voleuse,* although plenty reckoned it stood for *valois,* as though the name to which she aspired had somehow come to torture her. But perhaps even this gave her a kind of identity, and became something for us to remember her by. After all, the extraordinary thing about her is that she engineered her own infamy in order to secure even greater notoriety for the queen.★ If Mirabeau is right, then few can have invented romps with such dramatic consequences. Every creative detail about Marie Antoinette's desires—the opera about orgies with the Comte d'Artois and the Duchesse de Polignac; the painting in which she grabs a scepter from the king's lap while a snake writhes around her; even the line about the cake—made her execution more certain.

But other deaths, during the Terror as much as during the first throes of the Revolution, satisfied the people in different ways. There were moments when the rises and falls of fortunes had a briskness that would have stunned even the Romans, except that there was something more democratic about it: You could be fairly plebeian and still be worth executing, not least because you might have caused some executions yourself. So it was with Robespierre, the lawyer's son who unleashed the Reign of Terror of 1793–1794 as the leader of the Committee for Public Safety. As it happened, when events caught up with him, Robespierre's executioners did everything they could to make his end as inglorious as possible.

---

★ For more on this kind of faking, see chapter 10.

He helped by failing to shoot himself properly during his arrest, with the result that he mangled his jaw. He was taken with eighteen others and wanted to be the last to go. Of his batch, he was the penultimate victim.

To survive, you had to be one of the people: to be the people's people. The problem was that you had to keep those people in some kind of order, too. As we have seen in the cases of George IV and Louis XVI, no ruler could expect automatic love and loyalty. So how could the new lot command it?

A painting by Goya suggests an answer. He painted an official portrait of Ferdinand Guillemardet in 1798. Guillemardet was France's ambassador to Spain, at a time when the revolutionary period was as stable as it ever would be. This is an official portrait in some senses, at least: The sitter is at a desk, with two pens in an inkstand and some papers we can't see. He faces us, but his legs are crossed. The crossing is crucial: It suggests that he's halfway between his work and the viewer. Although one of his legs and the chair he sits on is pointing toward us, the other leg isn't—it's running alongside the desk. But still more significant, the pose suggests a studied informality. He doesn't mind looking comfortable for us. To sit with your legs crossed was seen as vulgar at the time. Perhaps out of desperation, Louis XVI's finance minister, Charles Alexandre de Calonne, had sat like that for Élisabeth-Louise Vigée-Lebrun in 1784.* But with Calonne, the gesture seems countermanded by the piece of paper he holds in his hand: *"Au roi,"* or "King," it says, in a grand copperplate.

Guillemardet would never be writing that. As an elected member of the Convention, he had voted for Louis XVI's execution, a fact that was well known in Spain. He was a man who had been intimately involved with the most impressive show of power imaginable—regicide—and yet Goya contrived to make him look like one of us. Unlike Calonne, he wears no wig. His hair is short

---

* This relaxed attitude did little to dismiss rumors that Calonne and Vigée-Lebrun were having an affair. They weren't, but the painter wrote of the allegations that they made her "feel disgusted by celebrity, especially when one has the misfortune to be a woman" (*Citizens and Kings*, 388).

and curly. His suit lacks the gloss of Calonne's silk. The only gaudy touches come in the reds, whites, and blues of the cockade and feathers on his hat, and his sash. But those colors aren't his colurs. They're the colors of everyone the Revolution wanted to make free.

Discussing this painting in his biography of Goya, Robert Hughes calls Guillemardet a "Burgundian country doctor," to stress his ordinariness even more than Goya did. This plays down the subject's sophistication. For a start, there was his medical degree, and then, he made quick work of entering Talleyrand's circle in Paris. Soon the servants of the state would start looking even more approachable.

Michel Gérard was another member of the National Convention. He was a Breton farmer, admired for his simplicity and loyalty; he was a member of the Jacobin Club before Robespierre turned it into a killing machine. It is in dispute whether a painting that hangs in a museum in Le Mans is of him. That fact in itself tells you something about Michel Gérard—people didn't remember what he looked like. We're not even sure if the painting is really of a member of the National Convention. For that matter, we don't even know who the painter was. For a while he (he?) was thought to be Jacques-Louis David, the man who strove so hard to give some kind of heroic, antique dignity to the horrors of the Revolution. The sitter might not be Gérard, and the painter definitely isn't David. Here, from around 1810, is a portrait of a family man, surrounded by his children. We don't know how much power he has in the state, but we know he has power within his family. This is a French glimpse at the "representative man" we met earlier in America. He looks even more settled in the household since there's no mother to upstage him.★ He is a father of four. His children look as though they could be aged from eight to eighteen. Either they resemble him, or else the painter didn't have many ways of doing eyes. In any case, they look as if they're going places: Both of the elder boys have high collars and fine coats; the daughter

---

★ The commentator in the *Citizens and Kings* catalog, Amar Arrada, raises the attractive possibility that the mother is the painter.

at the keyboard will make an accomplished wife, and the pretty blue dress with the modest frills on top already suits her. The youngest boy has been listening to his father reading. His open shirt collar is white, his waistcoat red, and his little jacket blue. He is the future of the Republic.

And the father himself? He's plonked himself down, fitting his sturdy frame between the piano stool, the wall, and a small table. The drawing room has all the right stuff in it, but it isn't big. Although he has a pleasing paunch, the man's clothes are loose on him. His sleeves are rolled up like a worker's. His hair is gray; he has a spare chin; his cravat is slack. If he's Michel Gérard, then he's had a hard day legislating. The whole scene presents a man who hasn't enjoyed many advantages in his own life, but whose labors have benefited his children. And, as the little boy's color-coded outfit suggests, those children are the viewer's children—*les enfants de la Patrie.*

The painter has his or her faults, but not many. Here is a picture of a civilization at a turning point. We are allowed to think that this is an age when people—men, anyway—are represented by people who are as much like them as possible, and who have their interests at heart. It is the beginning of the age that Roland Barthes could still recognize when he came to write *Mythologies* (1957), his essays on twentieth-century life that strove to expose the messages and manipulations beneath its surface. In a piece on election photography, he writes:

> *Needless to say the use of electoral photography presupposes a kind of complicity: a photograph is a mirror, what we are asked to read is the familiar, the known; it offers to the voter his own likeness, but clarified, exalted, superbly elevated into a type. This glorification is in fact the very definition of the photogenic: the voter is at once expressed and heroized, he is invited to elect himself . . .*

So *les grands* really are like us, only a little bit grander; and they come from among our ranks. Barthes suggests that a picture of a politician offers us "a style of life of which he is at once the product, the example and the bait."\* In theory, that bait could tempt us to want to be that politician; but, like all famous people, politicians are doing something on our behalf. They are undergoing mental fights so that we don't have to, and, in Barthes's view of it, for reasons we mightn't want to know about:

> Almost all three-quarter face photos are ascensional, the face is lifted towards a supernatural light which draws it up and elevates it to the realm of a higher humanity; the candidate reaches the Olympus of elevated feelings, where all political contradictions are solved: peace and war in Algeria, social progress and employers' profits, so-called "free" religious schools and subsidies from the sugar-beet lobby, the Right and the Left (an opposition always "superseded"!): all these coexist peacefully in this thoughtful gaze, nobly fixed on the hidden interests of Order.

By this description, politicians appear to transcend their mortal origins and gain their own kind of godlike understanding. It's a reminder of that eighteenth-century model of the human being that becomes the model of the state: reason governing passion. But the passion will emerge somehow. It's just that revolutions and elections give us still more ways of killing our gods.

### iii. All tomorrow's parties
Politicians *are* celebrities; the struggle to seem different from them is in vain. Politicians must be concerned with the same things that concern the rest of us, and if we complain that our representatives are preoccupied with ephemera, then we are going to have a long wait before Josiah Bartlet really does become president. Even so, our leaders get themselves in a pickle when they try to share our interest in them. It seldom goes well. For a moment, President Obama managed it with some panache when he called Kanye West a jackass, even though this distracted attention from the truth

---

\*Barthes uses "he" throughout his discussion; but then, the first time women could vote in France was 1945.

of West's message, that the video for *Single Ladies* was better than whatever it was that Taylor Swift's people came up with. He even manages to maintain some grace when the White House guest list reveals that there have been visits from Alicia Keys, Jennifer Lopez, Brad Pitt, and, poignantly, Tiger Woods. Even so, Republicans have eagerly derided Obama as a celebrity himself.

It seems unfair. There are times when you need celebrities, surely, and when George Clooney is the very person to keep you up-to-date on the situation in Darfur.* And anyway, Obama manages to trade on a friendship with Jay-Z while approaching the lyrics with caution. (Maybe this approach will start working soon with Benjamin Netanyahu.) It's especially unfair when it becomes clear how coy Obama is about schmoozing stars when compared to Tony Blair.

During his time in office, Tony Blair managed to seem cozy with the stars whose homes he'd visit on holiday—Sir Cliff Richard, Robin Gibb of the Bee Gees—and yet he was enthralled by the glamour of their lives. When he met one prominent musician, he asked where the man was jetting off to next, and was evidently disappointed to learn that there was no jet. This could reflect the fact that since Tony Blair, a Labour leader, could enjoy such facilities, private airplanes should be available for the many, and not for the few. Or perhaps he was recognizing that one day, he wouldn't have flights chartered just for him, and was basking in the moment with someone equally privileged. He took boyish delight, not only in the company of famous people, but also in the trappings of fame.

Shortly after he'd won his first election, Blair invited a slew of celebs to a party at Downing Street. When the magazine *Grazia* went to interview them about it ten years afterward, even the kindest of them were ambivalent about the bash. Piers Morgan told an interviewer, "It actually makes my skin crawl to think I was involved with it." By the time of the article, Blair was about to announce his much-trailed resignation, and most of the celebrities could content themselves that they were still doing what they'd been doing

---

* Before this, Clooney had to deny that he'd been giving Obama style tips.

a decade earlier. There's something Darwinian about this: In most cases, the celebrities have managed to survive better than Blair. There is a competition for longevity. The famous people, feeling that they still have their reputations and their integrity, allow themselves to judge, as though history will treat them better. This is why, when the British prime minister, Harold Wilson, gave John Lennon a "Show Business Personality of the Year" Award, Lennon said to Wilson, "Thank you, Mr. Dobson." Caesar, I am as little keen to please you as I am to know if you are black or white.

It gives us a jolt when it's the other way around: when somebody wants to lend glamour to the status quo. And it is still startling to read Elvis Presley's blue felt-tip scrawl on American Airlines notepaper, writing to Richard Nixon: "First, I would like to introduce myself. . . . The drug culture, the hippie elements, the SDS, <u>Black Panthers, etc. do not consider me</u> as their enemy or as they call it the establishment. <u>I call it america and I love it.</u> . . . So I wish not be given a title or an appointed position. I can and will do more good if I were made a Federal Agent at Large and I will help out by doing it my way through my communications with people of all ages." He met Nixon at the White House on December 21, 1970; the notes of the encounter show that Nixon thrice said to Elvis that he should "retain his credibility." This shows the master at work: Nixon knew that anything unsubtle, such as a speech from the stage, could lead to mutually assured dorkdom.*

Stars who become politicians show even greater commitment: They know that they will fail to achieve what's in their manifesto, and they take on the jobs anyway. Celebrities as civilians don't always ask to be accountable; they're allowed to have one talent, or even none. Although they fulfill many requirements we have of them, often unwittingly, and often painfully, they don't tend to present themselves as public servants. It seems extraordinary when they do. To see Arnold Schwarzenegger become governor of California

---

* And yet he might have gotten away with it: James Brown's reputation survived his performance at Nixon's inauguration, and even the reference to Gerald Ford as a "brand-new funky president."

was to see a shirt stuffed to the ripping point. To see the Hungarian adult-film performer Ilona Staller enter the Italian parliament as a deputy for the Radical Party was to see voters getting what they wanted: a pale, pouting woman who enhanced her left-wing credentials by exposing her enhanced left breast.★

### iv. The door to your right will now open

December 30, 2006, was the dawn of Eid al-Adha, or at least it was for Sunni Moslems. It is a festival that commemorates the moment when the patriarch Ibrahim didn't sacrifice Ishmael and slew a ram instead. The faithful can rejoice that he complied with Allah's call, and in exchange Allah showed mercy. At dawn that day, Saddam Hussein was executed.

In setting the date for the execution, the Iraqi prime minister Nouri al-Maliki was using the Gregorian calendar, rather than the Islamic one. Saddam had to be gone by the end of 2006. This in itself did little to convince Iraqis that their nation's court was acting independently of the occupying alliance.

As a result, the whole thing was rushed. Even George W. Bush said, "I wish, obviously, that the proceedings had gone in a more dignified way." He said this only once it had become clear just how undignified the execution had been. Before then, he had let it be known that he was asleep when it happened, which required a bedtime of around 9 P.M. in Crawford, Texas. He had been told that the matter was in hand before he retired for the night. This suggests that, however undignified things turned out to be in the end, the arrangements seemed just dignified enough for the president—not that he had any say over them.

The first images of Saddam's death were broadcast without sound, and without any glimpse of the moment when his neck snapped inside the noose. It all looked as serene as a hanging can look in a shed on a compound called Camp Justice filled with men in bala-

---

★ There is some indication that voters wanted La Cicciolina (to give her her stage name, which means "Little Dumpling"), but they preferred her when she stood for some agenda beyond sex. In the 1992 elections, her Party of Love attracted 1 percent of the votes.

clavas. The former dictator declined the offer of a black sack over his head, and mouthed holy words. He looked sleepy and bothered. Only when a later film appeared, recorded clandestinely on a mobile telephone, did it become clear that he was taunted in his last moments. "Go to hell, Insha'Allah," one man said, while others chanted the name of Muqtada al-Sadr, a Shiite leader. He replied by asking, "Is this bravery?" He died saying the words "There is no God but Allah, and Muhammad is the messenger of Allah."

So often in the story of fame, we find substitutes for bloodshed and actual killings of actual gods. Democracy is a substitute. But there are still executions, and they continue to reveal an instinct that has never left us; at least, it didn't leave those who were present at Saddam Hussein's death. It is hard to see how executions can be dignified. If the victim behaves calmly, the authorities look worse. And public figures, even evil ones, who have managed to maintain their positions through some kind of stagecraft, often know how to conduct themselves at the end. For them, the public nature of their deaths has a posthumous advantage. From the beheading of Charles I, to the use of the guillotine, to the video camera and the age of YouTube, the audience for these spectacles has grown, and dictators have understood how to work it. Charles I wore an extra layer of clothing so he would not shiver in the cold and appear frightened on the January morning in 1649, when he stepped out of Inigo Jones's banqueting hall to the block. He asked the axe man to strike only when he put out his hands: At that stage, the condemned could have a last moment of power. Louis XVI tried to have his hair cut in advance, so that he wasn't shorn at the scaffold. He failed, and when he reached what is now the Place de la Concorde, he addressed a crowd of twenty thousand. The drums began to roll before he could finish his last speech. When Marie Antoinette followed him ten months later, an actor rode in front of her cart through the streets shouting, "Here she is, the infamous Antoinette, she is *foutue* [fucked], my friends!" She stepped lightly up to the guillotine and declared that her death would end her torture.

Most leaders have been able to make some kind of a scene, with the massacre of the Romanovs in 1918 being a prominent exception.

Even in the gymnasium at Nürnberg, the ten Nazis who were hanged had a small audience and were arranged for photographs afterward. Beyond that, everything was brisk and official. A witness wrote that "to get the execution over quickly, the military police would bring in the man while the prisoner who preceded him still was dangling at the end of the rope." Although the men found guilty of crimes against humanity weren't taunted, they were asked to announce their names, as if to rob them of their renown. This riled Julius Streicher in particular, who snapped back, "You know my name well." Still, he was made to say it.

So throughout the history of revolutions and coups, the victors have taken more and more steps to make the process less personal, as if they are taking away the victim's identity as well as his or her life. One way of doing this has been to carry out the procedure in smaller, less public spaces. The thing must be seen to have been done, but the less pomp there is about it, the better for the executioners. The invention of the guillotine was a slip-up. One of the machine's many ironies is that Dr. Joseph-Ignace Guillotin designed it as a more humane way of dispatching a villain. Odd as it may seem, what he was after was intimacy. He meant for the death to be away from town, to keep the criminal's family removed from the suspicious and snatching crowd. Instead, the guillotine stood at the center of the city as both spectacle and deterrent. The victims would have been famous, if there hadn't been so many of them.

The execution of Saddam Hussein is part of these developments: It was at once secluded and global. It had many consequences, one of which was to further the divide between Sunni and Shiite communities in Iraq: To kill him on the Sunni day of sacrifice, when it is forbidden that humans be executed, was seen by many as a calculated insult. But one effect has been insufficiently discussed, and that is its impact on the world of entertainment.

Details of Saddam's death were still emerging in the days leading up to January 10, 2007, but by then things were pretty clear. In a compound somewhere near London (although it could have been anywhere), a group of unimpressive celebrities, selected almost indiscriminately and kept under twenty-four-hour surveillance, were summoned around a table. A female, faceless voice, smoothed out to sound as though it had come from a computer, intoned over an intercom—the voice of Big Brother. "Something's happening," said Cleo Rocos, the former sidekick of the late comedian Kenny Everett. She couldn't say what was happening: Nobody knew. Other housemates checked the precise time. Jackiey (*sic*) Budden arrived last in the diary room. She was appearing on *Celebrity Big Brother* because she is Jade Goody's mother.

What happened next was extraordinary. Jackiey was called into the diary room, her shirt only half on her. As she shuffled shoeless away, she turned her bare back to a camera. From the diary room—a small studio to the side of the house—her face was filmed and beamed onto a monitor that her housemates could see, and the nation could see. She didn't look good. "See how good we look on TV," one housemate said. A hard laugh suggested that this was taken ironically.

Big Brother began to narrate events that had led up to this moment. Jackiey showed that she was following, but the voice ignored these interventions. It was a complicated story, in which most members of the house lived in simple servants' quarters, while the plebeian Jade Goody and her entourage—her mother, Jackiey, and her boyfriend, Jack Tweed—lived it up in plusher accommodation, as though they were in a dream. These trappings had not brought out the best in Jade, nor in her man, nor in her mother. Now they learned that one of them was facing eviction. Jackiey now realized what she was doing in the diary room. For her, *Big Brother* was over. "No!" she bellowed, as if trapped in the body of a bull. As her eviction became clear, her housemates reacted in shock. "No!" echoed one. "They can't do that!" The anguish increased as the voice continued with her instructions: "You will not be able to say your good-byes. . . . The door to your right will now open."

Accounts of the Princesse de Lamballe's death talk about a judge directing her to a door. It was open by the time she got there. Those instructions were the last words she heard before she met her killers in the Abbaye prison. This was during the September

Massacres of 1792, when fourteen hundred prisoners were killed in a combination of national paranoia and contrived vindictiveness. Her head was placed on a pike and held under Marie Antoinette's window.

Back in the *Big Brother* house, Jermaine Jackson, brother of Michael, muttered, "It should have been me out there, damn it," with all the nobility of Sydney Carton at the end of *A Tale of Two Cities*. The howls continued. The priority was to comfort Jade, who sobbed, "She got no shoes on or nothing." One contestant, who had been saying, "Let's have courage" since the events unfolded, told Jade consolingly, "Let's get a grip on ourselves here. They're not going to send her home without any shoes," and repeated, "You must have courage."

How Jackiey looked was vital to Jade. Jade was already a star, and was now determined to elevate her mother to the same status. But Jackiey had been an embarrassment in the house. She had been an ungrateful mistress to her servants, and had treated Shilpa Shetty with a snide indifference—she regularly refused to pronounce the Bollywood star's name correctly. But Leo Sayer, who had had a string of hits in the 1970s, addressed Jade's worries: "She was fantastic in there. She didn't shame you or look bad or anything." Out of Jade's earshot, others were franker. Dirk Benedict, who played Face in *The A-Team*, was quick to call her a "vicious, mean-spirited person."

There was no crowd to greet Jackiey when she left. There was no crowd when Jade herself was evicted, following the outrage after she bullied the Bollywood star Shilpa Shetty and referred to her as "Shilpa Poppadom." As Shilpa retorted, "All you are famous for is this," and pointed to the ceiling of the *Big Brother* house.

Jade Goody faced a strong ostracism. Department stores and boutiques stopped selling the scent called Jade; her book, *Jade: My Autobiography*, was removed from shelves. An antibullying campaign decided that Jade wasn't such a good poster girl after all. Even she felt that there was a wheel of fortune whirring away, and she said that the fame that had begun in the *Big Brother* house would end there.

It's quite something to ostracize somebody from being famous. It's nothing like killing them, but it does fill its victims with a mortal dread. The Romans thought of the *damnatio memoriae* as their severest punishment. It was forgetting without forgiving. But the show managed to dismiss her from folk memory even as it was giving her more publicity than she had enjoyed before. Not for the last time, Gordon Brown had something to say about her. A community voted her out of recognition. It was fitting that her brief fame arose from an equality of opportunity through which anybody could become a celebrity; and that the show adopted the instruments, at once democratic and degrading, by which we rid ourselves of those people, more or less great, who place themselves above us. Jade Goody was scared of dying, as who wouldn't be; but she faced death with greater dignity than she faced her loss of fame. *Vox populi, vox dei*—the voice of the people is the voice of God. And these days, it's scarier.

9

We're All Individuals (Yes, We're All
Individuals): How the Scent of Mariah Carey
Had the Power to Make Us All
Part of Something Special

### i. *I will give out divers schedules of my beauty*★

> "A daub of scent automatically makes everyone,
> slave or free, smell alike; but the smells that
> come from the efforts of free men in sport call
> above all for strict training over a long period,
> if they are to be pleasing and worth of a free
> man."
>    "That may be so for the young," said Lycon,
> "but what about us who are too old for the
> gymnasia—what ought we to smell of?"
>    "True goodness, of course," said Socrates.

—XENOPHON
*Symposium* 2

Have you ever given someone "Intimately Beckham for Her"?†
Did you ever receive "Lovely" by Sarah Jessica Parker? If so, how
did you feel? Were we tempted by "Donald Trump, the Fragrance"? (And why the subtitle? Was it in case we mistook something in a scent bottle for some other attribute of Donald Trump;
or was it because we needed to be clear that what was in the bottle
was supposed to be fragrant?) What was the allure of "Mystique de

---

★ Olivia, *Twelfth Night.*
† This isn't so much a rhetorical question as an open-minded inquiry, I promise.

176

Michael Jackson" or "Only, Only Crazy," redolent of Julio Igle-
sias? We're talking about an evanescent age already, when famous
smells pulsed through ebbing breezes. We cannot summon back
those essences, but perhaps the marketing blurb for a scent bearing
Mariah Carey's name can help:

> *Mariah Carey M perfume has a rich and seductive base that lays*
> *like a second skin on the wearer and reveals darker facets with*
> *amber, patchouli flower and spicy woody accents of Moroccan*
> *incense. Mariah Carey M perfume is the perfect scent to express*
> *Mariah's sensuality, beauty and glamour.*

The "rich" is subtle enough, avoiding at least direct reference to the
part Venezuelan musician's wealth—subtler, in any case, than Paris
Hilton, who has sponsored scents for men and women called, respectively, "Heir" and "Heiress." "Seductive" is unsurprising: If
Vivienne Westwood is right to say that fashion is about eventually
being naked, then a smell is a promise of something that will remain after the wearer has removed everything else.* But the "second skin" does reveal darker facets. Does this second skin belong to
Mariah Carey? The phrase is more often used of tight clothing,
such as rubber, which follows the contours of human skin while
feeling quite different. It's something that is you, and also isn't you.†

This suggests a moment when you could be Mariah Carey to as
great an extent as possible, without assuming her identity. The
pitch was careful: M perfume doesn't capture or reproduce Mariah's
sensuality, beauty, and glamour, but merely "expresses" it. The
wearer was able to show an affinity to the star, as if joining her fan
club; but being Mariah Carey has always been Mariah Carey's
business alone.

---

\* The slogan for Christina Aguilera's perfume was "Sometimes it's all you need to
wear," perhaps in homage to Marilyn Monroe's answer to the question, "What do you
wear in bed?"

† This might not be the time for Frazer's reminder that "in ancient Mexico the human
victims who personated gods were often flayed and their bloody skins worn by men who
appear to have represented the dead deities come to life again" (Frazer, *The Golden
Bough*, 357); and yet some aspects that he describes more fully, such as the way in which
that skin can sometimes be divided into different parts, will detain us shortly.

In a way, though, this made her stingy. We can't be sure that the wording truly ever represented the singer's intentions, and we are surely able to expect much more. As one journalist put it, in the heyday of the celebrity perfume, when George W. Bush was president:

> *Ms. Lopez's fragrances, which have generated an estimated $250 million in sales, reflect [the manufacturer] Coty's strategy of picking stars who have a multifaceted persona—in Ms. Lopez's case, a pop singer, actress, glamour puss and budding fashion designer—and who are prepared to impart the secrets of their personality to fragrance and packaging designers.*

Now, in the case of Mariah Carey, we can count sensuality, beauty, and glamour as three separate facets, since one can be sensual without being beautiful, and can be both of those without being glamorous.* The important thing is that we can split her up into different aspects. The perfumers chose three to bestow upon the consumer. They didn't offer us Mariah Carey the dancer, or Mariah Carey the actress. We just get the best of her.

Or at least, that's the hope. In the two-way wrangle between Mariah Carey and the world, we might have gotten what we wanted to get, or else what Mariah Carey wanted us to get. In the end, it never mattered, because she permeates our environment, so that now there's a little piece of Mariah Carey in all of us, and a little piece of us all in her.

## ii. Every man is a piece of the continent

On the face of it, this seems fanciful, wishful thinking. There is only one Mariah Carey (only one celebrity called Mariah Carey, anyway). Even so, we can divide the world into two sorts of people: those who are Mariah Carey and those who are not. This would seem to reduce our chances of being Mariah Carey, when in fact it doesn't. We only know that she's Mariah Carey *because* we know

---

* Glamour is an enchantment that can, but doesn't necessarily, rely on beauty.

she's not Mike "The Situation" Sorrentino, or Jackie Joyner-Kersee, or anyone else who has a name.

This is to use the logic of structuralist linguistics, which could be seen as a way to prove all sorts of things. The idea, when applied to language, explains how words come to have meanings. "Cucumber" means what it does because all the other words in the language don't mean "cucumber." There is a cucumber-shaped gap in our linguistic system, and we know the very thing to put in it. These ideas were expounded by the Swiss linguistic theorist Ferdinand de Saussure (only without the cucumber) around the time of his death in 1913. Later, Claude Lévi-Strauss would use the same thinking to examine social units such as families and tribes: To put it at its most basic, somebody is a son because he has a father. Somebody is an aunt because she has a nephew. Our relationships with each other define who we are, and we fit into our communities as words do into a language.

So we are all part of something together, and all depend on each other if we are to be who we are. But our relationships are spookier and less logical than that. To understand how the famous interact with us, we need to go back to a time when our views of luminous, chosen people were quite different. In fact, our views of individuals were quite different, too.

The idea of each of us being unique and remarkable and special and needing not only to be ourselves but also to love ourselves, each with our own quite different iPod playlists and Facebook pages, would have struck our ancestors from the Stone Age, Bronze Age, or even Middle Ages as perverse. Yes, we were all people, and to some extent different people; but the qualities we had were decided by others, and we were defined by what we did for them.

This does allow for some conception of the *prominenti;* but these people are only any use inasmuch as they consolidate the group they're in. "Among Melanesian societies 'big men' are those who integrate the entire community for exchanges with another group," the anthropologist Chris Fowler tells us. "Great men, a sub-community of the clan different in kind to other members, may take several heterogeneous forms, including sorcerers and warriors." Even these characters are not greater than the parts of the society that create them: They belong to everyone. A part of them might belong to their families, in their roles as fathers or great-uncles or whatever; and a part of them might belong to the community, in their role as shaman. A useful illustration of how this works appears in Chinua Achebe's novel *Things Fall Apart,* set among Igbo tribes at the end of the nineteenth century. The hero, Okonkwo, is not just a belligerent yam farmer who won a wrestling match and beats his family; he is also an *egwugwu* who represents the authority of the gods:

> *Okonkwo's wives, and perhaps other women as well, might have noticed that the second* egwugwu *had the springy walk of Okonkwo. And they might also have noticed that Okonkwo was not among the titled men and elders who sat behind the row of* egwugwu. *But if they thought these things they kept them within themselves. The* egwugwu *with the springy walk was one of the dead fathers of the clan.*

Archaeologists continue to find evidence of the way in which people become things, and things people, and people become part of the earth, from which a tribe can see itself as having sprung. Few undertakers now would consent to remove part of the deceased's collarbone and replace it with a bone arrowhead. But they might have done so in Jutland, around 5000 B.C, where corpses were wrapped in animal hides. There they would also bury dogs with the same solemnity as they would people, and even they would not be individuated:

> *A red deer antler was laid along its spine and three flint blades were placed in the hip region, in precisely the same fashion as that in which such objects appear in male human graves. . . . A decorated antler hammer was laid on the dog's chest.*

All these procedures indicate that the dead belong in the earth, surrounded by the natural world of which they are a part. Their body parts are interchangeable with those of their pets. This can happen because they are what anthropologists call "dividual"—their body parts, or possessions, or attributes, don't belong to them alone, but can be shared by a whole community. Sometimes the whole process of burying was made as communal as possible: "Those who die in winter in parts of Siberia are left in platforms suspended in trees until the annual gathering where all that year's dead will be buried together." This wasn't the kind of communal pit into which Mozart is thought to have been thrown; it is another of the many rituals that bring people together.

As if to reinforce the idea that nobody is ever dead to the clan, bodies could be reclaimed and used as fertilizer. Parts of the departed could be made into objects and exchanged as gifts. "The body was therefore not treated as a whole, but broken up and redistributed to different locations and perhaps even different groups of people: we could say that bodies became gifts to be circulated." At parties in Bronze Age Britain, you never knew who would turn up in your goody bag.

It's this exchange of gifts that shows just how interknit societies were, or can be. Gifts are a part of the giver, even when the gift isn't somebody's bone that's become a pestle. From a study of gift exchange by the French sociologist Marcel Mauss, we learn that people give things to other people with every expectation of getting back something exactly equivalent. The implication of this is that nobody really loses anything by giving; which in turn has the implication that the giver's identity—what he or she owns, as much as who he or she is—isn't compromised. Indeed, the gift retains the identity of the giver; it is that person, only somewhere else.

And then, this has its own implications for the famous, who impart themselves so that these selves are celebrated. Although it might seem a reckless leap from ages and places in which the "self" was viewed so differently, we can conceive of a modern equivalent, in which the self *becomes* the currency. And anyway, it isn't such a leap, if Marcel Mauss is right about Native Americans:

> *Everything contains and confuses itself; things have a personality and the personalities are in some way the permanent things of the*

> *clan. Titles, talismans, coins and the spirits of chiefs are homonyms*
> *and synonyms, with the same nature and the same function.*

From this exhilaratingly French rhetoric, we can begin to see how interconnected we all are, in the sense that John Donne meant by saying that no man is an island, or that George Harrison had in mind in his song "Within You Without You." It also haunts a recent advertisement campaign for Orange, the mobile telephone company, who promoted the winner of the Orange Prize for Fiction (an award for the best female author of a novel published in Britain):

> *I am Lev, wounded hero of* The Road Home
> *I am Rose Tremain, winner of the Orange Broadband Prize for*
> *Fiction 2008 . . .*
> *I am who I am because of everyone.*

And, *mutatis mutandis,* we are Rose Tremain. Or not Mariah Carey.

Mariah Carey's perfume is everyone who ever wore it, and everyone who worked on it. Had you presented it as a gift, then you were presenting Mariah Carey, and offering your beneficiary the chance to smell like her. In this way a famous person becomes reproducible and has the power to be everywhere. This is something more pervasive and subliminal than other sorts of merchandise, such as the *Desperate Housewives* dolls or a Martha Stewart fitted sheet. Even so, it is successful precisely because it is fleeting. As we inhale it, we are aware of moments to be seized.

The scent industry can be a tribe itself, able to make its own sacrifices to a god, but also needing to ensure its own survival. Some profit from the glamour of the past, and perhaps an idea that smells from one generation can be re-created for a later one—Victoria Beckham has said that she cherishes Creed, because the bottles look grand, and it's the product of an old family firm. Similarly, the link between Marilyn Monroe and Chanel No. 5 is all the stronger because it seldom needs stating.

Given this sort of competition, the need of a celebrity to cling to a scent, rather than the other way around, feels just that—needy: It is as if they cannot stretch themselves further into time, so will let themselves drift out through space instead. Scents that are named after celebrities have sold well, but not for long; more established brands have continued to produce more stable sales figures in the long term. At least, that would be the case on a celebrity-by-celebrity basis; but if we take celebrities en bloc, then the vogue seems to have faded in its own turn, just as smells fade and so, too, must Mariah Carey fade. On the one hand, "The short attention span of young consumers works to the benefit of cosmetic companies, which view celebrity as an endlessly renewable resource." On the other hand, endlessly renewable celebrities might now have to find a less endlessly renewable medium through which we can celebrate them.

Jennifer Lopez has several perfumes to her name, and so has renewed herself by replacing one scent with another. We are more apt to replace one actual famous person with another. These essences of celebrities have permeated us as they have flown from the atomizer onto a body and then toward our olfactory canals. Victoria Beckham's advice shows how the process is at once intimate and vital: "Just a little dab on the back and sides of the neck and on the inner wrists, as those are the pulse points and emit fragrance best." The smells became part of us, and what's more, the packaging is recyclable.

### iii. Figures in perspective

The healer is at the center of the group, and those gathered around him are pretty much healed. There are other shots of the assembly meeting on this occasion, and they sit in comfortable chairs, discussing old times. They are at their best now, more like saints in an altarpiece: Nobody is too relaxed. Relaxing could lead to the days before they were reborn and washed.

Dr. Drew Pinsky is flanked by another pair of healers; when the others leave the set, they can continue the mission of which *Celebrity Rehab* is such a key part: Can they inspire others to clean up by their own examples?

Here is Jeff Conaway: The stick on which he leans is the symbol of the pain that has led him to the drugs that have led him to rehab.

Next to him is Mary Carey, who is grinning in a low-cut dress; as with Conaway, her appearance, which is pneumatic, is a clue to the problem that triggered the other problems—in her case it is the porn industry. Joanie "Chyna" Laurer looks like the bodybuilder and fighter she is; she looks as though she can fight addiction, but can she, really? Brigitte Nielsen is famously tall. Jaimee Foxworth is famously petite. The show's lineup offers characters who could represent many of us. Think of those characters in Hieronymus Bosch's painting *Ecce Homo,* with their leers and piercings, only now they've been in makeup and are in the presence of the man who has the patience and faith to remake them.

And then, just as we are defined by who we're not, so in this photo other celebrities are present by their absence: Daniel Baldwin has left, because he kept texting the porn star; Jessica Sierra has been banned from going within one hundred yards of a camera or a microphone (which sounds as unworkable as it is unconstitutional on many grounds, including cruel and unusual), so she can't show up to this reunion.

Group portraits are a useful way of testing where we are in a society: Are we really individuals, or are we parts of bigger building blocks, in which our feelings of difference are put aside so that we can fill more generalized roles? In the *Celebrity Rehab* shoot, we see individuals defined not only by one another but also by the light of Dr. Drew's wisdom. Here, he is not quite a celebrity, but not quite a noncelebrity. This is a problem for us if we are tempted to see the history of fame as a narrative in which all humanity starts as a bunch of nameless nebbishes until, one by one, we begin to twinkle each to each in a sparkly firmament. Is it as simple as that? When we come to see our social systems as wholes and to understand more elevated figures as members of those systems who are shared among us, we see that the process is more fluid than that. We can glorify our celebrities, but need to remind them constantly of where they stand in relation to us. And ultimately, that is alongside us. As the classicist Charles Segal writes of the victory hymns that Pindar composed for Olympic athletes, the poem "reincorporates the victor into the community and into the values of the community." The story is often one of proportion and perspective. Are the important people always the big ones, or is there a time when they come down to our level, until we're all equally prominent?

From our perspective, the Bronze Age looks like a procession of great men, all admired and served by countless, nameless menials. Brecht poses the question when he asks "who built Thebes?" in a poem. "In the books you will read the names of kings. / Did the kings haul up the lumps of rock?" Never mind them; this is the age of such heroes as Achilles, who kills so many people that Homer runs out of names for them. As ever, though, it is when Athens becomes a democracy in the late sixth century B.C. that the story seems less linear. The figures around it are individuated—each is doing something distinct, and each could be a portrait of an actual person. Still, these figures are designed to fit the architectural shapes available for them. And on the west pediment, in an isosceles triangle, we have Athene and Poseidon, who vied to found Athens, in the middle, with their heads nudging the apex; smaller than they come the figures of heroes, and smaller yet come the voters. Elsewhere is a parade of people processing to give Athene her cloak, or *peplos*. However dynamic and unique the mortals are, we see them here because of their relationship to a deity. They are central and comfortable, like the figures of Dr. Drew and his two assistants, Bob Forrest and Shelley Sprague, on the sofa; but they are huge.

Four centuries later, and we're in another sacred lineup. This is the Ara Pacis Augustae—the Altar of the Augustan peace—and the queue is for a sacrifice. There are faces of senators, wreathed and solemn, sometimes scowling, and the occasional priest among them, with a veiled head. One man has both a wreath and a veiled head. He is Caesar Augustus, the one-man ruler of Rome, who is both a political and religious figure, but he's as hard to pick out as anyone.

To read the poems of Horace or Virgil, you would think that Augustus was the most splendid man ever. The lengths to which both poets go to glorify him and weave him into the fabric of timeless, deathless myth might remind readers now of the way subjects have worshipped Stalin or Mao. But the Ara Pacis suggests other views. Augustus may be the *pater patriae*—the father of the fatherland—but he is also *paterfamilias*. Even when he's at his grandest, as in the forum he had already built, the imagery can be seen as domestic. It was the custom for patrician Romans to assemble lifelike heads of their immediate ancestors in their atria. In some sense, these were living characters, who would show up at funerals, borne by their descendants, and the cortège would form a kind of mobile group portrait. Similarly, in his forum, with its illustrious busts, Augustus traced his purported lineage, starting with Julius Caesar, through Romulus, and all the way back to Aeneas, the good father and devoted son.

And so, in the Ara Pacis, we have the whole family. His wife and daughter are elsewhere in the sequence as it shuffles about the altar. Little children are tugging togas, and a matronly woman raises her hand to shush them. Two of these darlings have been adopted by Augustus himself, and one of them, Gaius, who doesn't have so far to look up, is to be his heir. These children look so unspecial that some have doubted they are members of the Caesar family at all, and have suggested that they just happen to be there, or, given their foreign trappings, that they are guests or hostages. Still, if they are royal, their ordinariness is part of the point. They are on show, and identifiable, but only just.

This tells its own story about Augustus and fame, and about men and gods. We are in a different age, in which people are perhaps dignitaries, but could be anybody, too. It's not quite a situationist joke, but we can perhaps imagine the same kind of double take that Londoners had in 2009 when they dodged the traffic and pigeons of Trafalgar Square to see what the sculptor Anthony Gormley had done with an empty plinth. Among the statues of lions and Admiral Nelson, Gormley allowed volunteers from the public to occupy a space reserved for statuary and to mooch about in the sort of place where heroes would otherwise have been.

In Rome, conversely, the emperor carefully avoided prominence and charisma. Although he held immense global power, gaining it wasn't exactly in his manifesto. His stated mission was to stop civil war and to restore Roman values of peace. (Hence the name, Altar of Peace, even though it gives thanks for his safe return from military campaigns in Spain and Gaul.) So, to start with at least, he wasn't called an emperor—a title that would have had associations with martial law—but consul, a fine, civilian, elected way of running your state. It's a post that was usually held for a year. Augustus just happened to hold it for a lot of years on the trot. And so he appears to mingle, and he rubs shoulders with priests and senators, as if the honor is as much his as theirs; and they in turn are allowed to look as stern or plump or wrinkly as they would have done in earlier, Republican representations, when Rome was a sort of democracy, and *grandes hommes* didn't mind looking as though they'd just gotten out of bed.

All this shows the hazards of trying to mark a trend in the rise of the individual. Augustus allowed his own image to remain as human as possible, but this is as much a result of his peculiar political circumstances as it is of any intellectual developments shifting in the Roman subconscious. His acts were presented as being by the consent of the senate; and it was up to them whether he became a god on his death. Not many emperors later, and this kind of promotion to divinity became a matter of course. This is one reason why they become more removed from the rabble around them; another is the influence of eastern art, with its more iconic, static views of human figures, arranged more within a hierarchy than with naturalism in mind. In the Arch of Titus in Rome, built in A.D. 81, we see the emperor in a chariot, raised above his men; in A.D. 200, Septimius Severus appears similarly elevated. Everyone faces the front, like a school team photo.

Why did artists stop showing people as they really were? Why did the famous people end up being physically bigger and higher? One argument is that, for a long time, painters and sculptors weren't very good. This is unfair, but it's a view that pervades Giorgio Vasari's *Lives of the Artists*. Vasari's line is that artists depicted figures that didn't move and didn't look lifelike, until Giotto came along and freed us from static Byzantine iconography. It's hard not to see an East versus West thing going on here, along with a failure to see that iconography, and the veneration of godlike figures, can have an integrity and tradition of its own. Still, in Italy, there were artists experimenting with more three-dimensional forms, and Giotto is great (as were the unnamed artists in his workshop). And the result of this kind of art history is that artists themselves became famous: Vasari's pages present a succession of geniuses, each the object of praise and the subject of quirky anecdotes. Giotto was even well known enough to make it into Dante's *Divine Comedy.*

And, as the artists became famous, so their paintings began to show a chummier approach to superior figures such as Christ. Even in medieval times, Christ was looking less like a king and more like a man in extreme pain; he was allowed to show his human humility, too. He becomes one of us, but, unlike Dr. Drew, he is suffering and can bring to mind our own suffering, rather than showing how cleansed we can be. A contemporary of Giotto's, Duccio, showed something of this shift in his elaborate altarpiece for the cathedral in Siena, installed in 1311. It is made up of more than sixty scenes, and at the center is a monumental Mary, who holds aloft not such a baby Jesus—he's the size of the adult saints who stand at the foot of the Virgin's throne. So here, Christ may have become a man, but no man can match him for stature and presence. And yet, in a small panel on the other side is Christ washing Peter's feet. All the disciples are there, looking either at the action or else, in one case, directly away from it. All their heads are the same size, and their gold-embossed halos overlap. Although Christ is doing something so intimate for one of them, he is apart. As with the later godlike emperors (and unlike Augustus), he is distinguished; but here, he is distinguished by how lowly he can be.

That lowliness dares artists to paint Christ as less famous. His disciples have to share a space with the rest of us, too. (It would stretch the point, though, to compare this to the *Celebrity Rehab* episode in which the patients see how they can cope outside their retreat.) In Dieric Bouts's painting of the Last Supper, Christ is still central. Bouts has sat the disciples all around the table, and so his problem is to show us all their faces and keep them looking natural—anyone who has tried to photograph friends in a restaurant will sympathize. The effect has the sort of grace this ceremony requires. But peering out, as if through a hatch, or else from a painting (a trick on the eye makes it either), are two jollier faces. People have guessed at who they are—the painter's sons? Members of the church in Leuven who commissioned the piece? After all, plenty of bankers and benefactors have sought fame or redemption by showing up in the works for which they paid, riding on the robetails of the immortals. Look, they say, this is me, with Mary and Joseph and the baby Jesus.

As with the Ara Pacis, what matters to us is that we think we ought to be able to tell who Bouts's crashers are, but can't quite. In Tintoretto's *The Last Supper,* from about 1592, the extras start to dominate. Christ is quite a way from us. We know it's Him because he's breaking bread and has a bulb of a halo. But bigger than all of the disciples are the servants who dole out eggs and fruit, while a cat rummages around in a basket of provisions. They are picked out by the last rays of angelic light. Another looming figure is the schnorrer who must have come into the Passover seder through an open door.

Perspective, you would think, is made for artists to tell the story of fame. For example, Raphael uses it in his *The School of Athens,* a painting that assembles a range of philosophers. It was finished in 1511. Central to the scene are Plato and Aristotle. They are at the back, but long before the vanishing point (you can see the lines of perspective still going strong behind their feet). They are fully standing, with an arch about their heads. It makes them much more visible than anyone else. Epicurus, for example, gets a look-in on the far left. We want Epicurus, but, since we're in the Vatican, and Epicurus is often (mis)understood to be a good-time thinker, a pope might not want him too prominent. The most obvious figure apart from Plato and Aristotle is the fiery Heraclitus. His part is played by Michelangelo—it turns out that this is a double-layered portrait of fame, with luminaries of Raphael's own age appearing in roles of luminaries from a mishmash of times. Raphael has included himself, with some modesty, since he is nearly out of the shot, and he hasn't even cast himself as a philosopher but as a painter. Some modesty, but not much—he is here as Apelles, whom Pliny the Elder pronounced to be the best painter ever.

After the Renaissance, and into a time when half of England rose up against kings, and the Dutch snatched a republic from the monarchs of Spain, people wanted to appear in group portraits in their own right. There had been attempts before, but Holbein's late painting of Henry VIII giving the guild of Barber Surgeons their charter shows what a homogeneous lump of souls we were. All the surgeons are shown with their heads in lines and their names tagged next to them. At least they had names; but these, as the labels we wear on our lapels at work do, remind us that we are forgettable. The subjects are about as exciting as a convention of dentists, except that these characters didn't stop at teeth and never offered local anesthetics. Now these sawbones are in the great king's presence, and he lords it over them as Christ might over his angels in some medieval fresco.

That was in 1543. A century later (1642), Rembrandt painted *The Night Watch,*★ an astonishing piece depicting a bunch of Rotarians out on a prowl. These men are no longer sitting with their hands together before a king. They're in a kind of action, claiming the streets. Everyone is differentiated, and the genius of the painting is the way in which Rembrandt has given each of his subscribing burghers prominence in a display that still seems natural. After all, like patrons and donors, these fellows were paying for fame. An earlier shot at this genre, by Cornelis Ketel, shows how extraordinarily difficult this is to pull off. Another militia company, this time under the command of Captain Dirck Jacobsz Rosecrans, stands in an orderly line, some vaunting their paunches, others

---

★ Now that the painting has been cleaned it no longer deserves its nineteenth-century nickname (R. H. Fuchs, *Dutch Painting*, 95). Its full title is *The Militia Company of Captain Frans Banning Cocq.*

looking somewhere else. As the art historian R. H. Fuchs explains, the artist was unwilling to put some in the foreground, and some behind; this might well have implied varying status, and damaged the amour propre of his patrons. "His problem was his unwillingness to sacrifice the individual distinctiveness of each single portrait to a conception of the group as a whole." Fuchs calls the result a compromise. The age was posing challenges to which only Rembrandt could rise. He was a genius, after all, like Giotto, and, like Giotto, famous in his own lifetime.

Maybe this justifies the frequency with which he painted himself. Increasingly, the artists who offered us the chance of posthumous fame were bagging it for themselves. By the eighteenth century, artists could decide that they had their own club; since they could memorialize others, they deemed themselves worthy of the same memory. And, if we cast our minds back to the process we've seen—by which the artist becomes a visionary figure, sharing a unique vision of the world—then he or she is allowed to inch toward the center of the composition, on the sofa between the other healers.

Johann Zoffany's painting of the Academicians gathered in the Royal Academy was a prestigious project. The institution was founded in 1768; three years later it was patting its own back. Artists had their own aristocracy at last. And if the country's best painters were to be painted, how fine a painter would you have to be to paint them? Zoffany seems aware of the honor; he sits at the edge of the composition, holding a palette and drawing us in. This is an ad hoc composition, and the apparent randomness of the order is a way of sidestepping the issues of status involved. Still, it is a guide to who was in and who out, since three are omitted. One is Thomas Gainsborough, following a quarrel with the academy's president, Sir Joshua Reynolds. Gainsborough is the Daniel Baldwin or Jessica Sierra of the piece.

There are two odder, partial exclusions. Zoffany has represented the Academy's two female members, Mary Moser and Angelica Kauffman, with paintings of them. They are not allowed in the room because there are naked men present, ready for a life class. And even the paintings are positioned behind the posers. Moser does have a chance to catch a glimpse of male buttock, but she doesn't look like she'll take it. There are all sorts of ironies and awkward cultural negotiations going on here. On the one hand, the women are detached from a bulk of chaps, each of them distinguished, and so they're not in this cohesive club; but on the other hand, if you see it from the perspective of the men in the room, these women are already celebrated enough to have paintings on their own. The fact that they are outside might define the group inside; but then, the group characterizes itself by this coyly gallant gesture.

A later glimpse of the Academy shows how successful its members have become. In William Powell Frith's painting, the opening of the 1881 exhibition is a celebrity affair. This canvas has been seen as a satire on what will and won't last. Oscar Wilde and a bunch of kindred aesthetes stand enthusing, while red-faced formal types fulminate in their direction. To the center is an archbishop (William Thomson, of York) and next to him, the actress Lillie Langtry. Robert Browning's whiskery jowls bristle in the background. Above them all hangs a painting of the recently dead Benjamin Disraeli, who is clearly going to endure. After so many images of ordinary people inching their way toward fame, here is Frith, the master of the crowd scene, giving us an in-crowd on a trip to the gallery, just like us, and along with us.

It's the same idea that lies behind the Sgt. Pepper album cover. In his liner notes for the twentieth-anniversary reissue, Peter Blake writes:

> *The concept of the album was already evolved: it would be as though the Beatles were another band, performing a concert. Paul and John said I should imagine that the band had just finished the concert, perhaps in a park. I then thought that we could have a crowd standing behind them, and this developed into the collage idea. I asked them to make lists of people they'd most like to have in the audience.*

The lineup includes the famous among the living and the dead. Some are there as much because they are famous as for any other reason—Dr. Livingstone, Albert Einstein—but others are famous really because they are associated with the Beatles—Stuart Sutcliffe, a quartet of gurus George Harrison liked. Artists had long been the makers of fame, from time to time stepping forward to take the credit for it. But now the Beatles, fresh from John's "more famous than Jesus" brag, were appointing their own pantheon. The living members of that pantheon were honored to be included: Brian Epstein insisted on asking them. The Beatles themselves provided enough allure to induce some recalcitrant stars to cooperate. As Blake explains: "Mae West replied 'No, I won't be on it. What would I be doing in a lonely hearts club?' So the Beatles wrote her a personal letter and she changed her mind."*

Together with the Sgt. Pepper crowd, milling around in some municipal garden, the famous have been happy to switch places with us more and more. It takes us back to Augustus's self-presentation, that blip in the narrative, when Rome's finest would be arrayed as if in a family gathering, be it at the forum or the Altar of Peace. And in trying to pass themselves off as us, they simply identify themselves as more famous. Now we are used to seeing ourselves in group formations, and are identifiable not so much because of who we are, but whom we're with; and famous people can knit themselves together in similar groups, connected simply by their fame. As Fowler said, great men are "a sub-community of the clan different in kind to other members."

Back in *Celebrity Rehab*, Dr. Drew occupies a subcommunity within a subcommunity. He is a great man among greats: an innocent but determined rabbinical figure among some fairly special sinners. His guests are people who in a couple of cases have worked out more than the rest of us, in some cases have been in movies, or, in other cases (three if you count Jessica Sierra's sex tape), have been so good at having sex that they've done it on film. These people are not only talented, they're also fucked up, and are important to us

---

* But then, how can we avoid thinking that Mae West would always have said yes, but couldn't resist delivering the one-liner? Of all the others whom the Beatles approached, only the actor Leo Gorcey demanded a fee. He was painted out as a result.

because they offer us a means of defining ourselves; or at least, they help us gauge how fucked up we are in comparison.

Jeff, Mary, Brigitte, Jaimee, Seth (Shifty), Ricco, Chyna, and absent Daniel and Jessica are all personalities in transformation, struggling to rid themselves of the addictions that define them, just as walking sticks, height, or vital statistics define them. But in doing so—and in offering us, too, the chance to transform—they're defining us and our own identifying features. For better or for worse, however special or unspecial we are, we're not them.

# 10

# You Complete Me: How Celebrity Couplings Provide an Index on Celebrities and Ultimately on the Rest of Us

A small whinge: some men lie, deny true things,
and nobody admits he's had no flings;
If bodies say no, people touch the name,
and bodies, though untouched, bear the ill fame.

—OVID
*Art of Love* II.631–4

It's one thing to be special and famous and individual, but it's even harder to do it on your own. In the previous chapter, we saw how people are recognizable as much because of who they're not as who they are, and that these definitions come from the mesh of social networks that involves us all. But they also seek to define themselves by another kind of mesh—the entanglements they make with other celebrities.

To be clear—these enmeshings need to be with other celebrities. The most obvious explanation for this is that this reduces the risk of kissing and telling; the sense of complicity must guarantee less publicity. But then, if these things happen between a celebrity and a noncelebrity, something feudal occurs, and the old romantic plot of elevation comes into play: The noncelebrity member of the partnership attains the new rank of famous person, just as the wife of an ennobled man is able to call herself "Lady." It's like a fairy tale that can go two ways: Either the character who is elevated was actually a princess all along, such as Cinderella and Snow White;

or else a nobody got lucky, like the penniless soldier who ends up as king with a beautiful queen in Hans Christian Andersen's story "The Tinderbox."

It hasn't always been straightforward, though. Pericles became a figure of fun for his unrepentant relationship with the courtesan Aspasia (but he could have done worse: As we've seen, Cimon was mocked for how close he was to his sister). Madame de Pompadour gained power with her relationship with Louis XV; Louise O'Murphy did not. And before becoming Louis XV's mistress, Madame du Barry needed to be given a title. The Byzantine emperor Justinian did the same when he met the dancing girl Theodora—he raised her to patrician rank, but kept their relationship secret while the empress was alive. Louis XIV had a secret wife of lower caste, Françoise d'Aubigné, Marquise de Maintenon—they were married for forty years.

Relationships among the famous, although analogous, are more fluid. There is no anointing as such, and no guarantee of remaining famous in any case. But this makes the process many-layered; the distinctions between A-list, B-list, and so on, banned in the style guides of some newspapers, actually turn out to be helpful in this area. They help us establish the hierarchies within which celebrity matches are made. As with monarchies and aristocracies, it must be a ruthless and terrifying world, and the words "Without me you'd be nothing" must echo down many hotel corridors. They should chill anyone who has sought fame through another, and the idea of going single becomes an even greater test of an individual's charisma if it's a relationship, rather than a band, he or she's walking away from. Ryan Phillippe made the same point when he was presenting an Academy Award with Reese Witherspoon: He told her to open the envelope because "you make more money than I do."

The recent history of fame shows how tricky it is to negotiate these niceties. The linking of Eddie Murphy and Melanie Brown—Mel B of the Spice Girls—seemed as though it would be to the advantage of the Brit. For a British celebrity, breaking into America remains the ultimate challenge; it requires careful positioning and a lot of hard work, we're told.★ But how much easier is it on the arms of someone who's already well established there? Brown, née Blatt, had lived in Los Angeles for three years before newspaper reports began to circulate about her liaison with Murphy. The stories purported that they had paid tributes to one another in the form of tattoos and were even planning a wedding. Then Mel B became pregnant. "I can't wait to spend Christmas with [Eddie Murphy] and I can't wait to have this baby." Then the couple split. Then Eddie Murphy denied that the baby was his, pending a paternity test. Then Angel Iris Murphy Brown was born, and she turned out to be Eddie Murphy's baby. He has since acknowledged that he is the father. Contrary to what one might have expected, although Mel B emerged from the tryst with a beautiful baby girl, fame-wise Eddie Murphy is the winner—he became talked about, appeared in a music video, and was recognized as a stud for having sired his eighth child. Even Brown's slur of calling him the "Beverly Hills Cock" becomes a kind of compliment.

The case of Paul Sculfor seems clearer. Even as a schoolboy in Essex, southeast England, he was regarded as a looker, though he busied himself with boxing. When he left, he went to work on building sites, but gradually gained recognition as a model. Soon he would become one of those British men who become the envy of their compatriots by becoming the trophy of an impressive American woman, along with Chris Martin, or Guy Ritchie, or even Calum Best. When he moved to the States, he had the good fortune to become Jennifer Aniston's lover briefly, and then the even better fortune to find happiness with Cameron Diaz. The question here is, was this a promotion? The whole thing can look like a promotion of Paul Sculfor in the PR sense; but it also makes us ask, which is better, Aniston or Diaz? Given that no one had heard of him before, either option sounds terrific. From Diaz's point of view, there's some slight loss of kudos because she got to

---

★ It's a point Natasha Bedingfield was keen to make in interviews, anyway, about how she became famous in America. Natasha Bedingfield is a talented British singer; you may recognize her voice in the theme music for *The Hills*. Do keep up.

him second; but perhaps on this occasion, contentment is the greater concern.

In these matters, celebrity becomes property and can be passed around like a gift. It can either transfer between people of similar renown, such as when matadors in Spain go out with members of the royal family; or it can trickle down and be shared about, like gifts or relics. In Britain footballers don't go out with royals, and for them, the proper trophy is a pop star; but this doesn't stop them endowing passing mortals with their attention and lovemaking, almost like in a fairy tale. Ashley Cole, though married to the best-known member of Girls Aloud, Cheryl Cole née Tweedy, spent a night with a girl named Aimee Walton, and when he was sick in her car, told her that she was privileged. (She was underwhelmed by what happened next—by the account she gave to *The Sun,* he was little more than adequate.) When Wayne Rooney found himself in a bathroom with Charlotte Glover, described in *The Sunday Mirror* as "a call girl," he left a souvenir: a pencil-written note saying, "To Charlotte, I shagged u on 28 Dec. Loads of Love, Wayne Rooney." These jaunts into the world of noncelebrities, like Zeus wowing mortals, tend to have repercussions in Olympia; Rooney has to swamp Coleen McLoughlin with gifts; both Cole and Aimee found ways of telling Cheryl how sorry they were.

Even more than in our world, relationships in the celebrity world define people. But celebrities live more and faster than the rest of us, so that they can be part of multiple permutations. The effect is to make the individual celebrity all the more "dividual": a little bit of Paul Sculfor will always be associated with Jennifer Aniston, because, in two senses, she has made him what he is—she has contributed to his success and also defined him. And not just for a little while, either—she will always feature on his CV.

So it is that these matters come under the careful control of image makers, and anyone who opposes arranged marriages should campaign against the public relations community as much as any other. Given that our knowledge and understanding of stars is strongly colored by the other stars with whom they're linked, this aspect of their lives is as likely to be as real as their own names.

There are unnameable but fairly obvious examples of entertainers who are gay or bisexual but who feel the need to conceal this from their fans, perhaps because they worry that audiences won't buy them in a heterosexual romantic lead. They are part of a long tradition, including Rock Hudson and Dirk Bogarde.

The need here is to keep fans believing that the desires they see expressed on the screen are genuine, and could plausibly be reproduced in the real world. In short, fans have to keep fancying them. Nor is it a problem for homosexuals alone. It's a reason why we need to keep remembering that Tom Cruise is heterosexual, and to take comfort that any rumor to the contrary is definitively skewered in Andrew Morton's biography: Not that Tom Cruise minds, but it's important that audiences—that is, we—believe in the characters he plays.

Thus stars' narratives—their story arcs—can all too easily mesh with the story arcs of their onstage or on-screen personas. It makes us start suspecting even the happiest of couplings as shrewd product placement. We have now heard so much about Russell Brand's promiscuity that his only hope of settling down in a way that the public can tolerate is to link him with the woman who sings, "I kissed a girl and I liked it." Or else we can accept that the union between Russell Brand and Katy Perry is the result of two special people who have met through the medium of celebrity; so perfect together that, had they not been famous, they could have met only by stalking one another.

Judged by the standards of the ancient Greeks, celebrity couplings are fine and desirable. In Plato's *Symposium,* the comic playwright Aristophanes takes his turn to answer the question, What is Love (Eros)? His view is one of the best-known contributions to the debate, because it starts with an odd image of human beings: At first, we were spherical, and had eight limbs, which we would use to roll bouncily along. But when Zeus was displeased with us, he sent his lightning to rend us in two, and ever since we've been looking for our other halves. This can help us understand why Russell Brand's search was so thorough. Depending on the nature of the split, we could be men looking for a man or a woman, or women looking for a man or a woman. As Aristophanes goes on, he argues that eros—desire—is a good thing, because it leads older, distinguished men, such as generals and statesmen, to fancy younger ones, and to spend time with them and impart their noble qualities to a new generation.

This connection between patronage and sex strikes us now as distasteful, even more so when Aristophanes makes it sound as though it is in the interests of the youth's education. But does it really seem so different from the practical decisions made by, say, Madonna? We've already heard her say that losing her virginity was a career move. It wasn't, but she has said that her sexual encounters benefited both parties.★

Seen this way, series such as *Rock of Love* or *A Shot at Love with Tila Tequila* become meritocratic. If beauty or musical talent—or both—have always been ways of gaining fame in more feudal times, then it's a comfort that people who win that kind of fame can now audition among our own ranks for lovers with whom to share that fame. Tila Tequila has been especially progressive in allowing applicants of both sexes the chance to win the golden ticket to celebrity. But *Rock of Love* is even more helpful in reminding us that neither sex nor rock and roll provide a greater allure than fame itself: The woman who won a date with Bret Michaels didn't much want it, although at least her triumph was on television.

So fame can lead people into relationships. But can it survive? Do you have enough of it that you can keep it in your own right? There ought to be a kind of court that arbitrates this kind of thing. By the terms of some contract, Bret Michaels could surely claim some of his borrowed kudos back.

In *The Art of Love*, a three-part sex-tips poem that led in part to Ovid's exile from Augustus's Rome, the author is pretty free with his advice, and really doesn't draw the line at much, but he does disapprove of those who claim they've slept with people they haven't.

---

★ This is to say nothing of the Adonians, a Cambridge University male-only dining society at whose meetings older members are sat next to younger ones.

(As far as anyone knows, it might have been an incident like this in Ovid's own life that led to his exile by the Black Sea—how much did he know about rumors concerning Augustus's daughter Julia?) He suggests that this tends to happen when someone has said no to a fellow, but the fellow brags that the sex happened anyway. William Wycherley makes his female characters swap views about this in his play *The Country Wife* (1675). Young Dainty gibes at men because "they do satisfy their vanity upon us sometimes, and are kind to us in their report; tell all the world they lie with us." Lady Fidget replies, ambiguously, "To report a man has had a person, when he has not had a person, is the greatest wrong in the whole world that can be done to a person." On the surface, she's saying that it is a crime to slander someone for being light; but she's also saying that it is wrong for a man to talk as though he's bedded a woman without troubling to give her any pleasure.

As the *Rock of Love* denouement suggests, these days people can pass on such pleasures, because the pleasures are less likely to be the endgame. The éclat caused by remote possibilities becomes the climax now: The teasing snog between Angelina Jolie and her brother, James Haven, and his coquettish comments since, have helped preserve some mystery around both. As he said to the *Daily Mail* in March 2007, "I'm a perfectionist by nature. Then, because I'm so close to Angie it's like I've already got the perfect woman in my life and it's hard for anyone else to live up to that."

So nothing need happen; these things can be all froth and no Guinness. With celebrities, fake trysts sometimes have the consent of both parties, or else the famous can allow exaggerated accounts to flourish of things that are sort of true. Robbie Williams occupies a peculiar position in this, and as his biographer notes:

> It's such an easy way for people to get reflected publicity and try to elevate their importance, in some weird manner, by claiming that they have been propositioned by, but have knocked back, someone famous. "I'm going to start telling loads of people I've knocked people back," he seethes. It's all absurd. "J Lo, I've

> *knocked back. Cameron Diaz, it got so bad I had to get a re-straining order."*

Williams genuinely did have something going with Rachel Hunter, but conspired with her to give the paparazzi an easy glimpse of them making out. On the other end of the scale, it clearly matters to him that he didn't sleep with Courtney Love.★

It matters to us that celebrities date celebrities, just as it unsettles us when they don't. As we saw with gods, something strikes us as amiss when stars take mortal lovers. In *Mythologies,* Roland Barthes tells us that the French were surprised when Sylviane Carpentier, Miss Europe 1953, married her childhood sweetheart, Michel Warembourg:

> *Thanks to her title, Sylviane would have been able to pursue the career of a star: to travel, be in the movies, make lots of money; sensible and modest, she renounced ephemeral glory and, faithful to her past, she married an electrician from Palaisseau. The young couple here appears in the post-nuptial phase of their union, in the process of establishing the routines of their happiness and to settle themselves into a modest little comfort. . . . They have breakfast, they go to the pictures, they go to the market . . .*

What bothers us? Is it jealousy? Do men think that, under the right circumstances, they, too, could have been on the arm of a Miss Europe? What are they, stalkers? Give it up already. If you get stuck in a lift with Scarlett Johansson: That's something even Benicio Del Toro has to dream about, and anyway, the elevator wasn't big enough. If anything, there's likely to be a more wide-spread jealousy, coming from the feeling that we're not in on it anymore: that the couple are enjoying what David Hare has called "the secret rapture." The rapture remains secret in part because the

---

★ On Rachel Hunter and Geri Halliwell, see Chris Heath, *Feel,* 26–29. Of Courtney Love, Heath writes, "[Williams] has a request for me. 'Can you ask me the question "Did you sleep with Courtney Love?"' he asks. 'And I can say, "Fuck off, I'm a good-looking lad."'" (42). His former songwriting partner Guy Chambers refers to Williams's "celebrity fuck-tree" (24).

French are so much better at privacy than we are in the English-speaking world. No matter whom they marry, our celebrities are public property, and we need to see this cottage with its split kitchen so that we can see how it stacks up alongside our own homes. Then we can be happy for Sylviane Carpentier, just as we can for Cameron Diaz and the unexpected Paul Sculfor; and in this way, we can be content for ourselves, too. Our own homes can become fairy castles, just as Michel Warembourg becomes a character in a fairy story, only luckier: He gets the girl, but misses out the troublesome business of being king.

## Too Much Information: How Well Do We Really Know Famous People?

Demi Moore lies with her eyes shut next to her dying mother, Virginia, who strokes a small dog under the chin. The dog is called Ray.

The photograph is one of a collection taken by Véronique Vial called *Women Before 10 a.m.* The rules of the project are to take photographs of normally glamorous women, only without makeup, posing, or artificial lighting.

The results are fairly convincing; and yet the no-makeup, no-posing rule was surely impossible to enforce. However vulnerable these women look as they light up, or play with their children or dogs, or fix themselves, most of them can't help being beautiful, and so it's hard for the viewer to avoid feeling that the vulnerability is staged. And then there's Demi Moore.

Demi Moore could only be photographed at her mother's house, and her mother was dying. She asked Vial if they could be photographed together. Vial published two of these images in her book. They are extraordinary, for all sorts of reasons—really, for as many reasons as the viewer wants to find. In the one we've mentioned, the actor has her eyes shut, and the lids are shaded, though it's hard to say if this is because of cosmetics or the shape of her skull. In the other, the two are in a steamy bathroom. We can see Virginia's knees while her daughter tends to her, and we can see her reflection in the mirror. There's every chance that she's on the loo.

Whatever we learn of Demi Moore from the pictures, we can safely conclude that this is how she wants to be seen, and she has gone to some trouble to arrange the session with a photographer. After all, this is the same Demi Moore who exposed her bare, pregnant tummy on the cover of *Vanity Fair,* a shot that was considered so revealing at the time that some newsstands declined to display the magazine. Even the photographer, Annie Leibovitz, hadn't thought that this picture would be published. And it is the same Demi Moore who was comfortable enough with her body to appear in *Striptease.*

Is this different? We are allowed into an intimate space, presumably with the consent of both subjects. In the text that accompanies these images, Vial reflects on the intensity and intimacy of the experience. And now we can all share it. This is a public death, though not as public as some that will follow—of Jade Goody and John Paul II.

Photography, publishing, printing, and broadcasting this feel like a new phenomenon. Maybe it is; or at least, maybe we feel that these glimpses of the famous, in which they do the kinds of things we might be doing, take us closer to those we want to admire or judge. But in no age have celebrities been careless of how they have presented themselves; otherwise, how would they have been celebrities? It's like that perhaps apocryphal press release from the 1997 general election, saying, "Mr. Blair will be spontaneous at 1.30 P.M."

So it's worth exploring those moments when the famous have allowed us to feel close to them, as though we know them. How do they do it? More important, why do they do it? Has the process changed over time? And have the motives depended on historical circumstances, or are all famous people "giving till it hurts"?

In ancient Rome, particularly in the late republic, and even in the early days of the empire, men and women allowed themselves to be portrayed as they really were. There would be no concealing of bumps, balding, or fine dryness lines; everyone, from senators to slaves, would be depicted in this way, and scholars have occasionally muddled up which is which ever since. It is odd, now, to look back through centuries of emperor portraits in which men are idealized as gods, and when power was something fetishized in itself, and find aristocrats looking so at ease with their own imperfections. The context of these portraits matters, too—these were glimpses of characters at home. Many of these sculptures came into being as funerary busts, portraits of the recently departed, to add to the group portrait you could see in the atrium of a Roman house. These were family gatherings that extended back in time. Again, you were really sitting with these people, and yet it was absolutely impossible that they could be there.

It seems odd to us now that a senator or an aristocrat could have looked ugly; and it's easy to take the idea of "warts and all" as a bold innovation of Oliver Cromwell's. We assume that we are looking at the busts of people who aren't beautified, or even beautiful, because they matter to us in some other way; that somehow these jowly characters are presenting their experience or their *gravitas*. But in the late Roman republic, when every leading figure went about claiming he was trying to save the constitution of the Senate and People of Rome (SPQR), it wasn't so bad to look more like the rest of us. In according them fame, we separate them from the rest of humankind. So, no matter how these people look, we are interested in them for some other reason than that they're wrinkly or balding.

It is the same with memoirs. The French historian and critic Paul Veyne puts the matter fairly clearly:

> Public figures have the right to publish their memoirs; they will be of interest to everyone because they are history. Unknown people also have the right to some publicity if they become the heroes of some extraordinary incident or occasion. Even the most banal of incidents can be of interest if it happens to some well-known person. But what of the rest? It can be turned into literature on condition that what is told is deemed of interest in the society in question.

So we're interested in boring people if interesting things happen to them, and in boring things if they happen to interesting people. Either way, we must be removed from our own experience of the world, assuming, that is, that we are boring people to whom boring things happen.

Few people in the history of the world have thought themselves as interesting and worthwhile as Marcus Tullius Cicero. We're lucky to have a letter he sent to Lucius Lucceius, who was writing a history of Rome that was to cover Cicero's time as consul. It's a remarkable insight into the relationship between a *grand homme* and his ghostwriter, Roman style. Cicero's theory on what ordinary people want out of a memoir or biography is revealing. He urges Lucceius to "bring out the perfidy, intrigues and treachery of many people towards me":

> *For nothing is better fitted to interest a reader than variety of circumstance and vicissitudes of fortune, which, though the reverse of welcome to us in actual experience, will make very pleasant reading. . . . To the rest of the world, indeed, who have had no trouble themselves, and who look upon the misfortunes of others without any suffering of their own, the feeling of pity is itself a source of pleasure.*

Cicero wasn't alone among the Romans for thinking that we gain pleasure from the suffering of others. Lucretius put it as kindly as possible:

> *It's sweet, when sea plains swell with rolling winds*
> *to be on land and watch somebody struggle,*
> *not because you delight that someone's vexed,*
> *but you can see the suffering you don't have.*

So is Cicero telling the historian to show him at his lowest ebb, and to reveal his weaknesses? Not on your nelly. Cicero's purpose in writing the letter is something that even he's embarrassed about it, and he begins, "I have often tried to say to you personally what I am about to write, but was prevented by a kind of almost clownish bashfulness. Now that I am not in your presence I shall speak out more boldly: a letter does not blush." What he wants to do is to find out if Lucceius was planning to work Cicero's achievements into an account of the age, or whether he's going to give Cicero a chapter of his own. Cicero is clear that he wants the latter; not only that, but he wants it fast. And not only does he want the first

draft of history to happen as soon as possible, but to be as finished
as possible. Not only that—he doesn't mind if the historian makes
stuff up:

> *And so I ask you outright again and again, both to praise those*
> *actions of mine in warmer terms than you perhaps feel, and in*
> *that respect to neglect the laws of history. I ask you, too, in re-*
> *gard to the personal predilection, on which you wrote in a certain*
> *introductory chapter in the most gratifying and explicit terms . . .*
> *not to go against it, but to yield to your affection for me a little*
> *more than truth shall justify.*

To start with the business of exaggerating Cicero's role in
history—Cicero was perfectly capable of doing that himself. Once
he had seen off Catiline's rebellion of 63 B.C., he delivered a speech
to the senate in which he ranked himself alongside Romulus: After
all, wasn't the man who saved Rome as praiseworthy as the fellow
who founded it? And in an execrable line of Latin verse, he yelled,
"O lucky Rome, born when I was your consul."★ So why couldn't
he do this bit himself? Well, for one thing, Cicero was an orator.
He was best known for making speeches at the time, or in court,
and although he would polish these up to make himself look even
cleverer to posterity, part of that cleverness relied on his ability to
write to the moment. To do so as a historian would have been as if
Churchill had called his six-volume history not *The Second World*
*War* but *How I Saved the World*. And for another thing, Cicero really was bashful:

> *But if I fail to obtain my request from you, which is equivalent*
> *to saying, if you are by some means prevented—for I hold it to*
> *be out of the question that you would refuse a request of mine—I*
> *shall perhaps be forced to do what certain persons have often*
> *found fault with, write my own panegyric, a thing, after all,*
> *which has a precedent of many illustrious men. But it will not*

---

★ The line, which survives to us because Juvenal quoted it as an example of poetry that
is at once vain and awful, manages to offend the Latin ear every which way in thirteen
syllables: *"O fortunatam natam me consule Romam."*

*escape your notice that there are the following drawbacks in a composition of that sort: men are bound, when writing of themselves, both to speak with greater reserve of what is praiseworthy, and to omit what calls for blame.*

Get the chutzpah. You wouldn't decline me any sort of favor, would you? Not unless there were the sort of conspiracy the Clintons constantly had to deal with. No, I can't write it, Cicero argues, because I wouldn't show off enough. And there's a lot about which to show off. Still, there's clearly not so much showing off to be done that a bit of bullshit wouldn't go amiss.

Even if we allow for all the cultural differences between the late Roman republic and now, the similarity between Cicero and the modern celebrity ego is striking, especially when the famous require others to write their stories for them. A recent feature in *The Guardian* introduced us to seven of them. All of them felt that they were very close to their subjects, and that they could ask them anything. Some were candid about how much embroidering celebrities can tolerate. Here's Mark McCrum, who is best not known for his work with Robbie Williams:

*From the transcript of a very long interview, I build up a richer narrative. Mostly it's done by asking a load of subsidiary questions, but sometimes you just have to let your imagination free and try to become your subject. Strangely, these are often the bits they like the most. I heard one of the people I'd written for interviewed on* Woman's Hour, *recounting a specific detail I'd invented to make her story come alive. I felt strangely flattered.*

Now, it could be that the teller of the story had come to believe it, or that it fitted neatly into the world of her head and adventures. But the anecdote allows us to question how well we really know the celebrities who offer us such intimate confessions, and why they're imparting so much information. The rule for all of us is one known to schoolteachers everywhere: The more they tell us, the more they're hiding; from this it follows that the more we think we know them, the less we do.

The life of Dirk Bogarde gives us a clear example, and his biographer, John Coldstream, explains the tactic precisely. He begins with a definition of "chaff":

> *sb. 6. b. Strips of metal foil or similar material released in the atmosphere to interfere with radar detection* (Oxford English Dictionary, 2nd ed., 1989)

> *It was the American military which first coined the term at the end of the Second World War. The radarscope operator's screen would glitter with the promise of targets in the air, but the purpose was only to distract and confuse. By the time the word came into general currency during the Falklands conflict of 1982, Dirk Bogarde had been releasing his own variety of chaff onto the printed page for several years. He would tell interviewers, with an unmistakeable finality: "It's all there in the books, if you know where to look. The lines are wide enough to read between."*

The difficulty for Bogarde was that, on the one hand, he had a long and sustaining relationship with Tony Forwood, who was both his lover and his manager, while on the other, he had devoted fans who would send him presents and knit things for him. This helps us to understand how the celebrity love lives we saw in the previous chapter are the flashiest, most energy-intensive forms of chaff out there. But the candor of the memorialist has always had some other, sometimes higher purpose. Dirk Bogarde wasn't the first or last to tell us that it's all in the book, and the phrase has become something authors have to say for marketing reasons. But Bogarde offered that nuanced qualification, "if you know where to look." As Coldstream argues, what Bogarde most wanted to steer us away from, his homosexuality, "informs Dirk's life, some of his most important work in the cinema and—even if by omission—his writing."

Why would people even want to pretend that they are revealing themselves when they're not? One suggestion is that those who are taking us into their confidence are able to do so wittily or elegantly, as Bogarde did. Like the figures in the Parthenon Frieze, they look vividly human to us, but when we stand back we see that they're standing that way to fit into a premade shape. The means by which people present themselves—a portrait, a memoir, a novel, a newspaper column, or a television show or a Web site—may make us reach conclusions about how close we are to the truth about somebody; but even if one genre feels more revealing than another, each will be equally adaptable to taste and concealment.

Cicero wasn't alone in expecting history to provide a good and flattering read, rather than the complete truth. We don't get much candor from the early Roman emperors, if we can count Julius Caesar's *Commentaries on the Gallic Wars* or Augustus's *Res Gestae Divi Augusti* as autobiography. The latter, which title translates as *The Deeds of the Divine Augustus*, is a lengthy tomb inscription that explains how carefully the author ruled and how well he rebuilt Rome. In his book on Roman love elegy, Paul Veyne shows how the poets reveal much more, but that they do so as if they were using stage names. Still, a poet such as Propertius is at least pretending to help others when he offers his own intense experience of love as a guide and warning to others:

> Then you'll reflect that I'm no rhyming hack—
> you'll rate me more than any Roman brain;
> youths mourning at my grave won't hold this back:
> "Here lies Propertius, poet of my pain."

Propertius doesn't give much away, though, that doesn't harmonize with the style and precedents of other love poets. From more than a century later, Veyne quotes a second-century orator, Aristides, who is content to give us an alarming amount of detail about his health, not with fame in mind, but to impress us with the power of Asclepius, god of healing:

> How many friends have asked me or urged me to tell about it,
> to write it down! . . . Here are the considerations that led me
> to confide myself to the god as to a physician, in order to do

> *absolutely what he wanted. I am now going to tell you what was the status of my lower abdomen. I will give you a day-to-day account.*

Aristides doesn't tell us this because he thinks he's important, and so is his abdomen; he's telling us because he wants others to trust the miracle cures from which he has profited. His thoughts would be less likely today to go into the memoir part of a bookshop than under self-help. If he establishes the right to tell us about his innards, it is in the name of public interest.

So altruistic a genre was just waiting for the Christian treatment, and at the very end of the fourth century, Saint Augustine provided it. In his *Confessions,* he, too, is generous with his own experiences, and, like Aristides, he rummages through the difficulties of the past to show us how the grace of God can work on anyone; it's just that now God is working on the spirit rather than the abdomen.

Views differ on his *Confessions.* Some hold that all the things he confesses aren't real sins so much as symbolic ones that lead to a generally Christian outcome. "Modern man errs if he thinks he can already discover the Self in the *Confessions,*" says the philosopher Pierre Hadot, and Veyne adds, "His autobiography is just a theology written in the first person." For example, there's the time when he and a gang of friends raid a pear tree: "As it was not the fruit that gave me pleasure, I must have got it from the crime itself, from the thrill of having partners in sin."

For sure, there was a motivation to the *Confessions* that was different from appearing on chat shows and saying, "It's all in the book." There's an irony about it: It's addressed to God, and God already knows the plot. As the saint explains:

> *I need not tell all this to you, my God, but in your presence I tell it to my own kind, to those other men, however few, who may perhaps pick up this book. And I tell it so that I and all who read my words may realize the depths from which we are to cry to you. Your ears will surely listen to the cry of a penitent heart which lives the life of faith.*

But that doesn't mean that the book isn't a personal and revealing exploration. One of his translators is of the opinion that Augustine presents himself as such a rotter for a reason: If I'm this bad, Augustine's argument is supposed to run, then think how great God is, to turn me around. In wondering why Augustine is so hard on himself, his translator R. S. Pine-Coffin suggests, "Perhaps his training as a teacher of rhetoric accounts for this. He was, after all, trying to make out a case against himself before an audience which was predisposed to believe him a saintly man."

This is pretty convincing. We can conclude from it that Saint Augustine's real problem was that he was famous. His readers clearly didn't know him well enough; at least, they were unlikely to believe that he had ever been anything like them. And fame is a real bother for him. In fact, after his preoccupation with sex, the quest for glory is the thing he most wants off his chest.

To deal with the sex first: It's a constant theme, in Augustine's adolescence and beyond. An early intimation of it is when his father takes him to the swimming baths and notices what a little man his Gussy is already; he even brags to his wife about it when he comes home.★ And then there's the famous teenage prayer, "Give me chastity and continence, but not yet." Revealingly, this line comes, not in chronological sequence, but when the writer is thirty-two, and about to accept God into his heart. It's a flashback to a phase from which he is emerging only now. In a passage that shows what a persuasive preacher he must have been, he compares the experience of recognizing the intellectual value of Christianity, but not embracing it, to the experience of sleeping in. You know you have to wake up soon, but for now the slumber is too agreeable to cast off.†

As things to confess go, sexual desire is one of the most personal—or at least it seems so now—and it doesn't necessarily fit the pattern offered by Genesis. At least it's not as biblical as taking

---

★ "One day at the public baths he saw the signs of active virility coming to life in me and this was enough to make him relish the thought of having grandchildren" II.3.
† VIII.5. Cf. John Ford, *'Tis Pity She's a Whore*: "But those who lie in lethargies of lust / Hug their confusion, making heaven unjust, / And thus did I."

fruit from a forbidden tree. So Augustine digs inside himself to show quite specific weaknesses, and there *is* something genuinely autobiographical about the exercise. What's more, he doesn't present himself as an out-and-out rake, but says that he was bad to such an extent, and no further. For example, when he admits that he lived in sin with his girlfriend, he's clear that he never cheated on her. And anyway, bragging about sins you haven't committed is a sin in itself, as Augustine tells us.

But then, there's the problem of fame and earthly glory, which is another sin of Augustine's youth that he's determined to avoid now. How can he, though, when the whole point of the book is to explore himself as an example of the way redemption works? Sacrifice is how. In his old life, he had won praise and admiration as a speaker: "By now I was at the top of the school of rhetoric. I was pleased by my superior status and swollen with conceit. . . . It was my ambition to be a good speaker, for the unhallowed and inane purpose of gratifying human vanity." But when he complains about others who have been similarly vain about their achievements, he is clear and withering. Of successful astronomers he writes:

> *They lapse into pride without respect for you, my God, and fall into shadow away from your light, but although they can predict an eclipse of the sun so far ahead, they cannot see that they themselves are already in the shadow of eclipse. This is because they ignore you and do not inquire how they come to possess the intelligence to make these researches. Even when they discover that it was you who made them, they do not submit to you so that you may preserve what you have made, nor, such as their own efforts have made them, do they offer themselves to you in sacrifice.*

St Augustine does, though:

> *Accept my confessions, O Lord. They are a sacrifice offered by my tongue, for yours was the hand that fashioned it and yours the spirit that moved it to acknowledge you.*

This sets the bar high for later authors of their memoirs. Augustine is doing the complete opposite of what a modern celebrity does. As Mark McCrum reports, these days, "From the publisher's welcome party to the signing at Waterstone's Piccadilly, it's the celeb who's the centre of attention" rather than the writer; whereas Augustine is doing everything he can to make his work belong to Somebody Else. If Saint Augustine had had a launch party, it would have been a *sacrum convivium.* No drinks at Elaine's for him.

Jean-Jacques Rousseau was someone else who might have shunned a big do: King Louis XV came to an opera he wrote, *The Village Soothsayer,* and even liked it, but the philosopher, wearing an "ill-combed wig" and an untidy beard, declined the offer to meet him at court. He was, after all, the author of *The Social Contract,* which argued that rulers were there to serve the people, rather than the other way around. The rights of the individual and the freedom of self-expression were everything to him. So when Jean-Jacques Rousseau came to write his own *Confessions,* he had Saint Augustine's in mind, but whereas Augustine's were about something greater than the self, self is the dominant theme of Rousseau's. His book did a lot to enshrine our developing idea of the self as something indivisible and markedly different from other selves. The tone of the opening was daringly presumptuous, and can still sound so now:

> I am commencing an undertaking, hitherto without precedent, and which will never find an imitator. I desire to set before my fellows the likeness of a man in all the truth of nature, and that man myself.
>
> Myself alone! I know the feelings of my heart, and I know men. I am not made like any of those who are in existence. If I am not better, at least I am different. Whether Nature has acted rightly or wrongly in destroying the mould in which she cast me, can only be decided after I have been read.

The imitator part didn't work out that way, as we'll see all too soon. But he thought it so at the time. Rousseau is making it clear that he is more interesting than the rest of us, and that is why we should read his story. There's even more conceit between the lines, which sound oddly like the opening of the *Odyssey:*

> *Make man my subject, Muse, a resourceful man*
> *who suffered much, knew many people, sacked*
> *a lot of towns. . . .*

Not only is the author making himself a Homeric hero, he is also sidestepping God, and unlike Augustine, is making Nature his guide. This is the way I am, he tells us, with the implication, Get over it. When Rousseau does mention the Almighty, it's to tell even Him that it's all in the book:

> *Let the trumpet of the Day of Judgement sound when it will. I will present myself before the Sovereign Judge with this book in my hand. I will say boldly, "This is what I have done, what I have thought, what I was . . . I have neither omitted anything bad, nor interpolated anything good. If I have occasionally made use of some immaterial embellishments, this has only been in order to fill a gap caused by lack of memory. . . ."*

He does stand naked in front of his maker, as Augustine did, but that isn't his main objective:

> *I have unveiled my inmost self even as you have seen it, O Eternal Being. Gather round me the countless host of my fellow men; let them hear my confessions, lament for my unworthiness, and blush for my imperfections. Then let each of them in turn reveal, with the same frankness, the secrets of his heart at the foot of the throne, and say, if he dare, "I was better than that man!"*

If we read the last line literally, he really does seem to want imitators, and his confessions are a study in how to examine yourself. Like Saint Augustine, he is encouraging us to try it at home; even so, Rousseau is fairly confident that we won't do it as well. He wrote these words in 1766, when Goethe was a little boy; Beethoven and Wordsworth were four years away from being born. This is a clarion call to geniuses everywhere, that they should express themselves fearlessly, relentlessly. For six hundred pages if they have to. (Even six hundred pages takes us only as far as Rousseau's early fifties.)

So the book comes from an age of genius, and really is a spontaneous overflow of powerful feelings. If Rousseau is famous for one thing—apart from *The Social Contract,* the novels, and the un-shakeable belief that children are the future, even though he left five of his own to a foundling hospital—it's for his propensity to burst into tears. His opening words of *The Confessions,* and all that follows, he writes instinctively. There is some sign-posting when he approaches something particularly shameful, but he plows on anyway, and takes us way beyond the orator with the abdomen. As a boy he peed in saucepans. He likes being spanked. He is oddly shy in the presence of women—or, as he puts it, "Too bashful to declare my taste, I at least satisfied it in situations which had refer-ence to it and kept up the idea of it."

Emboldened by this, Rousseau tells us fully and stylishly of his feats and errors. He gets a maid sacked by letting it be believed that she stole some spoons; he desires married women; he fathers five children, whom he abandons. He doesn't spend so much time on this, but it does haunt him, and he confesses it to at least one woman he meets later in the story. He tells us a little of his think-ing behind this most alarming of his deeds—that he would have been happier in a foundling hospital himself, that "I thought I was behaving like a citizen and a father, and considered myself a mem-ber of Plato's Republic." Plato's Republic was never going to be such a lovely place, and men much, much worse than Rousseau have been inspired by it. He admits candidly that he was wrong, in his motivations, anyway—he doesn't tell us that the hospital in ques-tion had a scarily high mortality rate—and spares us more self-justifying, with a revealing consideration:

> Since [my reasons] were strong enough to mislead me, they might
> mislead many others, and I do not desire to expose young people,
> who may read my works, to the danger of allowing themselves to
> be misled by the same error.

It's an odd moment, in which he suddenly becomes aware of his influence, not only as a thinker, but also as a celebrity and role model; it is a rare example of this confessor holding back, if only for a little while.

Modern celebrity would be unthinkable without Rousseau. The idea that we really can know someone completely through his writings and reputation finds fulfillment in *The Confessions*. Even so, commentators thought they could find gaps. One reader, Mikhail Lermontov, author of *A Hero of Our Time,* quipped, "The problem with Rousseau's *Confessions* is that he read them to his friends." One could quip back that, by the time he wrote his *Confessions,* Rousseau had hardly any friends.★ In fact, although he tells us at one point that the book isn't an "apologia," a self-defense, still, he does give special attention to those moments when rivals or adversaries—Diderot, Grimm, Voltaire, Rameau—screwed him over. Some have seen and even diagnosed paranoia in all this; they may be right, but that doesn't make him wrong. As the graffiti joke has it, just because you're paranoid, it doesn't mean they're not out to get you.

Lose friends though he did, Rousseau won loving readers. Not long after his death, his admirers could even go to Ermenonville, north of Paris, and have the Rousseau experience. It was at Ermenonville that the Marquis de Girardin gave Rousseau his last home, and the patron opened up the estate so that Rousseau's admirers could come and weep for their lost hero. Its highlights were Rousseau's cabin, a little hamlet, much visited by "faithful lovers," as one travel writer recorded, and then dramatic effects of nature: a forest; a wilderness complete with what Simon Schama calls "craggy outcrops and cascades"; some ruins; and finally the great man's tomb, where admirers could read the inscription

> *Among these poplars, beneath their peaceful shade*
> *Rests Jean-Jacques Rousseau*
> *Mothers, old men, children, true hearts and feeling souls*
> *Your friend sleeps in this tomb.*

At this point you had to cry. Not only is this what Rousseau would have done; it's also what he would have wanted.

---

★ He did read them to his friends, until one Madame d'Épinay tipped off the police, who made him stop.

It's customary to take the homes or birthplaces of great men and women and turn them into museums, as well as to memorialize the objects they used to create their works of genius—you can see the violin Mozart played or the pen with which Hardy wrote *Tess*. (He used a different one for *Jude the Obscure*—we know because he wrote the titles on his pen.) It offers us the hope that we pilgrims can absorb the influences of our heroes and live the rest of our lives having some share in their world. It's odder when the living let us do this. Country and Western singers have had a habit of erecting museums to themselves, such as Conway Twitty's Twitty City and Johnny Cash's House of Cash; and then there is Dollywood, to which millions come every year, and where they can inhabit a world of Dolly Parton. It has a fairground. It is a concert center. And you can see local people practicing rural crafts, including dulcimer making and moccasin sewing. The plot isn't exactly where Parton grew up in east Tennessee, but at least it's in the same county.

The resulting clash between a humble background and glitzy celebration must be as striking as the difference between Saint Francis of Assisi's teeny chapel and the vast, Vatican-style basilica that houses it. In all these cases, there is an encounter that is on the one hand up close and personal, and on the other carefully manipulated, complete with landscape gardening. Even the geography of such places ends up being changed to tell a particular story. Add to this the wildly different impressions that each visitor will bring, and the result is anything but a journey to the heart of an artist.

Still, Rousseau's legacy remains the benchmark for celebrities now when they are purveying their innermost selves to the rest of humanity. A glance at any memoir shows us how much the writers, or ghostwriters, have learned from the master. Here are three different examples:

> *Whether I'm a good man is, of course, for God to judge. I know that I am not as good as my strongest supporters believe or as I hope to become, nor as bad as my harshest critics assert.*

*Now you can make up your own minds. This is my story, and I've held nothing back: not the parts I'm ashamed of, nor the things I regret. It's all here. My life is in your hands. Judge for yourself.*

*I have been reviled, prosecuted, imprisoned, and shot. I have spent half my life, it seems, in court. I have survived years of the worst physical pain any human can endure. I have accomplished much and triumphed against the odds. But one thing I have not done. I have not looked back. I couldn't; I was too busy living my life. Perhaps it is time.*

These characters are, respectively, Bill Clinton, the British glamour model Jordan, and Larry Flynt. It becomes clear that there is a house style to these productions—not only that, but there are often thematic or narrative links, too. In a time when the misery memoir is such a success, some childhood trauma is essential. So Bill Clinton had a violent stepfather; Jordan met a creepy photographer and had some obnoxious boyfriends; Larry Flynt grew up in rural Kentucky. Let's not mention the business of the chicken, except to quote Rousseau, on his own solitary pastimes: "It is easier to admit that which is criminal than that which is ridiculous and makes a man feel ashamed." Flynt's candor shows how far we have come along that road.*

What would Cicero have made of all this? For a start, he would have felt himself all the more justified in saying that to feel pity is a source of pleasure. And then it would have endorsed another of his ideas: If the historian *can* yield to Cicero "a little more affection than truth shall justify," then Lucceius would have "matter worthy of your genius and your wealth of language." A modern way of saying this is, "Fiction sells." We're always happy for books and films to be "based on a true story," but we want them to have the

---

* *Confessions*, Book 1. For a comparable crime, see Book 3: "I would look for dark alleys and hidden passages, where I could expose myself further to women in the state in which I would have wanted to be in their presence. It wasn't an obscene thing they saw—I didn't even dream of it; it was a ridiculous thing."

shape of something an author would have crafted if he or she had been able to give the imagination full scope.

It's a conflict that Clinton recognizes: He even lets us in on the possibility that he might not tell us everything: "It was even harder to learn which secrets to keep, which to let go of, which to avoid in the first place. I am still not sure I understand that completely. It looks as if it's going to be a lifetime project." This reads as though it's a confession about confessions, and that, for whatever reason, we shouldn't expect the absolute truth all the time. The clash between a narrative pattern and the truth is one the author acknowledges from the start: "As for the great book, who knows? It sure is a good story." It had better be. By the time he writes, "As I said, I think it's a good story, and I've had a good time telling it," we're on page 957.

The lines between fiction and fact have always been blurry. Is *Robinson Crusoe* a novel or a ghostwritten memoir? Alexander Selkirk became famous for having survived on a desert island for years, and after his rescue, it was said:

> *Being illiterate himself, he told every thing he could remember to Daniel Defoe, a professed author of considerable note; who, instead of doing justice to the poor man, is said to have applied these materials to his own use, by making them the ground-work of* Robinson Crusoe; *which he soon after published, and which, being very popular, brought him a good deal of money.*

This quotation comes from an essay from 1783, by James Beattie. Beattie was writing at a time when readers would divide prose fiction into the genres of romances and novels. As one (seventeen-year-old) writer put it, "The fiction of romance is restricted by no fetters of reason, or of truth; but gives a loose to lawless imagination, and transgresses, at will, the bounds of time and place, of nature and possibility." Fantastical tales of knights running errands for ladies fall into this category. Novels were meant to be truer to our own experience. As an early, self-styled novelist wrote:

*Novels are of a more familiar nature; Come near us, and repre-*
*sent to us Intrigues in practice, delight us with Accidents and odd*
*Events, but not such as are wholly unusual or unpresidented*
*[sic], such which not being so distant from our Belief bring also*
*the pleasure nearer us.*

*Robinson Crusoe* became a huge success because it managed to fall into both categories. Beattie considered it to be a romance, because it is set on a desert island and deals with the powerful passion for self-preservation. But it also satisfies the definition of a novel, because it is sort of true. It's worth saying that one of the most obvious liberties that Defoe took with Selkirk's story was to have the unlettered sailor write a diary; as a result, the passages that are the most realistic are the least real.

Defoe tried the trick again three years later with *Moll Flanders,* the tale of a pickpocket and whore who marries five times before repenting of her crimes, which include incest and bigamy. Here, again, the truth is stretched, and Defoe strives to give the tale what he calls "infinite variety." His preface, though a fabrication, could be read today as a definition of ghostwriting:

*The world is so taken up of late with novels and romances, that*
*it will be hard for a private history to be taken for genuine, where*
*the names and other circumstances of the person are concealed. . . .*

*The author is here supposed to be writing her own history,*
*and in the very beginning of her account she gives the reasons*
*why she thinks fit to conceal her true name, after which there is*
*no occasion to say any more about that.*

*It is true that the original of this story is put into new words,*
*and the style of the famous lady we here speak of is a little al-*
*tered; particularly she is made to tell her own tale in modester*
*words than she told it at first. . . .* ★

So the novelist looks like the editor of a memoir. Today, the

---

★ Some ghostwriting pretends to elude this definition: In Jade's book, we're to believe that it is as she spoke it, and to help the reader, there's a glossary at the back to help us with words and phrases such as "lala," "East Angular," and "Barry Big Time."

author of a celebrity autobiography must rival the novelist for what Defoe calls the "abundance of delightful incidents"—the romance of fame, with the extreme ups and downs that it brings. This means that it's no surprise that Jordan's novels and her autobiography, *Being Jordan,* are written by the same author, Rebecca Farnworth. We need to remember, too, that Jordan, whose real name is Katie Price, sees Katie and Jordan as two separate entities. Counterintuitively, she publishes her fiction under her real name.

Has there been an age when we could have said that we really did have an intimate knowledge or understanding of the famous?

You would think that it would be now. Celebrities can choose to share their lives with you on blogs, or invite you to go to their Facebook sites, as Lily Allen has. The Internet would appear to give every user as much information as he or she would want, and to allow celebrities to show you as much as they like of themselves, as the stories of Pamela Anderson or Paris Hilton demonstrate. But there are (at least) two reasons why the Internet doesn't promote a thorough familiarity with stars; it's because of them and because of us.

To deal with them first: The business of sex tapes shows celebrities simultaneously giving and withholding. About the actual content of these documents, I've nothing to say; it's the pragmatics of their existence that concern us here. On the one hand, this is about as much as you can know about a person. On the other, there is something close to an established etiquette about how to leak these things. The formula is that the wronged party should deny leaking or making the recording, but still profit from it. Jenna Lewis, a model, advanced her fame by appearing on the reality television show *Survivor,* and then furthered it by appearing on a video of her wedding night. Never mind the Mediterranean custom of showing stained sheets, or the Roman practice of having the act take place during the speeches: This wedding night went global. Did she mean this to happen? As the mother of twins, she protested strongly that she didn't; but some reports have her taking 70 percent of the $100,000 the leaked recording earned on the Internet.

The questions this raises are the same problems that magazines such as *OK* or *People* or even *US Weekly* pose. When the cameras show that an actor might have some cellulite or some blisters from where a high-heeled shoe has chafed, then we learn something about them that they would rather we didn't know—we have gone beneath the surface of their shiny image and discovered that they are more like us than they'd want us to realize. And yet, the fact that we've taken something from them against their will actually means that we *don't* know them. If we get to know people in real life and decide we like or don't like them, much of this will be based on how they are with us—what they tell us about themselves, what we feel we can say to them in return, and how we interact. If we go through their trash cans and make judgments about them based on discarded receipts from the drugstore, we're not seeing them as they would like to be seen.

This might seem as though we're getting to know them better; indeed, it helps us to know them better than others do. But getting to know someone, really, is about allowing them to act on their own decisions about what they do when they're with us. If someone wants to impress us at a party by wearing a sporty tie or a cloche hat, that's who they are. They are the person who's made that fashion decision. If, at a dinner party, someone has opted to serve us lamb curry rather than beans on toast, that's who they are. They are the person who wants you to have lamb curry. Freud devised a way of accounting for these different layers of the personality by dividing the mind into three parts. Just to exhaust this dinner-party analogy: If you're the host, then the aspects of yourself that you want to project makes up the superego; the ego is the part that sorts out what impression you're trying to make; and the third part of your brain, the id, is the part that wants to cut to whatever it thinks might happen after the coffee.

Now, it could be argued that the best way to know someone is to know the id, the secrets of the subconscious mind, and to weigh these up alongside the superego, the top layer of the tripartite mind, so that we can see what that whole editing process tells us about a person. But the result of this really is too much information. James

Joyce knew about this. When a fan approached him in Zurich and asked, "May I kiss the hand that wrote *Ulysses*?" Joyce replied, "No, it's done a lot of other things."

If we apply this to the way in which technology has apparently revealed more to us about Jenna Lewis's *thalamos* or, say, Sienna Miller on the streets between her house and the baker's, then we see that we learn less. In 2008 Sienna Miller kept the debate about consent going when she accepted an out-of-court settlement from a newspaper that printed pictures of her topless, taken clandestinely; some have criticized her for seeming so *pudique* when she has been willing to expose herself elsewhere.* If anything, the portraits of her by Nick Knight are closer to the real Sienna Miller, because she's taken some trouble to appear in this way. How people want to be seen is the most crucial question of all. The ultimate example of this is the late Diana, Princess of Wales. Jeannette Walls discusses her strange case at the end of her book *diSh,* an expert examination of who makes the news these days, and how. Here is a glimpse of the holiday Diana took in July 1997 with Dodi Fayed:

> *Some of the media horde were already surprised by Diana's behavior. Until that point, she seemed quite happy to be photographed. "She would flash a complicit smile towards the photographers whenever she appeared or left," one of them said. She had "delighted" the photographers, noted* Hello! *"Aware of the lenses but, for once, totally unfazed by them."*

Walls's sources for this concur that Diana was trying to knock Camilla Parker-Bowles out of the newspapers, and this would account for her displays of diving from a yacht. However plausible this sounds, it matters that we don't really know. Are these snapshots from an idyllic holiday with a princess's new love? Are they signs of smoldering jealousy, and therefore not so idyllic? Well, the mere fact that a gesture could be seen in such opposing ways, and the idea

---

* At least, it's a cretinous argument that someone was happy to advance on some "21st Century's 100 Worst Celebrity Moments" style of program. The logical extensions of this don't really bear thinking about.

that she sort of wanted to be photographed and sort of didn't, shows that the abundance of information makes the most basic, most significant conclusion impossible: Did she want the press there or didn't she?

In this instance, technology becomes the means for disseminating chaff rather than information; in much the same way, we know less about celebrities, rather than more, when they've appeared on *MTV Cribs*. A revealing sidelight on the phenomenon comes from Jason Schwartzman, in the extras of the DVD version of Sofia Coppola's film *Marie Antoinette*. In the role of Louis XVI, whom he plays in the film, he takes the viewer around the Palace of Versailles as if it were his home. Echoing the MTV cliché, he says at the key moment, "This is the bedroom, where it all happens." As we know from the film, the bedroom is where, for a long time, not a lot happens. What with all the ladies-in-waiting, and the bishop of Chartres, brought into the chamber to bless the acts that could produce a royal heir, this bedroom should be able to reveal everything that a *Hello!* reader or an *MTV Cribs* follower would want to know. In fact, it tells us the opposite of the truth. We would be as off the mark to think "it all happens" there as were the *libellistes* who would devise romps around the personage of Marie Antoinette.

So these glimpses are misleading, not only because of the celebrities disinforming us but also because of our role in the relationship. We bring our own expectations to these insights and end up with our own stories, rather than the real ones. And in addition, the more information is available about the more people—and the more swamped we are by celebrity gossip—the more we struggle to make sense of them. We make patterns out of them, and make tales of the famous fit the structures of fables. We've already seen how early novels emerged from items we might read today as ghostwritten memoirs, and that truth was more pleasing if it fit into a narrative shape. Another celebrity from the early days of printing, Doctor Faustus, made such a pleasing story that he became a myth shortly after his own lifetime, and became the template for a certain sort of fame ever since. In a wildly different way, we feel we know a lot about Jessica Simpson because we saw her on a reality television program about her marriage. It's entertaining stuff and purports to give us a whole new level of access to the subject. As Simpson herself has said of the show, "I let people in on who I am and how I react to my husband. That's a big deal. Celebrities don't do that." As so often with a remark of Simpson's, the best use we can make of it is to assume the opposite to be the case. This is precisely what celebrities—Carmen Electra, the Gotti family, Bobby Brown and Whitney Houston, David and Victoria Beckham—do all the time. In fact, an insight into the Beckhams needed a legal disclaimer advising viewers that some scenes had been reconstructed—a sure indication that life ends up consciously imitating art.

The logic of this would lead us to conclude that the *less* we know about a celebrity, the greater the possibility of knowing him or her intimately. It seems true, and at the heart of Jessica Simpson's remark is a truth. Although, as it turns out, celebrities do make a play of letting us in on who they are, still, as Simpson hints, they shouldn't; or at least, if Jessica Simpson thinks she's an exception, then she has a sound view of how celebrities ought to behave (even if she doesn't behave in that way). By her definition, all celebrities could establish the right to conduct themselves like Sylviane Carpentier (Miss Europe 1953)—to hunker down in their cottages with their electrician husbands and to shut the doors. The dignity and excitement of fame relies on the moments when we're not let in.

"Celebrity" doesn't seem the right word for King Ashurbanipal, who ruled the Assyrian empire in the seventh century B.C. In many respects he was typical of the rulers who lived thousands of years before him, in the early days of writing. If you received a letter from a king in Bronze Age Mesopotamia, and (as would have been likely) you couldn't read, a scribe would bring the letter to you and read it. As he did so, he wouldn't just be bringing the words of the king; he would be bringing you the king. As the scribe opened his mouth, it would have been as though the ruler were talking to you. So, in the library of Ashurbanipal, there was a letter from another king, which bore these words, just for the scribe:

> *Whoever you are, scribe, who is going to read this letter, do not*
> *conceal anything from the King, my lord, so that the gods Bel*
> *and Nabu should speak kindly of you to the King.*

The point of this furniture to the letter proper is that you, the listener/reader, can relax in the knowledge that everything you are learning about the great man's thoughts is free of chaff; that the medium of the scribe isn't even a medium. There you are, listening to a godlike being who has a message just for you. This was such an important idea that when Hammurabi, king of Babylon, decreed that those who bore false witness would suffer the penalty of death, he had scribes particularly in mind. This was in the eighteenth century B.C. Even seeing the face of Hammurabi would have been unthinkable enough, let alone the prospect of a tour around his ziggurat; his subjects' understanding of him would have in no way resembled our idea of what it is to understand or know about another human being. And yet their technology could bring them this experience of him that felt firsthand. They could cast aside the fact that this was a tablet and somebody else's voice reading it. Unrestricted by webcams or buffering or conference calls, their imaginations could take them to the inner chambers of majesty.

# Shades: Can the Famous Ever Shed Their Fame?

*Superstar d'un soir ta vie redevient normale*
*après*
*Pas besoin de lunettes noires pour te cacher personne te*
*reconnaît*

—YELLE
*"Je veux te voir"*

---

I am very fond of the good soldier Schweik . . . I
am convinced that you will sympathise with
this modest, unrecognised hero. He did not set
fire to the temple of the Goddess at Ephesus,
like that fool of a Herostratus, merely in order
to get his name into the newspapers and the
school reading books.
And that, in itself, is enough.

—JAROSLAV HAŠEK,
*The Good Soldier Schweik*

Greta Garbo didn't exactly say, "I want to be alone"; not as herself,
anyway, and not publicly. In the film *Grand Hotel,* she said, "I want
to be let alone." And, as she's supposed to have told people in private, "There is a whole world of difference." There is. The big,
defining quality of how to be famous is the way in which stars
turn their starlight on and off. When they stop becoming famous,
is that really what they want? In saying, "I want to be let alone," or
at least, in correcting the quotation and applying it to her own life,

Garbo was telling us that if she did want to be alone, it would be on her own terms—that she wanted to regain control of who found out what about her and when. So maybe she didn't want us finding much out, if anything; the crucial distinction is that she sought to regain control of the situation. We can hear her doing it in an interview she gave to Mordaunt Hall for *The New York Times:* She gives solitude a mention, and then tries to change the subject. When asked what she did on her first evening in New York, she replies that she dined alone. All alone?

> *Yes, quite alone, and I loved to look at the—what you call—shyscrapers— No, what it is?*
> *Yes, skyscrapers. Let's not talk about me, let's talk about New York and the skyscrapers.*

The more we look at why people want fame, the the more mysterious their motives for attaining it seem considering how we've treated them when they've become famous. Yes, this has a lot to do with our own needs as nonfamous people, and whether those needs have changed according to our historical circumstances. But what about when people don't want to be famous? This is surely understandable, if remaining famous is a primrose path that leads celebrities to be kebabbed as human sacrifices. So is there a way around this grim fate?

When I've told people what I've been writing about and what conclusions I've been reaching, some have said, "But what about people who are just cool or good at what they do, and they get on with it, and we like them?" It's true. There are some celebrities who manage not to look ridiculous, because they have the kind of integrity that prevents us from mocking them. The idea of faulting Chesley Sullenberger seems anathema; to accuse Cate Blanchett of car-crash couture, or to know too much about her private life, would seem disrespectful. David Bowie is cooler than the rest of us, and can do what he wants. If Helen Mirren admits that she used to take cocaine, she manages to do it in a good way.

So there are, even among us, people who manage to avoid the horrors and pratfalls of exposure. Everyone can think of plenty more, or else we can cherish those celebrities who can do no wrong in our own eyes. Still, not everyone has been so lucky, and their attempts to deal with their fame and at the same time establish some peace of mind for themselves have shown us as much about fame as our responses have.

When the comedian Peter Cook did his impersonation of Greta Garbo, he went about the streets in a tank declaiming "I vont to be alone" from a bullhorn. Sometimes when celebrities try to slip back into what Liz Hurley would call "civilian life," they end up attracting more attention to themselves; or else we accuse them of seeking celebrity by their peculiar behavior. The example of the anchorite shows how this works. If you lived in a medieval town or village, you might well have had an anchorite living in your community. Living in a community was never really the point of being an anchorite. Anchorites were supposed to be solitary souls who would devote their thoughts and lives to the quiet, untroubled contemplation of God. But because they sat in one place for extraordinarily long periods of time, passersby knew where to find them and would give them a bite to eat or maybe stop for a chat. Lots of people passing by and stopping for chats made anchorites a rich source of information and even gossip; the more withdrawn they were supposed to be, the better known they became. Saint Simeon Stylites took this principle to an extreme. In the early fifth century, he withdrew to a mountain to be nearer God, and managed to fast for whole Lents. His feats and solitude attracted too much attention, so he withdrew to remoter desert still. Near Aleppo, in Syria, he put himself on a pillar four meters high—high enough to be away from the crowd. For, sure enough, a crowd came, just as they would for David Blaine, and marveled that a fellow could stand on a post for so long, and go so long without food. Even the emperor Theodosius showed up to ask for advice. Some kind helpers built him an even taller post, fifteen meters high.

It's an odd image of our relationship with the famous, this. It's as if the crowd is saying, We like you so much that we want you farther away from us, even nearer the sky. Not only that, but although you want to be alone and to be spared from us bothering you, we want people to be able to see you from farther away. Garbo's coinage seems right for people who are celebrated in this way—shyscrapers.

Throughout the ages, running away from fame has become part of the celebrity repertoire. It's so strongly associated with the famous that the idea of dark glasses has become a cliché. As Yelle raps in the song quoted above, "Superstar for a night, your life becomes the everyday / No need to wear sunglasses no one knows you anyway." They want fame, they don't want fame; what they really want is for you to know they don't want fame.

Printmakers in the eighteenth century found themselves caught up in these crises of the ego. When Sir Joshua Reynolds painted his portrait of the actor Sarah Siddons, posed as the Tragic Muse, a printer named Valentine Green wanted to publish it. In a letter to Reynolds, Green dropped a hint about the "particular support of the party," meaning that one way for him to make his money up-front would be for Siddons to pay for the work. As Tim Clayton points out in his essay on these processes, "For obvious reasons this was done discreetly and evidence has not usually survived."

It's hard to think of a more peculiar or extreme case of trying to cheat fame than T. E. Lawrence. On the face of it, he was desperate not to be Lawrence of Arabia. He had a key role in the campaign against Turkey in the First World War: Because he knew Arabic and Arabia, he became the man responsible for persuading the Arabs to revolt against their Turkish rulers (who were allies of the Germans). His book about it, *Seven Pillars of Wisdom,* throbs with guilt at his part in what he considered to be a deception—that some of the liberated lands fell to Britain and France, and not to King Faisal as promised. So throughout his memoirs, he either finds spurious ways of justifying what he was up to or else disowns his achievements. In addition, he turned down a knighthood, having accepted other awards.

Some have argued that he exaggerated his part in the uprising. As ever, the self-lacerating Lawrence was ahead of his critics, and in his introductory chapter, almost urges them to bring it on:

*This isolated picture throwing the main light upon myself is unfair
to my British colleagues. . . . My proper share was a minor one,
but because of a fluent pen, a free speech, and a certain adroitness
of brain, I took upon myself, as I describe it, a mock primacy. . . .
In these pages the history is not of the Arab movement, but of me
in it.*

By this account, he gains primacy, not because he's done more than
anybody else but because he's cleverer than they; and he's mortified by it. One of the odd, even attention-grabbing things about
the book is its extreme candor in other areas. There's the notorious
chapter 80, in which he enters Deraa, disguised, and is rounded up
and presented to the bey governing the town. The bey tries to
have sex with him; Lawrence kicks him in the groin; the bey has
him beaten; at one point, through all the pain, Lawrence records
that "a delicious warmth, probably sexual, was swelling through
me." That take-it-or-leave-it objectivity of the "probably" is another sort of disguise from the man who would appear in Arab
dress and, on one occasion, as an Arab woman. It suggests that
there's nothing to be lost by telling us absolutely everything about
himself—after all, we wouldn't understand. (Every now and then
he tells us how different he is from the rest of us: "Indeed, I saw
myself a danger to ordinary men. . . .")

If he was reckoning that the more he told us, the less we would
know of him, he was onto something. Some have doubted that the
assault-and-battery episode ever took place, and the relevant page
of his diary was torn out; others, in spite of Lawrence's frankness
here and elsewhere, have denied that he was a sexual being at all.
He clearly knew his audience and had worked out that the best
way of hiding himself was to be as revealing as possible.

After the campaign and the honors, he tried to slip into obscurity again. It was difficult, because the American war reporter
Lowell Thomas had made a film about him. He hated it. He saw it
maybe five times. Then he worked in the colonial office, with Winston Churchill, where he hoped that the government could find
some way of honoring its pledges to the Arab rebels. After that, he

played extreme games with his identity. The smaller jeux d'esprit of 1932 involved him writing letters to Sid Abrahams, a swimming instructor in Southampton, in which he pretended to be his own uncle Ted Lawrence (not much of a pseudonym from Thomas Edward Lawrence). In them he urged the teacher to be harsh with a young swimmer, who turned out to be himself:

> *Please show him some of the slave-driving which you tell me is your reputation. . . . These swimming lessons are not his idea, but mine, for his own good. . . . Keep him hard at it all the time, and insist upon his trying again and again until he satisfies you. He will not give you much trouble if you handle him firmly from the first. . . .*

When Lawrence showed up, the staff at the pool recognized him but didn't let on. As Abrahams told a local paper years afterward, "I decided to do exactly what the letter said." Lawrence used a similar tactic when he persuaded a man from the Tank Corps to beat him.

By this time, Lawrence had tried to disappear from view, by joining the Royal Air Force at the lowest rank. Even this was with a view to writing about it. He sent a characteristic letter to Sir Hugh Trenchard, the chief of air staff:

> *I see the sort of subject I need in the beginning of your Force . . . and the best place to see a thing is from the ground. It wouldn't "write" from the officer level.*
>
> *I haven't told anyone, till I know your opinion: and probably not then, for the newspapers used to run after me, and I like being private. People wouldn't understand.*

The project was scuppered when the newspapers did find out. Later he would rejoin the Force, where he would work on a translation of Homer's *Odyssey* and a book about his experiences in the ranks. *The Mint* appeared twenty years after his death.

Although the book really is about his immersion in the ranks and rings with compassion, there are clues throughout that the author isn't at all ordinary, and that his nom de plume—the rank and number 352087 A/c Ross—is as pseudo as a pseudonym can be. At one point, he finds a photograph of himself and discreetly burns it. (It's hard not to think that someone in Trenchard's office had it placed in the barracks at Uxbridge for a joke.) And early on he tells us, as straight as possible, his truer reasons for going undercover:

> *Could a man, who for years had been closely shut up, sifting his inmost self with painful iteration to compress its smallest particles into a book—could he suddenly end his civil war and live the open life, patent for everyone to read?*
>
> *Accident, achievement, and rumour (cemented equally by my partial friends) had built me such a caddis-shell as almost prompted me to forget the true shape of the worm inside. So I had sloughed them and it right off—every comfort and possession—to plunge crudely amongst crude men and find myself for these remaining years of prime life. Fear now told me that nothing of my present would survive this voyage into the unknown.*

The idea of the extraordinary figure going in disguise among ordinary ones is an ancient one. It surfaces in Shakespeare's *Measure for Measure*. One of the sources for the Duke, the ruler of Vienna who dresses as a friar to see what he can do about his tottering state, is the late Roman emperor Alexander Severus, although James I, who had just succeeded to the throne when Shakespeare was writing, was just as capable of showing up incognito and dispensing justice. The example of James I convinces us that these things really happen, and are more than an extension of the creepy feeling that Zeus and Hermes might be passing by. The idea is so slinky and instinctive that when people do see celebrities in their midst, they find it hard to believe. Here is an instance from the life of Robbie Williams:

> *A young and evidently attractive woman walks by.*
> *"Hello!" he says. "What's your name?"*
> *She chats for a moment, from a distance. She says she's off to work.*
> *"You know who you look like," she says.*

> "Who?"
> "Robbie Williams," she says.
> "Yeah?" he says. "If only I had his money. And his good
>    looks."

In talking to this woman, is Robbie Williams seizing an opportunity or blending in? It seems like the latter, because he asks her whom he resembles. Even then, this could be to satisfy his ego, but this is Robbie Williams—of course people recognize him. He's clearly enjoying the appearance of being normal.

The rule is that it's only when the famous divest themselves of celebrity that they learn things. It's an obvious rule, and it applies principally to flatterers. There's a reason why celebrities don't learn the truth. Machiavelli advises princes that they shouldn't seek too much frankness too obviously:

> *The only way to safeguard yourself against flatterers is by letting people understand that you are not offended by the truth; but if everyone can speak the truth then you lose respect.*

Similarly, if a person of glamour takes too many insults from his or her entourage on the chin, he or she will inevitably lose some of that glamour. Disguise, or anonymity, is the only way to make progress. A thought experiment that demonstrates this is the terrific play *Insignificance*, by Terry Johnson. The characters are called the Professor, who is really Einstein; the Actress, who is really Marilyn Monroe; the Senator, who is really Joseph McCarthy; and the Ball Player, who is really Joe DiMaggio. Monroe flees the crowd and calls on Einstein, but Einstein doesn't know who she is. Joe DiMaggio follows her, but thinks Einstein is her psychiatrist. The next morning, McCarthy arrives at Einstein's apartment and finds that Monroe has stayed over, but takes her to be a call girl whom Einstein has hired because she looks like Marilyn Monroe. The resulting confusions show how the glare of fame can be so bright it can end up blinding us to who people are, even when their identities are extremely obvious.

So, like Lawrence, celebrities need, if not crave, the chance to find the worm within the caddis shell, and they do their sloughing in solitude; at Promises, for example. The moment Jonny Wilkinson kicked the winning drop goal in the last minute of the 2003 Rugby World Cup, the sense of deflation began, and a series of injuries followed. "I was afflicted by a powerful fear of failure and did not know how to free myself," he has said: "Quantum physics has helped me to realise that I was creating a destructive reality." His studies of Buddhism have endorsed this. In her memoir, *The Other Side of Nowhere*, the British soap actor Danniella Westbrook opts out of celebrity. It ends shortly after she walks off the set of *I'm a Celebrity, Get Me Out of Here!* and decides that from then on she will only appear in television programs that she can imagine herself wanting to watch.

It seems banal to point out that famous people often err—after all, that's one of the main reasons why we take such an interest in them—but when they do, should they be punished by ceasing to be famous? One hopes, for example, that Lindsay Lohan can cope with being famous but without being wrecked after a hearty night out, but some might argue that obscurity is just the thing to solve her problems. This argument is intuitive rather than logical, but it is at least the one that Giles Fielder-Civil advances. He thinks that a boycott of his daughter-in-law Amy Winehouse's music would "send a message." Amy Winehouse's father, Mitch, disagrees.*

It's not such an original idea. In Rome, when an emperor died, he either became a god or else was given the memory punishment, the *damnatio memoriae*. This meant that statues of him could be defaced, and coins with his head on them restamped. It was impossible to do this completely, especially in the case of emperors; but Tiberius tried to give the ambitious schemer Sejanus the same kind of treatment Stalin gave to Trotsky—to have him erased from the book of life. The Athenian practice of ostracism is its own punishment for fame or too big an ego, but at least offers the chance of a comeback after ten years, or sooner, if the state requires. Herodotus

---

\* It seems in character that Mitch Winehouse doesn't think exposure is the problem, since he has done so little to avoid it himself.

wields the same power over his subjects as he writes his histories. As one of his editors points out, "It is not uncommon for Herodotus to say that he knows something but will not state it. . . ." Among the reasons for this is an "unwillingness to 'immortalize' (by inclusion in the work) scandalous behaviour that does not deserve fame. . . ." We find similar things in the court of Haile Selassie:

> *His Most Benevolent Highness no longer hurled people into dungeons, but very simply sent them home from the Palace, and this sending home meant condemnation to oblivion. . . . Everything disappears in a second. You stop existing. Nobody will mention you, nobody will put you forward or show you any respect.*

Two cast members of *Celebrity Rehab*'s first season experienced the *damnatio memoriae:* not only Jessica Sierra, who, following charges of possession and assault, was banned from going within one hundred yards of a microphone or a camera (soon after she made a sex tape), but also Jaimee Foxworth, the actor who played one of the Winslow children in *Family Matters*. She was the third child; then she was dropped. It turned out that the Winslows had only ever had two children; nobody ever mentioned Judy Winslow again.

Still, these days, we don't often lose our stars. Although the present generation can allow people to remain famous while they're being rehabilitated, this must baffle those who, in 1963, watched John Profumo, the philandering British defense secretary, tuck his bat under his arm and take the walk from the crease to the pavilion. He returned to private life and did good works in east London. Today, sex cheat Bill Clinton is venerated as one of the world's elders; Watergate plumber G. Gordon Liddy is a surprise turn on talent shows. The whole premise of *Celebrity Rehab* suggests that celebrity itself is a vice we can pardon if its followers truly want to repent.

This continual parading of fallen stars feels like a new development in the history of fame, and could be a peculiarly British contribution to our dealings with personalities, with its unique blend of fair play and sadism. Certainly it's different from historical equivalents in commemorating people who have done bad things. There are still signs that Herodotus's principle of withholding fame from the wretched applies. In America recently, when a youth killed people in a mall and said that he did it to become famous, newspapers united in declining to print his name. The same nearly happened in Ephesus, where Herostratus burned the temple of Artemis. The authorities banned any mention of him, but his name survives, and has given posterity the notion of Herostratism, the urge to be remembered for bad deeds.

In his poem *The House of Fame*, of about 1379–80, Chaucer works through the permutations of our response to Fame, who appears personified as a noble queen in the house and doles out her favors arbitrarily to different crowds of petitioners. After she's dismissed the first group, she summons Aeolus, who appears in the *Odyssey* as the keeper of winds. He has two trumpets, one for praise and one for slander. Crucially, there remains a third option—not blowing either trumpet. Here are the categories of her supplicants:

| GROUP | WANTS | GETS |
|---|---|---|
| 1 | Good fame for good deeds | No fame |
| 2 | Good fame for good deeds | Infamy |
| 3 | Good fame for good deeds | Good fame |
| 4 *(small)* | No fame for good deeds | No fame |
| 5 | No fame for good deeds | Good fame |
| 6 | Fame for nothing | Fame |
| 7 | Fame for nothing | No fame |
| 8 | Good fame for bad deeds | No fame |
| 9 *(includes Herostratus★)* | Bad fame for bad deeds | Infamy |

It is now routine for commentators to assume that the problem with society these days is all the shmendriks in groups 6 and 7: They appear on *The Hills* or seek glory through *Jersey Shore,* and if that's what our kids get to be like it's no wonder that the free West

---

★ Sort of. Chaucer's sense of irony leads him not to name the blighter, and to record that he burned the temple of Isis at Athens.

is going to the dogs.* This is so often presented as a moral crisis that we forget about the more glaring issue of the scumbags in groups 8 and 9, who are openly committed to being scumbags. When pundits say, "People will do anything for fame nowadays," they need to remember that the fickle canons of celebrity have always been ready for such finks, and that posterity has dealt with them, even if willy-nilly.

But, to conclude our journey from fame hell to fame paradise, there is a place for those exceptional souls who fall into groups 4 and 5. However much preachers and educators complain that our children look to their role models and see that fame can come for next to nothing, even in Chaucer's time this was an easy point to make; his way of addressing it is to make groups 4 and 5 small, and to put everyone else into the remaining seven categories of people who want fame on their own terms. To look over the people we've met, not everybody is a clear case of a 4 or 5. For example, it's hard to gauge whether T. E. Lawrence thinks he's in this type, but is secretly more of a 3; and the whole idea of group 5 means that Greta Garbo and Saint Simeon Stylites can fit into it whether they want to or not. In Chaucer's account, the common motive for such people is service to the greater glory of God:

> We have done well with all our might,
> Although we haven't kept our fame.
> Hide our achievements and our name,
> For love of God; it's certain we
> Have done it for prosperity
> And for no other sort of thing.

To 4 she gives renown, but to 5 she says:

> "What?" said she; "And are you crazy,
> You who do good, with none to praise ye?

---

* You can hear this in Britain at least once a week from any of a number of speakers on "Thought for the Day" (Radio 4, *Today Programme*; the slot is at 7:48 daily, except Sundays).

*So is that what you think of fame?*
*You've no respect, then, for my name?*
*No, each of you will have fame. So*
*Straight away, my trumpets, blow!"*

As even these portions show, the delight of this extended passage lies in the vehemence with which Fame pronounces completely opposing sentences.

If it is true that fame is a cross the famous carry, and yet that it is something so worth having that those sometimes cruel types, the Romans, thought it a punishment to take it away, why, why on earth, would anyone want it? As Bertolt Brecht wrote in a song that considers how those defining traits—Solomon's wisdom, Caesar's courage, and Socrates' honesty—proved their keepers' undoing, "How fortunate the man with none." It's a feeling that besets the shade of Achilles in the Underworld, where his old rival and ally Odysseus finds him. As T. E. Lawrence (or by then, T. E. Shaw) translates it:

> *"How I envy your lot, Achilles, happiest of men who have been or will be! In your day all we Argives adored you with a God's honours: and now down here I find you a Prince among the dead. To you, Achilles, death can be no grief at all." He took me up and said, "Do not make light of Death before me, O shining Odysseus. Would that I were on earth a menial, bound to some insubstantial man who must pinch and scrape to keep alive! Life were better than King of Kings among these dead men who have had their day and died."*

Even dead, though Achilles doesn't want fame, he sort of wants it—he wants to hear from Odysseus that his own son is famous.

Odysseus himself has a lot to learn about fame, and one of the strongest themes in Homer's poem is identity. Odysseus plays with it constantly and goes about in disguises, to the point where his defining characteristic becomes his ability to rid himself of character. In his most famous adventure, the encounter with the Cyclops, he gets around the monster by telling him that his name is "Nobody," so that when he gouges the one big eye out and the Cyclops yells, "No-body is killing me!" the neighboring Cyclopes mooch away because they don't think they can be much use. (In the exchanges, the word for "nobody" ends up needing to be the same as the word for "cunning," for which Odysseus is famous.) What happens next shows that Odysseus can still be reckless with his renown. He yells at the Cyclops and reveals who he is. This enables the Cyclops not only to locate the vaunting voice and to lob a huge rock perilously close to its source, but also to have a name so that he can bring a potent curse down upon him.

Later, Odysseus lands on an island, where he appears naked—another example that shows how when you're most exposed, you can't be taken for who you are. Here he is rescued by the beautiful Nausicaa, and protected by King Alcinous. Again, he goes about pretending to be a nebbish, but one who is suspiciously good at Olympic field events. The pretense breaks down when a bard starts singing about the Trojan War, and the hero at the dinner table breaks into sobs. The talk of famous deeds has rumbled him. He reveals himself: "I am Odysseus, son of Laertes: a name which among men spells every resource and subtlety of mind: and my fame reaches heaven."

When Odysseus finally comes home, he comes crudely among crude men. His task is to dispel the scoffing, schnorring suitors from his craggy island on the wrong side of Greece, and he does so dressed as a tramp. He reveals himself selectively, but not to his wife; still, in an interview with her, he pretends to be someone who knows Odysseus. He offers a detailed description of himself, and furnishes it with the kind of information only his wife could know about, down to the design of his brooch. Best of all is the observation that this Odysseus has a tunic that fits him as smoothly as the skin of an onion, hinting at the layers of disguise. (Lawrence translates this as a "dried onion," which makes the outer skin all the easier to crackle off.) When he finally tells his wife who he is, it is her turn to test him. She asks him to move the bed. He says it can't be moved. He knows she knows. This leads us to a cadence of the most ordinary intimacy. They go to bed; he tells her about his adventures. He's been away a long time; she's so glad he's back.

As ever, what's intriguing about these tales from Homer is what the Greeks made of them. To Aristotle, the *Odyssey* was recognition throughout. Unlike modern readers, the ancients took the Underworld episode as part of the whole package, although it is now consistently identified as an add-in. We should pay more attention: It is among the shades that Odysseus learns the most about fame. After all, this is the episode that began a genre adopted by Virgil and Dante, and which Chaucer mimics in his *House of Fame*: the processions of memorable dead souls, those shades which, though they won't come back to the earth, have achieved immortality there. At the very end of *The Republic*, Socrates spends some time talking about this Homeric hero, even though he spent a while earlier in the dialogue pooh-poohing Homer.

Throughout *The Republic*, Plato argues that we should want justice, and that we should want justice because justice is good. But at the end, he caves in and shows that we might also want to be just because, by and large, it does us good in the afterlife. And he tells a story about how a certain kind of wisdom pays off. In the story, souls can choose the forms in which they would like to return. The problems are, first, that there is a finite number of souls from which to choose, and second, we don't make the right choices anyway:

> For the most part they followed the habits of their former life. And so he saw the soul that had once been Orpheus choose the life of a swan; it was unwilling to be born of a woman because it hated all women after its death at their hands. . . . The twentieth soul to choose chose a lion's life; it was the soul of Ajax, son of Telamon, which did not want to become a man, because it remembered the judgement of the arms. It was followed by Agamemnon, who also because of his sufferings hated humanity and chose to be an eagle. And Atalanta's turn came somewhere about the middle, and when she saw the great honours of an

*athlete's life the attraction was too great and she chose it. . . . And
so it happened that it fell to the soul of Odysseus to choose the
last of all. The memory of his former sufferings had cured him
of all ambition and he looked round for a long time to find the
uneventful life of an ordinary man; at last he found it lying
neglected by the others, and when he saw it he chose it with joy
and said that had his lot fallen first he would have made the
same choice.*★

Before these souls are reborn, they must drink from Lethe, the
river of forgetfulness.

So Odysseus learns from fame; but can we? If Chaucer put the
number of people who didn't want fame at a handful, and Plato reduces the number to just one, it seems hard to be optimistic that
people will stop hankering after celebrity for themselves. It also
seems unlikely that we will stop wanting to know about famous
people, because the needs they fulfill are hard to shift. In the latter
case—the case of the fame we want others to have—this is surely not
such a bad thing. If the demands we make of the famous do bear any
relation to the manifestations of our more bestial impulses from earlier times, then heck, we could be doing a lot worse. In the former
case—the case of the fame we want to have—the soundest principle
is the adage carved at the temple of Apollo at Delphi: "Nothing to
excess."

In some ways, this inscription couldn't be less relevant to fame.
After all, excess is something worth being famous for; luxury and
feasting are the very treats sacrificial victims enjoy throughout *The
Golden Bough*. How can you have fame without excess? Isn't Cham-
pagne the very symbol of celebrity? Would Faust have signed on the
line if Satan had offered him a lifetime's gym membership and a gift
card to The Vitamin Shoppe†? But maybe, for a moment, there will

---

★ Plato, *Republic* 10.620, trans. Desmond Lee (Penguin, 1955). In life, Orpheus was torn
apart by Bacchant women; Ajax went mad with rage when Odysseus inherited the arms
of Achilles (at least, he does in the play by Sophocles); for Agamemnon, see chapter 1;
Atalanta was a huntress who didn't want to marry, and would settle down only with a
man who could beat her in a footrace.

† The boutique's own spelling suggests it's hoping to attract customers of Faust's vintage.

be a little moderation. Maybe a global financial crisis will have something to do with it, although this seems unlikely in the long term. A greater corrective may come from information technology, thanks to which everyone with access to the Internet can become a little bit famous to groupuscules of like-minded folk. In either case, we might end up becoming better known, and even better appreciated, in smaller communities, whether they're local or virtual.

It's a lot to expect the candidates on *American Idol,* those plumbers for whom the public vote on a Tuesday night is the big ticket out, to be content with clogged pipes the following Monday; but the day job might end up offering more intimacy and gratitude. If this is worth having, then Odysseus looks like a better role model than Achilles; or, failing that, there's always Damon the mower, the bucolic nebbish from a poem of the same name by Andrew Marvell. He cuts grass. When the shepherdess he loves rejects the gifts he offers, of toothless snakes and chameleons, he comforts himself by claiming as much fame as he can:

> *I am the Mower Damon, known*
> *Through all the Meadows I have mown.*

# NOTES AND CREDITS

## INTRODUCTION

p. 1  Jade Goody remembers her encounter with Mariah Carey in *Jade: My Autobiography* (HarperCollins, 2006).

p. 4  For the oxygen chamber, see J. Randy Taraborrelli's comprehensive *Michael Jackson: The Magic and the Madness* (Pan Books, 2003), 356–60.

p. 4  Cimon's death: Plutarch's Life of Cimon, trans. Robin Waterfield, *Plutarch's Greek Lives* (Oxford University Press, 1998).

p. 4  Katie Couric is quoted in the *Washington Post*, January 11, 2005.

p. 7  The Chaucer passages are updated from *The House of Fame*, vv.1730–39 and 1771–86. Chaucer really does mean to write "jaws."

p. 8  Hierius: Augustine, *Confessions* 4.14, trans. R. S. Pine-Coffin (Penguin).

p. 10  *Katie Holmes*: quotation from Andrew Morton's *Tom Cruise: An Unauthorized Biography* (St. Martin's, 2008), 267.

## CHAPTER 1: WHAT WAS BRITNEY TELLING US WHEN SHE CUT HER OWN HAIR?

Walter Burkert's *Homo Necans: The Anthropology of Ancient Greek Sacrificial Ritual and Myth* has influenced this chapter, as have sections of James Frazer's *The Golden Bough*. Vanessa Grigoriadis's article on Britney Spears in *Rolling Stone* is an invaluable summary of the situation in early 2008; Britney and Lynne Spears's collaborative *Britney Spears' Heart to Heart* seemed pathetic when it first appeared in 2000, and is pathetic in a different sense now.

p. 12  *Hormonal moment*: The quotes from Esther Tognozzi are in Marcus Errico, *Britney's Mane Event, Day 2: Hair for Sale?* (eonline.com).

p. 12  *Big payday*: Grigoriadis, *Rolling Stone*, February 21, 2008.

p. 13  *Durkheim*: Walter Burkert, *Homo Necans,* trans. Peter Bing (University of California, 1982) 24, quoting from *Les formes élémentaires de la vie religieuse*, 598 and 610.

p. 14  *fama: Lewis and Short's Latin Dictionary,* ad loc.

p. 14  *Foul fame*: Virgil, *Aeneid* 4.174–7, 181–3, 195.

p. 16    *tribute:* Euripides, *Hippolytus*, 1423–7.

p. 16    Pausanias 2.32, and Lucian, both quoted in John Ferguson's edition of *Hippolytus* (Bristol Classical Press, 1984), 104.

p. 16    Hair in rites of passage: Ibid.

p. 17    *Get me out of here!:* by Britney and Lynne Spears, *Britney Spears' Heart to Heart* (Hodder and Stoughton, 2000), 122.

p. 19    Deuteronomy: Chapter 22, vv.13–21.

p. 19    Russell Long was working for UPS when he spoke to J. Randy Taraborrelli (*Madonna: An Intimate Biography* [Pan Books, 2008], 25–26).

p. 20    *Why the Greeks put them through it:* Burkert begins *Homo Necans* with an account of sacrifice in ancient Greece, drawn from a range of sources, not least Homer's *Iliad*, Book 1. This account, and much of what follows, is indebted to Walter Burkert's vital book, *Homo Necans*. Denniston's account is his Oxford edition of Euripides' *Electra* (1939, 147). The passage in question begins at line 791.

p. 22    *you may justly sacrifice:* Burkert, *Greek Religion* (Blackwell, 1987), 56 n.

p. 22    *Shall thousands:* Euripides, *Iphigenia at Aulis,* trans. R. Potter.

p. 23    *The modern world:* Burkert, *Homo Necans*, 297.

p. 24    *more likely to die:* This is demonstrated with scientific credibility in Mark A. Bellis et al., "Elvis to Eminem: Quantifying the Price of Fame Through Early Mortality of European and North American Rock and Pop Stars," *Journal of Epidemiology & Community Health* 61, no. 10 (2007): 896–901.

p. 25    *decided by lot:* James Davidson, *Courtesans and Fishcakes* (Fontana, 1998), 15.

p. 26    *hardens into custom:* Burkert, *Greek Religion,* 56.

p. 27    This view of Frazer comes from Peter Metcalf, in *Anthropology: The Basics* (Routledge, 2005), 118.

p. 27    *Lhota Naga:* James Frazer, *The Golden Bough*, ed. and abridged by Robert Fraser (Oxford World's Classics), 445.

p. 27    *dance followed:* Ibid., 443.

p. 27    Achilles' human sacrifice: *Iliad* 23.174–6.

p. 28    *sacred impulses of aggression:* Burkert, *Homo Necans,* 41.

p. 29    *Man in fact created gods:* Frazer, *The Golden Bough*, 224.

p. 30    *misfortunes of the people:* Ibid., 583.

p. 31    *religion and morality:* Burkert, *Greek Religion*, 248.

p. 32    Albert Stanburrough Cook, "Ibn Fadlan's Account of Scandinavian Merchants on the Volga in 922," *Journal of English and Germanic Philology* 22(1923):54–63.

p. 32    *Crystal:* www.mtv.com/ontv/dyn/i_want_a_famous_face-2/series.jhtml.

p. 34    *For the savage believes:* Frazer, *The Golden Bough*, 187.

## CHAPTER 2: TEMPORARY LIKE ACHILLES

For much of this chapter, I am indebted to Nigel Spivey's *The Ancient Olympics* (Oxford, 2004)—a short, invaluable introduction to the Greek world, and a lot more. Tim Adams's interview in the *Observer* is the principle source for Linford Christie.

p. 36    *poor a show of sportsmanship:* Ben Fenton, *Daily Telegraph,* July 29, 1996.

p. 36    *You always know; nandrolone:* Interview with Tim Adams, *Observer,* September 4, 2005.

p. 37    *react to a stimulus:* see BBC Sport, August 2, 2000, and Roger Highfield in *Daily Telegraph,* May 17, 1999.

p. 37    *Son of luck:* Sophocles, *Oedipus Tyrannus* 1080.

p. 38    *Megacles:* Pythian 7.

p. 39    *My child:* Homer, *Iliad* 1.414–16.

p. 39    *My mother Thetis:* Homer, *Iliad* 9.410–16.

p. 39    *Nobody will escape:* Homer, *Iliad* 21.103–13.

p. 40    *youthful armor ("sumptis Priamus iuvenalibus armis"):* Virgil, *Aeneid* 2.518.

p. 40    *He did it easily:*

p. 41    *Without a word . . . short of its objective:* Virgil, *Aeneid* 12.896–900; 905–7, trans. C. Day Lewis (Oxford, 1998).

p. 42    *the fifth-age men:* Hesiod, *Works and Days,* vv 170–85.

p. 43    *Our parents' time:* Horace, *Odes* 3.6.45–8.

p. 44    Sarpedon's speech to Glaucus: Homer, *Iliad* 12.310–328; Goldhill's *The Poet's Voice* (Cambridge, 1991) offers a discussion of this passage (78–79).

p. 45    *King of the Ring:* Spivey, *The Ancient Olympics,* 125–6.

p. 46    *As in a dream:* Homer, *Iliad* 22.199–200.

p. 46    For the link between athletics and war, see Spivey, *The Ancient Olympics,* Chapter 1.

p. 46    *Any kind of violence:* Ibid., 106.

p. 48    Juvenal on Gracchus: *Satire* 2, 143.

p. 50    *Abu Ghraib:* Scott Shane, "Grueling Duties in Prison, Rounds of Golf on Its Roof," *Baltimore Sun,* May 7, 2004.

p. 51    David Rousset, quoted in Perec, *W, or the Memory of Childhood,* trans. David Bellos (David R. Godine, 2003),163.

p. 51    *this huge machine:* Ibid., 161.

p. 52    For a discussion of Pandarus and his death, see James Tatum, *The Mourner's Song* (University of Chicago, 2003), 124–5

p. 52    *spindles:* Thucydides, *Peloponnesian War* 4.40.2. I'm indebted to a fine piece of coursework by Scott Pearce, which steered me toward Thomas Nelson Winter's essay "The Place of Archery in Greek Warfare."

p. 53   *a light sniff of gas:* Hervey Allen, *Toward the Flame* (1934), quoted in Denis Winter's *Death's Men* (Penguin, 1978), 121.

p. 53   Dave Grossman's *On Killing,* quoted in Tatum, *The Mourner's Song,* 127.

## CHAPTER 3: AND WHAT BECAME OF LAST YEAR'S SNOW?

The two most significant encounters with Kate Winslet here are her appearances in *GQ,* February 2003, and *Vogue,* January 2007, in which she is interviewed by Alex Bilmes.

p. 58   Coco Rocha, interviewed in the *Daily Telegraph* magazine, May 23, 2008.

p. 58   Photoshop: *Sunday Times,* April 20, 2008.

p. 59   *portraiture in vase-painting:* Kenneth Dover, *Greek Homosexuality* (Duckworth, 1978), 116.

p. 62   *the best fragrance of all:* Xenophon, *Symposium* 2.

p. 62   For the gymnasium and military training, see Spivey, *The Ancient Olympics,* Chapter 2, "In training for beautiful goodness."

p. 62   *I didn't get any further:* Plato, *Symposium* 217c.

p. 62   *with their fists alone:* Fragment from Euripides' satyr play *Autolycus,* quoted by Spivey, *The Ancient Olympics,* 26.

p. 62   *Lydia, by the gods:* The Sybaris ode is I.8.

p. 63   Rhetoric 1361b, quoted in Spivey, 68.

p. 64   *That activity of all the senses: Within a Budding Grove,* in Marcel Proust, *Remembrance of Things Past,* vol. I, trans. Terence Kilmartin (Penguin, 1983), 528.

p. 65   *unarmed gums: Satire* 10, 196–200.

## CHAPTER 4: SYMPATHY FOR THE DEVIL

I have consulted David Hawkes's occasionally penetrable book, *The Faust Myth.* An article in *The Great Composers and Their Music* intrigued me early on with its tales of virtuosos (Issue 12—"Like Men Possessed"). Clive James's "Point of View" deserves a fuller consideration than the one offered here; it contrasts Amy Winehouse favorably with Snoop Dogg.

p. 68   *spirit should be subservient: Historia and Tale of Doctor Johannes Faustus,* 2.

p. 68   *The parlour was full of blood:* Ibid., 44

p. 69   *David Leipziger:* David Hawkes, *The Faust Myth: Religion and the Rise of Representation* (New York, 2007), 41.

p. 70   *bewitching:* Thomas Heywood's *Apology for Actors,* and antitheatrical writing, discussed in Hawkes, *The Faust Myth,* 50–51.

p. 72    *Ah, happy he: Faust* Part I—"Outside the City Gate," trans. Philip Wayne (Penguin 1949), 66–67.

p. 73    *limitations of the human faculties:* Kant, quoted in Coleridge, *Biographia Literaria,* Chapter 12.

p. 74    *triumph o'er a secret:* Browning, *A Toccata of Galuppi's,* 32

p. 74    *When that young woman sings:* "A Point of View," Radio 4, May 2, 2008.

p. 75    *The sufferings of the central character:* David Cairns, *Berlioz,* vol. II: *Servitude and Greatness* (Allen Lane, 1999), 356.

p. 76    *The excitement he created:* Alan Kendall, *Paganini* (Chapel, 1982), 27.

p. 78    *May the artist of the future:* Derek Watson, *Liszt* (Oxford University Press, 1989), 59.

p. 81    *the heart and cranium:* MacCarthy, *Byron: Life and Legend* (John Murray, 2002), 519.

p. 81    *Mariah Carey's riders:* David Rowan, *Evening Standard,* April 4, 2002.

p. 82    *Mark Bellis and others:* Bellis et al., *Elvis to Eminem.*

p. 82    Germaine Greer on Heath Ledger, *Guardian,* February 11, 2008.

p. 83    On Dasius and the Saturnalia, see *The Golden Bough,* 630–32.

p. 84    *arse: The Letters of Mozart and His Family,* 3rd ed., ed. and trans. Emily Anderson (Macmillan, 1966), 741.

p. 85    *Surely the vanity would have kill'd me:* Jonathan Bate, *John Clare: A Biography* (Picador, 2003), 178.

p. 86    *He came across Giotto:* Vasari, *Lives of the Artists,* vol. I, trans. George Bull (Penguin, 1987), 57–58.

p. 87    *Wilfrid Mellers:* Derek Taylor, *It Was Twenty Years Ago Today* (Bantam, 1987), 46.

## CHAPTER 5: DIVAS AND DIVINITIES

Robin Lane Fox's *Pagans and Christians* has guided me through this and the next chapter. His chapter "Seeing the Gods," an impressive survey of epiphanies throughout the pre-Christian ancient world, is most relevant to the present topic. E. R. Dodds's chapter on shamanism in *The Greeks and the Irrational* is good value on how mysterious the mysteries of Orphism are. Kay Turner's collection of dreams in *I Dream of Madonna* provides a modern perspective on intimate experiences of a revered figure.

p. 89    Metzstein on Angelina Jolie: Quoted by Alexandra Shulman, *Vogue,* November 2008, 246.

p. 89    Yannis Ritsos, quoted by Anne Carson in her edition of Sappho, *If Not, Winter* (Virago, 2003), 362.

p. 91    11,340 years earlier: Herodotus, *Histories,* II.142, trans. Aubrey de Selincourt (Penguin, 1954).

p. 91    Pisistratus's entry into Athens: Ibid., I.60.

p. 93    Paul and Barnabas: Acts 14, 8–15.

p. 93    Lane Fox on icons, Hero of Alexandria, etc., *Pagans and Christians* (Penguin, 1986), 136–37.

p. 94    *bees share in the godly mind:* Georgics 4.219–227.

p. 95    Iamblichus: Lane Fox, *Pagans and Christians,* 126.

p. 95    Pan's cave: Achilles Tatius, *Leucippe and Cleitophon*, Book 8.

p. 95    *"host and guest":* Lane Fox, *Pagans and Christians,* 124.

p. 96    Babylonian gods: David Rosenberg, *Abraham: The First Historical Biography* (New York, 2006), 34.

p. 96    *Ram and Hanuman:* BBC News, December 7, 2007.

p. 97    *"Your Angel":* Peter Brown, *The Cult of the Saints* (University of Chicago, 1981), 51.

p. 97    James Davidson on Phryne: *Worshipping Women,* TLS, October 5, 2007, 5. Davidson is reviewing Joan Breton Connelly's *Portrait of a Priestess*, and takes issue with Connelly's view that sacred prostitution is a myth.

p. 98    *bustin' with bounce: Daily Telegraph* obituary, October 5, 2004.

p. 99    Madonna as Pandora, Aphrodite, Artemis, Athene, Mary, and so on: Kay Turner, *I Dream of Madonna: Women's Dreams of the Goddess of Pop* (Thames and Hudson, 1993), 9.

p. 99    *the two are really friends:* Ibid., 15–16.

p. 104   Ammianus and the Roman senatorial ranks: See de Ste Croix, *The Class Struggle in the Ancient Greek World* (Duckworth, 1981), 378–9.

p. 105   Haile Selassie's ministers: Ryszard Kapuściński, *The Emperor* (Penguin, 1978), 153–4.

p. 107   *mists and clouds of ignorance: The Golden Bough,* 223.

## CHAPTER 6: ETERNAL FLAME

In addition to *Pagans and Christians,* I have found Peter Brown's *The Cult of the Saints* enlightening on the hierarchies from heaven downward in late antiquity.

p. 110   *O blessed and valiant martyrs: The Passion of Saints Perpetua and Felicity,* 21.

p. 111   Philip the Asiarch: Lane Fox, *Pagans and Christians,* 485.

p. 112   Rufinus: Ibid., 467.

p. 113   *but we an incorruptible:* 1 Corinthians 9, 24–25.

p. 113   *an ill-favoured Egyptian: The Passion of Saints Perpetua and Felicity,* 10.

p. 113   Pammachius: Brown, *The Cult of the Saints,* 36.

p. 113   Lampadius: Ibid., 46.

p. 115   acclaimed throughout the Christian world: Ibid., 47.

p. 115   daimons: Ibid., Chapter 3.

p. 116   *They were just women:* Proust, *Remembrance of Things Past*, 460.

## CHAPTER 7: I WANT TO BE LIKE YOU-HOO-HOO

p. 118   *SAFE SEX:* Madonna, *Sex* (Secker & Warburg, 1993), early on. (She doesn't really do page numbers.)

p. 123   Homer's advice on chariot racing: see, for example, Xenophon, *Symposium,* Chapter 4.

p. 123   *masters of all forms of skill:* Plato, *Republic*, X.598, 599, translated by H. D. P. Lee (Penguin, 1955).

p. 123   Plato on gods setting a bad example: *Republic* III.388–91.

p. 125   *No Alice bands:* Ovid, *Ars Amatoria* I.31–4, not too loosely.

p. 125   Messalina's 25: Juvenal, *Satire* 6; Pliny the Elder, *Natural History* X.83. The latter is reported in the interest of science, to distinguish human desire and monogamy from that of birds.

p. 125   The information about Marie Antoinette here comes from Caroline Weber, "Queen of Fashion: What Marie-Antoinette wore to the Revolution," as extracted in U.S. *Vogue* (September 2006).

p. 127   Information on *Woman's Hour* and Hollywood Cake comes from Marguerite Patten's *Victory Cookbook*. Oddly, she doesn't do page numbers either.

p. 128   Garbo, Dietrich, etc.: Georgina Howell, *In Vogue: Six Decades of Vogue Fashion* (Allen Lane, 1975), 109.

p. 129   *you feel, like, good in yourself:* Beverley Skeggs, "A Good Time for Women Only," in *Deconstructing Madonna*, ed. Fran Lloyd (Batsford, 1993), 73.

p. 130   *My week's stay in rehab:* Danniella Westbrook, *The Other Side of Nowhere* (Headline, 2006), 107–8.

p. 131   Durkheim, *Le Suicide*: un etude de sociologie, 1.4.1.

p. 131   Martin and Koo's study into suicide: "Celebrity Suicide: Did the Death of Kurt Cobain Influence Young Suicides in Australia?" in *Archives of Suicide Research* 3, no. 3 (September 1997), 187–98.

p. 132   Christine von Lassberg: see Michael Hulse's introduction to his Penguin translation (1989), 12; the other information in this paragraph comes from the same essay.

p. 133   Jade and Jackson: Goody, *My Autobiography*, 237

## CHAPTER 8: IF YOU WANT TO EVICT JADE, VOTE NOW

This chapter draws on, among other texts, Simon Schama's *Citizens;* Peter Thomas's biography of Wilkes, *John Wilkes: A Friend to Liberty;* Daniel Walker Howe's *Making the American Self;* and Jade Goody's first volume of memoirs.

The discussion of ostracism I have found most helpful is by Rosalind Thomas. Robert Darnton discusses the problems and possibilities of reading history through pornographic libel in *The Forbidden Bestsellers of Pre-Revolutionary France,* particularly in part 3. The exhibition *Citizens and Kings: Portraits in the Age of Revolution 1760–1830* at the Royal Academy brought together the paintings discussed here, and I acknowledge a debt to the accompanying catalog.

p. 136  The details of Jade's eviction come from *Jade: My Autobiography*, mostly from Chapter 6.

p. 141  *Aristides the Just:* Plutarch, *Greek Lives.* Here the translation is Dryden's.

p. 142  *the poet Eupolis:* Plutarch, *Greek Lives*, Cimon 5, trans. Robin Waterfield (Oxford University Press), 133.

p. 148  *designed to placate:* Plutarch, *Alcibiades,* 13.

p. 149  Abraham Lincoln quoting Gray's "Elegy": Daniel Walker Howe, *Making the American Self* (Oxford University Press, 1999), 138

p. 149  John Edwards's Buick: see Andrew Young, *The Politician: An Insider's Account of John Edwards's Pursuit of the Presidency and the Scandal That Brought Him Down* (Thomas Dunne, 2010).

p. 149  *all these go to make up the assembly:* Xenophon, *Memorabilia*, quoted by Paul Millett in his lecture "Elitism and Participation in Classical Athens."

p. 154  *fireproof against rumour:* Peter Thomas, *John Wilkes: A Friend to Liberty* (Oxford University Press, 1996), 12.

p. 155  *monks of Medmenham:* Julie Peakman's inventory of regular and less regular visitors to the ruins, in *Lascivious Bodies* (Atlantic, 2005), becomes speculative after a while, and perhaps fanciful; but since her discussion of it makes the sound link between sex and power, she's convincing enough.

p. 155  For the *North Briton* affair of 1763, see Thomas, *John Wilkes,* Chapter 3.

p. 157  E. A. Smith on Caroline: *ODNB*, ad loc.

p. 161  *Hercules in the form of Adonis:* Antonia Fraser, *Marie Antoinette: The Journey* (Anchor, 2006), 175.

p. 162  *What rapture!:* Simon Schama, *Citizens: A Chronicle of the French Revolution* (Penguin, 2004), 210.

p. 166  election photography: Roland Barthes, *Mythologies*, trans. Annette Lavers (Vintage, 1993), 91–92.

p. 168  Noel Gallagher: "Bye Bye Blair!," *Grazia*, July 2, 2007.

p. 170  *a more dignified way:* CBC, January 5, 2007.

p. 171  *foutue:* Quoted by Antonia Fraser, *Marie Antoinette,* 525.

p. 172  *to get the execution over:* Kingsbury Smith, International News Service, October 16, 1946.

## CHAPTER 9: WE'RE ALL INDIVIDUALS
## (YES, WE'RE ALL INDIVIDUALS)

The discussion of individuality and dividuality owes much to Chris Fowler's *The Archaeology of Personhood*; Jamie Coreth pointed me toward it, and it pointed me toward Marcel Mauss's *Essai sur le don* (1923–4). I'm grateful to Sorcha Carey, who commented on the section about group portraits.

p. 176    *Xenophon:* trans. Tredennick and Waterfield (Penguin, 1990), 231.

p. 178    *Ms. Lopez's fragrances:* Cathy Horyn, "The Sweet Smell of Celebrity," *New York Times,* June 30, 2005.

p. 179    *Among Melanesian societies:* Chris Fowler, *The Archaeology of Personhood: An Anthropological Approach* (Routledge, 2005), 74.

p. 180    *A red deer antler:* Lars Larsson, quoted in Fowler, *Archaeology of Personhood,* 145. It appears that dogs were singled out for these honors.

p. 181    Siberian burials: Ibid., 134

p. 181    *gifts to be circulated:* Ibid., 40, drawing on Joanna Brück.

p. 183    *short attention span:* Cathy Horyn, "Sweet Smell of Celebrity."

p. 183    For Victoria Beckham on scents, see *That Extra Half an Inch* (Michael Joseph, 2006) with Hadley Freeman, 285.

p. 184    Segal on Pindar: *Aglaia,* 3, quoted in Spivey, *The Ancient Olympics,* 138.

p. 185    Ara Pacis: I have followed Paul Zanker's readings and identifications in *The Power of Images in the Age of Augustus* (University of Michigan, 1998), 217.

p. 187    Titus and Septimius Severus: Sir Mortimer Wheeler brings these two images together in *Roman Art and Architecture* (Thames and Hudson, 1964).

p. 191    *distinctiveness of each single portrait:* R. H. Fuchs, *Dutch Painting* (Thames and Hudson, 1978), 95.

p. 191    Gainsborough versus Reynolds: This information comes from Simon Macdonald's entry in the *Citizens and Kings* catalog, 397. He cites Horace Walpole as a source for the dispute.

## CHAPTER 11: TOO MUCH INFORMATION

Geoffrey Day's *From Fiction to the Novel* has helped me to connect some of the ideas in this chapter.

p. 204    *Women Before 10 a.m.:* New York, 1998.

p. 205    *giving till it hurts:* Sandra Bernhard made this the title of her one-woman stage show in 1993.

p. 206    *Public figures have the right:* Veyne, *Roman Erotic Elegy: Love, Poetry and the West,* trans. David Pellauer (University of Chicago, 1988), 169.

p. 207    Letter to Lucius Lucceius: Cicero, *Ad familiares,* 10.

p. 207    *It's sweet:* Lucretius, *De Rerum Natura,* II.1–4.

p. 209    Mark McCrum: "Ghostwriters Spill the Beans," *Guardian Weekend*, November 22, 2008.

p. 210    *chaff:* John Coldstream, *Dirk Bogarde: The Authorised Biography* (Weidenfeld & Nicolson, 2004), 5.

p. 210    *Informs Dirk's life:* Ibid., 9.

p. 211    *Propertius:* I.7.21–24.

p. 212    *my lower abdomen:* Aelius Aristides, quoted in Veyne, *Roman Erotic Elegy*, 176.

p. 212    Veyne on Augustine: Ibid., 171

p. 212    *partners in sin:* St. Augustine, *Confessions,* II.8.

p. 212    *I need not tell all this to you:* Ibid., II.3.

p. 213    *a saintly man:* See the 1961 Penguin edition of *Confessions,* 11–12. The subsequent quotations are from this translation.

p. 214    Augustine on bragging: Ibid., II.3.

p. 214    *By now I was at the top . . . human vanity:* Ibid., III.3, III.4.

p. 215    *They lapse into pride:* Ibid., V.3

p. 215    *Accept my confessions:* Ibid., V.1

p. 215    *I am commencing an undertaking:* Ibid., Book 1.

p. 217    Rousseau and crying: for more on Rousseau, Ermenonville, and the Cult of Sensibility, see Schama, *Citizens,* 155–62.

p. 217    *Too bashful:* Ibid.

p. 219    *Dollywood:* see Stephen Miller, *Smart Blonde: Dolly Parton, a Biography* (Omnibus Press, 2006), 223ff.

p. 221    *The fiction of romance:* George Canning, writing at Eton in 1787, quoted in Geoffrey Day, *From Fiction to the Novel* (London, 1987), 3. Beattie's essay is quoted *in extenso* in Day's second chapter.

p. 222    *Novels are of a more familiar nature:* Congreve's preface to *Incognita: Or, Love and Duty Reconciled. A Novel.* It is quoted in Day, 1.

p. 225    *Some of the media horde:* Jeannette Walls, *Dish: How Gossip Became the News and the News Became Just Another Show* (Avon, 2000), 306.

p. 228    *Whoever you are, scribe:* Steven Roger Fischer, *A History of Reading* (Reakton Books, 2003), 27.

## CHAPTER 12: SHADES

p. 230    *Yes, quite alone: New York Times*, March 24, 1929, quoted in *The Penguin Book of Interviews,* ed. Christopher Silvester (Penguin, 1993), 262.

p. 232    Tim Clayton on Sarah Siddons: "The Role of Prints and Printmakers in the Diffusion of Portraiture," in *Citizens and Kings* (London, 2006), 50–56.

p. 233    *danger to ordinary men:* T. E. Lawrence, *Seven Pillars of Wisdom*, Chapter CIII.

p. 234    *handle him firmly from the first:* John Vincent, "Lawrence of Arabia's Tortured Fantasies Laid Bare," *Daily Telegraph*, July 21, 2001; the letters came up for auction the year after Sid Abrahams died.

p. 235    *Could a man: The Mint*, Chapter 4. In the first paragraph, Lawrence is referring to the labor of writing and rewriting *Seven Pillars*, a draft of which he had lost at Reading Station.

p. 235    Robbie Williams anecdote: Chris Heath, *Feel: Robbie Williams*, 12.

p. 236    *safeguard yourself against flatterers:* Machiavelli, *The Prince*, trans. George Bull, Chapter 23.

p. 237    Wilkinson studying Buddhism: "Quantum Physics Puts New Spin on Jonny Wilkinson's Life," *Times*, September 19, 2008.

p. 238    Herodotus on scandalous behaviour: John Marincola, in the Penguin edition of *Herodotus: The Histories*, 627.

p. 238    His Most Benevolent Highness: Ryszard Kapuściński, *The Emperor*, 81.

p. 240    *Hide our achievements:* Geoffrey Chaucer, *The House of Fame*, vv 1694–9.

p. 240    *"What?" said she:* Ibid., 1713–1718. ("Wood" = nuts, meshuggeh)

p. 241    *How fortunate:* Bertolt Brecht, "Solomon's Song." Actually, the poem ends up attacking ordinary folk for their equivalent flaw, their faith in God.

p. 241    *How I envy your lot:* Homer, *Odyssey*, 11.482–91.

p. 242    *my fame reaches heaven:* Again, the translation is Lawrence's (the opening of Book 9).

# ACKNOWLEDGMENTS

I would like to thank the colleagues, pupils, and friends whose insights and support made this book possible: Lorna Bradbury; Zsófia Botos; Martin Brooke; Sorcha Carey; Paul Carling; Toby Clements; John Coldstream; Jamie Coreth; Mark Corfield-Moore; Rebecca de Pelet; Sarah Drury; William Duggan; Simon Eliot; Lorraine Foster; Hugo Gent; Peter Graham; Bernard Holiday; Richard Hudson; Alex Latham; George Mackintosh; Barty Martelli; Murrough O'Brien; Jean-Marc Pascal; Scott Pearce; Lucia Quinault; Philip Rogerson; Kate Summerscale; Gary Tarn; Harriet Vyner; Mark Waldron; Sara Wheeler; and Josh White.

This book owes its existence to a number of people: its sharp and sensitive editors in London were Beth Coates and Liz Foley; my agent, Karolina Sutton, has guided and protected me throughout the project. It was Kate Jones who first saw that this could be a book; who nurtured it from its first inklings, through proposals, to its first drafts. My experience of her kindness, patience, shrewdness, humor, and warmth has given me a share of the great loss felt by all who knew her.

The debt to David Rogers at Picador, New York, is formidable. He took the book on, and ever since I've delighted in his advice and support. I've learned a lot from him, and at times working on the book has felt less like revision and more like collaboration; translating British references into American ones has been a joy under his guidance. He has also been behind the creation of the Web site www.popcropolis.com. At Picador, I am grateful, too, to Nicholas Richardson, Amy Rose-Perkins, Sara Sarver, Nancy Inglis, and David Logsdon.

*Acknowledgments*

All this would be nothing without the love and support of my family: the encouragement of my mother and the ample example of my late father. "Quiet consummation have; / And renowned be thy grave!" My three small daughters have been surprisingly patient. My final thanks go to my wife, Louise. Her early response to the idea led to the book's eventual publication, and she coped amazingly with everything that happened in between—not least the long spells of writing and researching that demanded more of her than of me. She has also saved me from foibles and faiblesses; without her, the book would have been worse, as well as impossible.

# INDEX